Apocalyptic Shakespeare

D1447912

Apocalyptic Shakespeare

*Essays on Visions of
Chaos and Revelation in
Recent Film Adaptations*

Edited by
MELISSA CROTEAU *and*
CAROLYN JESS-COOKE

McFarland & Company, Inc., Publishers
Jefferson, North Carolina, and London

LIBRARY OF CONGRESS CATALOGUING-IN-PUBLICATION DATA

Apocalyptic Shakespeare : essays on visions of chaos and
    revelation in recent film adaptations / edited by Melissa
    Croteau and Carolyn Jess-Cooke.
        p.   cm.
    Includes bibliographical references and index.

    ISBN 978-0-7864-3392-6
    softcover : 50# alkaline paper ∞

    1. Shakespeare, William, 1564–1616 — Film and video
adaptations.   2. Apocalyptic literature — History and criticism.
3. Film adaptations — History and criticism.   4. End of the
world in literature.   I. Croteau, Melissa.   II. Jess-Cooke,
Carolyn, 1978–
PR3093.A56   2009
791.43'6 — dc22   2009005072

British Library cataloguing data are available

On the cover: (left to right) Leonardo DiCaprio in the 1996 film
Romeo + Juliet; Operation Castle Romeo detonation on March 26, 1954,
near the Bikini atoll (NNSA); Chandos portrait of William Shakespeare
(National Portrait Gallery)

Manufactured in the United States of America

*McFarland & Company, Inc., Publishers
    Box 611, Jefferson, North Carolina 28640
    www.mcfarlandpub.com*

For all the friends, family, and colleagues
who steadfastly have listened, advised, and
encouraged me along this apocalyptic journey.
— Melissa Croteau

For Jared, Melody and Phoenix, with much love.
— Carolyn Jess-Cooke

Acknowledgments

We would like to thank the following people warmly for their assistance in producing this book: Evita Cooke, Jared Jess-Cooke, Diane Sutton, and Joyce Renshaw. In addition, a special word of thanks goes to each of our contributors. It has been a genuine pleasure to work with each of you.

Table of Contents

Introduction:
Beginning at the Ends

Melissa Croteau

And I saw a new heaven and a new earth: for the first heaven and
the first earth were passed away.   — Revelation 21.1

Not mine own fears, nor the prophetic soul
Of the wide world, dreaming on things to come,
Can yet the lease of my true love control,
Suppos'd as forfeit to a confin'd doom.
The mortal moon hath her eclipse endur'd,
And the sad augurs mock their own presage.
                              — Shakespeare, Sonnet 107 (lines 1–6)

Like the love of Shakespeare's speaker in Sonnet 107, the human race
and the earth it inhabits have endured innumerable cataclysms and prophesies of their "confin'd doom." Yet, we live on and continue to be obsessed
with apocalyptic narratives. From the ancient eschatological doctrines of
Zoroaster in Persia, through Judaic and Christian visions of the End, to the
fourth film in the *Terminator* series, *Terminator Salvation: The Future Begins*
(premiering in 2009), people have been drawn to the apocalyptic in one
form or another, unrelentingly, for well over three thousand years of recorded
history. That apocalyptic impulse has translated into diverse representations
in all forms of art. Although film is not much more than a century old, it
vigorously embraced the apocalyptic from the start and now, arguably, produces more widely disseminated apocalyptic narratives and images than any
other medium on the planet.

Although both the apocalyptic and Shakespeare have had an immea-
surably powerful and persistent life (or after-life) on film, none of the many
book-length studies of Shakespeare on film written in the past dozen years

has examined in depth the increasingly apocalyptic investments and concerns prevalent in contemporary Shakespearean cinema. This volume seeks to provide a comprehensive examination of the ways in which recent Shakespeare films — in particular a body of predominantly late twentieth century and post–9/11 productions — register cultural concerns toward a global wasteland of literal nothingness, technological alienation, spiritual destruction, and the effects of globalization. The most salient feature of the apocalyptic is *transformation*. Our world is embroiled in the swift and disorienting evolution of technologies, and, like civilizations of the past, we turn to apocalyptic narratives to order our experience, to make sense of seeming chaos. Turning to Shakespeare's well-known, sequential diegetics could be perceived as conciliatory and comforting in this environment of swirling fragments in which "master narratives" have been abandoned. However, many contemporary filmmakers adapting Shakespeare's work to film have chosen apocalyptic *mise-en-scènes*, imagery, and redesigned plots to interrogate, rather than ameliorate, apocalyptic concerns regarding rapid revelation and impending dissolution. By considering apocalypse as a theoretical and thematic lens through which these issues can be examined in terms of their current cultural currency, *Apocalyptic Shakespeare* charts new scholarly territory while offering original and critical insight to an area of popular significance.[1]

This introduction provides a brief account of the complex array of concepts surrounding *apocalypse* and *apocalypticism*, focusing specifically on the multivalent approaches to cinematic apocalypse that are presented in this volume. As opposed to limiting the apocalyptic to a checklist of requisite characteristics, we seek to offer several lenses through which the reader or viewer might fruitfully interact with the texts. A look at various hermeneutic approaches taken by creators and consumers of apocalyptic narratives, along with an investigation of the functions of the apocalyptic, will reveal the significance and profusion of these sorts of narratives, which traditionally privilege linear time, an inherently conservative way of viewing history. Many of the films discussed in this collection, such as Baz Luhrmann's *William Shakespeare's Romeo + Juliet* (1996), Jean-Luc Godard's *King Lear* (1987), Michael Almereyda's *Hamlet* (2000), and Alex Cox's *Revengers Tragedy* (2002) are spectacularly postmodern, placing Shakespeare's plays in disorienting, sometimes post-apocalyptic, urban landscapes which warn us of some sort of impending destruction in our own world, whether that destruction be textual, relational, or material. Ironically, whereas these films are considered avant-garde, counter to conventional cinema, they do embrace the conservative logic of "the end." By choosing to adapt Shakespeare's narratives, these filmmakers are able to comment simultaneously on the Bard, narrational modes, the apocalyptic, and contemporary cultures. This mix of influences offers a fantastically rich intertextual experience, one which is captured by the diversity of approaches to Shakespeare, cinema, and the apocalyptic contained in this volume.

"It's the Second Coming for the first time, again!"[2]

One has only to look at the films of the past, present, and future to discover that humanity is captivated by apocalyptic narratives. Film scholar Mick Broderick points out that "the cinematic antecedents of millennial beliefs can be traced right back to the origins of film, usually represented by violent cosmological interventions in such films as *The Comet* (1910) or *End of the World* (1916) or drawing on projected technological means for mass destruction as in *The Airship Destroyer* (1909)" (254–55). One of the most striking silent films in this genre is renowned director Fritz Lang's fantastical masterpiece *Metropolis* (1927), set in a dystopic world tragically divided between "workers" and "thinkers," in which a beautiful robot woman, who is flagrantly cast as the biblical Whore of Babylon, ironically exhorts the oppressed laborers to destroy the machines they work on, demonically screaming "Death to the machines!" over and over.[3] By obeying the techno-"whore," the naïve workers destroy their own world in "the depths," yet they are redeemed in the end by making peace with their formerly heartless and exploitative, now properly chastened boss. Their corrupt social order has been destroyed; the hope of a new world is before them. *Metropolis* is classically apocalyptic in that it clearly displays the traditional "eschatological pattern of crisis, judgment, and salvation" (McGinn 15)—it even quotes from the definitive apocalyptic text, St. John's Book of Revelation (17.1–6). However, it also depicts a profound fear of the trajectory of technology, which is seen as a juggernaut capable of swallowing the quotidian lives of the masses, who find themselves slaves to "the machines," as well as cataclysmically destroying their world in one fell swoop.[4] The genre of science fiction, since its literary inception, has been concerned with the threatening potential of technology. It is not surprising that *Metropolis* was made between the two twentieth century wars that proved to the world that the bright prognostications of scientific and human progress propounded during the Enlightenment had not materialized, or at least had a terrifying, diabolical underbelly.

Predictably, apocalyptic film increased in popularity between the World Wars, after the technologically inspired horrors of World War I. Following World War II, with its apocalyptic visions of the Holocaust and the dropping of the atomic bomb, Cold War fears fueled another period of cinematic fascination with catastrophic ends and the promise of new worlds. The 1950s spawned the explosion of the genre of cinematic science fiction, which continues to provide some of the most potent images of technological terror as well as redemption. While the technology of the cinema itself was expanding into Cinemascope, Cinerama, and 3-D, American film audiences flocked to see films like *The War of the Worlds* (1953), *Earth vs. The Flying Saucers* (1956), and *Forbidden Planet* (1956), an adaptation of Shakespeare's *The Tempest*. By 1964, the world was ready for a burlesque of the nuclear threat, Stanley Kubrick's mordant yet eerily gleeful *Dr. Strangelove, or, How I Stopped Worrying and Learned to Love the Bomb*, which perversely highlights "the irony of a society living in fear of the very weapon it sees as its salvation" (Stone 65). Notably, *Dr. Strangelove*'s macabre jocularity stood in stark contrast to Stanley Kramer's solemn, and perhaps maudlin, big-budget tale of nuclear annihilation, *On the Beach* (1959), made just five years earlier, and tellingly remade for television in the year 2000.

As the century slouched toward the year 2000, developments in science and technology inspired more trepidation as computers continued to take over the jobs of humans and the natural environment languished under the burden of industrial poisons. This escalating destruction was brought to the public's attention rather starkly by Rachel Carson's 1962 exposé, *Silent Spring*, which predicted, in apocalyptic terms, an "ecological 'meltdown'" or "environmental holocaust" (Stone 66; Weber 201). Science fiction films like *Soylent Green* (1973) and *Logan's Run* (1976) provide post-apocalyptic visions of a future in which humans have decimated our planet, but the latter film, unlike the former, does offer hope to the suffering human race. Although the hope of a renewed world, salvation, and a new life are crucial to traditional apocalypticism, postmodern apocalyptic narratives do not always include the redemptive aspects of the genre. Quintessential and popular apocalyptic films of the last three decades include Australian director George Miller's *Mad Max* series — *Mad Max* (1979), *Road Warrior* (1981), and *Beyond Thunderdome* (1985) — which depict a bleak and brutal post-apocalyptic world, and the three extant *Terminator* films — *Terminator* (1984), *Terminator 2: Day of Judgment* (1991), and *Terminator 3: Rise of the Machines* (2003) — which depict a devastating struggle between humanity and the machines it has created. The Wachowski brothers' celebrated *Matrix* trilogy — *The Matrix* (1999), *The Matrix Reloaded* (2003), *The Matrix Revolutions* (2003) — is decidedly post–Cold War, focusing not on nuclear threat but on cyber subterfuge perpetrated by machines that enslave and pacify humans by putting them in a virtual simulacrum of a pre-apocalyptic world. Rife with biblical and philosophical allusions, the *Matrix* films feature an unadulterated messiah figure, Neo, whose name reveals his calling to establish a renewed human world. The phenomenon of the apocalyptic film series is particularly ironic because the end never is the end: the narrative is resurrected and reincarnated in successive sequels, creating "a new heaven and a new earth" with each film. That we love to witness our own (fictional) devolution and destruction, or the threat or aftermath thereof, is made exceedingly apparent by films like *Blade Runner* (1982), *Brazil* (1985), *Twelve Monkeys* (1995), *Strange Days* (1995), *The Postman* (1997), and genuine blockbusters like *Armageddon* (1998) and the re-remade *War of the Worlds* (2005).

There has been a continual onslaught of apocalyptic movies since the turn of the millennium: *Artificial Intelligence: AI* (2001), *28 Days Later* (2002) and *28 Weeks Later* (2007), *The Day After Tomorrow* (2004), the *Resident Evil* series (*Resident Evil* [2002], *Resident Evil: Apocalypse* [2004], and *Resident Evil: Extinction* [2007]), *V for Vendetta* (2005), *Doomsday* (2008), and *The Happening* (2008), not to mention the vast majority of movies adapted from comic books, which inevitably feature a superhero of some kind saving the world from imminent extermination.[4] It is interesting that the American actor Will Smith has managed to star in five popular apocalyptic films in about twice as many years — *Independence Day* (1996), *Men in Black I* and *II* (1997, 2002), *I, Robot* (2004), and *I Am Legend* (2007) — making a career of rescuing the planet and surviving the utter ruination, attempted or accomplished, of Earth. It is an equally fascinating turn of events that Smith's foremost rival in this genre, Arnold Schwarzenegger, who starred in the *Terminator* series as well as *End of Days* (1999) and *The 6th Day* (2000), has translated art into life by landing another apocalyptic role: attempting to save the Golden State from economic and ecological ruin as the governor of California. In 2006, Mel Gibson released his cataclysmic epic *Apocalypto*, which depicts the last days of the Mayan civilization. One cannot help but wonder if Gibson's vision of the end is a warning to *our* civilization.[5] More recently, Cormac McCarthy's bleak and haunting post-apocalyptic novel *The Road*, which won the Pulitzer Prize in 2007, has been made into a major motion picture set to be released in 2009.[6] The film industry loves a well-woven tale of the end of the world and the beginning of new worlds, whether penned by Cormac McCarthy in the last decade or by William Shakespeare over four hundred years ago. St. John's Revelation is replete with stunning imagery begging to be used on film (conflagration, plague, war, oceans of blood, and so on), and Hollywood will continue to mine that treasure trove. Even the apostle Peter's millennial words could be used to pitch a film project: "But the day of the Lord will come as a thief in the night; in which the heavens shall pass away with a great noise, and the elements shall melt with fervent heat, the earth also and the works that are therein shall be burned up" (2 Peter 3.10). Undeniably, this is prime action film material. It is clear that apocalyptic narratives have much to offer cinema: a veritable visual feast of destruction, masses of people in dire crisis, and messianic heroes.

It seems that no matter what package Hollywood puts its apocalypticism in, the genre sells and the audience clamors for more. Many of the films I have named above are distinctly post-apocalyptic, and it is important to note that this collection treats post-apocalypticism as an aspect of the apocalyptic, rather than a separate genre. In his exceptional monograph *After the End*, James Berger argues that incomprehensible destruction is the provenance of the apocalyptic narratives we create and consume.

> A disaster occurs of overwhelming, disorienting magnitude, and yet the world continues. And so writers imagine another catastrophe that is absolutely conclusive, that will end this world. The initial disaster ... is not an apocalypse in that is does not reveal [and so] requires imagining a second disaster that *is* apocalyptic and thereby gives the first disaster retrospective apocalyptic status [6–7].

Therefore, Berger contends, "[a]pocalyptic writing itself is a remainder, a symptom, an aftermath of disorienting catastrophe" (7). The fictional apocalyptic text imbues the inscrutable cataclysm with sense and meaning after the fact. The work of distinguished apocalyptic scholar Bernard McGinn qualifies Berger's position by asserting that apocalypticism is not entirely crisis-driven: "It is not so much crisis in itself, as any form of challenge to the established understanding of history.... These challenges may be positive as well as negative, unexpected strokes of good fortune as well as terrible disasters" (31). However, the principle remains the same: apocalypticism results from a perceived or actual threat to individuals' and society's well-being, way of life, or worldview. Whether a disaster has taken place or looms large in the imagination, collective or personal, the human mind seems to be motivated by fear and consumed with plots for surviving in the aftermath. It is in this way that "apocalyptic thinking is almost always, at the same time, post-apocalyptic" (Berger xii–xiii). The proliferation of anxieties that has generated these various types of apocalyptic texts has resulted in a challengingly diverse menagerie of films that scholars and viewers have dubbed *apocalyptic*.

Apocalypse How?

> [I]f one wanted to unmask the ruses, traps, trickeries, seductions, machines of war and pleasure, in short, all the interests of the apocalyptic tone today, it would be necessary to begin by respecting this differentially proliferating division ... of voices and tones that perhaps takes them beyond a distinct and calculable plurality.—Derrida, "Of an Apocalyptic Tone Recently Adopted in Philosophy" [27]

There is a daunting number of definitions for the terms *apocalypse* and *apocalyptic*. Literally, the Greek roots of these words mean "to uncover" or "disclose" ("Apocalypse"). The first entry under *apocalypse* in the *Oxford English Dictionary* refers us to St. John's Book of Revelation, the final book of the New Testament, in which the saint receives angelic visions of the "end times," Judgment Day, and the redemptive era of the Millennium. Of course, even that statement is simply one reading of St. John's cryptic revelation. This book has been a devilish hermeneutical challenge from its inception, and scholars, pastors, cultural critics, and a host of other interested parties continue to battle over and "reckon what it did and meant" (Donne 10). Although *apocalypse* also refers to "a genre of visionary literature that emerged during the Hellenistic period of Western antiquity (c. 200 BCE-200 CE)," which deals with "the revelation of heavenly knowledge through means of a heavenly journey or ... visitation of a heavenly messenger," we have come to see *apocalypse* as nearly synonymous with catastrophic end-of-the-world scenarios because of the eschatological focus of the Book of Revelation (Stone 79). In his 1991 book *Contemporary Apocalyptic Rhetoric*, Barry Brummett gives a useful and succinct look at the many divergent approaches to the terms surrounding the "apocalyptic" (7–10). F. A. Kreuziger has lamented that even in the academy, "scholars have been stymied in their efforts to reach a consensus on what apocalyptic is and what it means" (qtd. in Brummett 7). Historian Bernard McGinn remarks that "[t]he variety of forms under which apocalyptic doctrines have been presented has led one foremost Old Testament theologian, Gerhard von Rad, to deny that it is possible to determine a genre peculiar to apocalyptic" (4–5). Furthermore, McGinn and other prominent scholars of the apocalyptic have disagreed on many aspects of the tradition. For instance, Norman Cohn, in his influential study *The Pursuit of the Millennium*, has argued that millenarian beliefs were the province of the poor, oppressed, and uneducated during the Middle Ages (15–18; 281–83), whereas McGinn and others contend that millenarianism always came from the top, the educated and privileged, down to the masses (McGinn 29–32).[7] This distinction is of great importance as it examines the immense socio-political power wielded via apocalyptic rhetoric. Were the masses who staged millenarian revolutionary movements in the Middle Ages and early modern periods being manipulated by clerics and literate men of wealth, or were they responding in an authentic, grass-roots fashion to their oppressed condition, justifying their rebellion with apocalyptic narratives? As this is a question of agency and power, an apposite analogy can be made between McGinn's position and Max Horkheimer and Theodor Adorno's claims in *The Dialectic of Enlightenment* that the "technology of the culture industry" has suppressed and homogenized the "individual consciousness" of the general populace, thereby manipulating the masses into prodigal, blind consumption that fills the coffers of the controllers of media (95). Their position can be contrasted to that of scholars like Camille Paglia, who argues that the masses choose the content of what the media feeds them; people consume the media that resonates with them, rather than being controlled as passive consumers.[8] The history and overwhelming popularity of apocalyptic narratives in visual media over the past century reveal that this genre has been and will continue to be used both as an instrument of social control and fear-mongering as well as an emancipatory, redemptive vehicle of hope and revolution.

Film scholars have encountered similar problems in their efforts to define what *apocalyptic* means, and how the concept can be used, when applied to cinematic texts. What one might call more orthodox or conservative scholars, like Jon R. Stone, assert that films labeled "apocalyptic" must display the "five identifying features common to all apocalypses," as defined by prominent apocalypse scholar John J. Collins:

> [A]pocalypses typically feature a supernatural source from which a secret knowledge comes ... often ... through visions, dreams, angelic visitations, heavenly journeys, and the opening of a heavenly book or sealed scroll. A second identifying feature of apocalypses is their interest in otherworldly forces, usually angelic and demonic.... A third characteristic feature ... is the firm belief in divine intervention in human history, usually culminating in the end of an evil person or power, or sometimes the end of time itself. Also characteristic ... is the restoration of paradise on Earth ... [including] the termination of the old world and its transformation into a new world order. A final feature of an apocalypse is the dispensing of rewards and punishments to men and women in the afterlife...[, which is] determined by the degree of faithfulness to God that a person showed in this life [Stone 79–80; cf. Collins 1–32].

These very specific criteria would exclude many of the films I have mentioned above. Indeed, most scholars of apocalyptic film use a far more liberal working definition of *apocalyptic*, much to Stone's chagrin. In fact, he harangues others, such as Conrad E. Ostwalt, for "lumping" films "haphazardly under a catchall metaphorical category called 'apocalypse'" (80). Ostwalt's major criterion for inclusion in his study of apocalyptic film is that the texts, "although not necessarily about the end of time, must project apocalyptic themes and images," which may include "traditional apocalyptic characteristics, such as mystery, revelation, dualism, and imminent destruction," while emphasizing a "twentieth-century attitude toward the cosmic cataclysm that marks the end of the world" (56). Certainly, these are broad parameters; yet, ironically, Ostwalt refers us in his notes to the same passage in Collins's work that Stone uses as the source for his criteria, and Ostwalt claims that "modern film bases its own apocalyptic themes" on the principles laid out in Collins's distinguished book *The Apocalyptic Imagination* (Ostwalt 164).

While Ostwalt may seem like the other end of the "pure apocalypse" spectrum from the conservatives, still other film scholars dismiss traditional apocalyptic ideas almost entirely. For instance, at the opening of an article in *CineAction* subtitled "Placing Apocalypse in Millennial Cinema," Diane Sippl declares, "I would like to define apocalypse as simply as this: the end of the world as we know it" (5). In light of the wide divergence of opinion on this matter, it perhaps is evident that we all see through a glass darkly when it comes to defining the apocalyptic genre. That being said, a defining effort must be made if one is to make any cogent arguments regarding apocalyptic film. The key, it would seem, is to introduce straightforward criteria at the onset of one's study and not to deviate from them. As for my own work, and that of this collection, I cannot claim anything nearly so consistent as that statement implies. Although this volume examines cinematic adaptations of Shakespeare's work, the films covered here appear generically to have very little in common: Baz Luhrmann's colorful *William Shakespeare's Romeo + Juliet* (1996) is a creative, MTV-style spectacle aimed at teenagers; *The Lion King* (1994) is an animated Disney classic; Michael Almereyda's *Hamlet* (2000), Julie Taymor's *Titus* (2000), Christine Edzard's *The Children Midsummer Night's Dream* (2001) are art house films with very disparate *mise-en-scènes* and directorial sensibilities; and *The King Is Alive* (2000) is a Dogme 95 film, a product of a Scandinavian, idealistically retrogressive yet postmodern film movement. While their Shakespearean provenance connects these films, they are also joined by their apocalyptic themes, imagery, and function. Although the authors in this volume do not adhere to a single definition of *apocalyptic*, their essays reveal that each film forges its own unique and compelling connections to the apocalyptic that may not fit neatly into any monolithic presentation thereof.

The apocalyptic is such a multivalent and versatile phenomenon that several scholars have developed hermeneutic rubrics or taxonomies to "bring order to the reigning confusion" surrounding the subject (Robinson, *American* 26). In his preeminent study of fiction and the apocalyptic, *The Sense of an Ending*, Frank Kermode divides apocalyptic hermeneutics into two types: the "naïvely predictive" approach, which embraces a literal view, expecting a historical End, and "implie[s] a strict concordance between beginning, middle, and end" (30); and "clerkly skepticism," which attempts to deny or resist this sort of "concord" and tends to read the apocalyptic allegorically (10). The foremost "clerkly skeptic" is the great fourth and early fifth century church father St. Augustine, who was the most incisive opponent of the apocalyptic interpretation of history in the patristic period.... [He] shied away from any reading of canonical apocalyptic texts that would attempt to find in them a source of information about current events...; rather, he tried to interpret them as a message about the perennial struggle between good and evil in the souls of men [McGinn 26].

Because Augustine was one of the earliest theologians to oppose a "predictive" hermeneutic and embrace an allegorical and personal approach to the apocalyptic, many modern and postmodern scholars have referred to his hermeneutic as a model for their own.[9]

While Frank Kermode's dichotomous hermeneutic division is fairly simple, Douglas Robinson offers a relatively sophisticated rubric of "five interpretive stances or topoi by which the apocalypse might be understood," as presented in his monograph *American Apocalypses* (26) and in *The Encyclopedia of Apocalypticism* ("Literature" 360–91).[10] Furthermore, Robinson's book opens with a chapter on "Apocalyptic Hermeneutics" that gives an excellent summary of numerous other approaches to apocalypticism that pertain to literary studies (*American* 1–29). Indeed, it would be a lengthy project to give an exhaustive list of the many hermeneutic approaches to apocalyptic, and it is not within the scope of this collection to do so. However, the several taxonomies through which apocalyptic texts can be read and analyzed can clarify the elusive idea of apocalyptic and help one avoid essentializing this extremely complex phenomenon.

These hermeneutic modes, which are not mutually exclusive (or comprehensive), apply to both the author of the text being read and the reader/audience of the apocalyptic text. The author presents his or her interpretation of apocalypse, and we, in turn, filter the author's reading of apocalypse through our own revelatory lenses. In his discussion of Augustine's hermeneutics, Robinson points out that the church father's approach is "double-layered: it is a hermeneutical stance on John's hermeneutical stance [in Revelation]" ("Literature" 366). He goes on to connect this concept to all hermeneutics: "the interpretation of another text always involves writers in a dual stance, simultaneously attempting to represent both *their own* interpretation of another text and *that text's author's* interpretation of the world and still other texts" (366). When applied to film adaptation, this point is particularly apropos and escalates in complexity. An audience of a Shakespearean film, for instance, is experiencing several hermeneutic layers, including Shakespeare's reading of his own environment, the screenwriter's and director's approaches to the play, the generic stance of the film, and one's own worldview and experience with Shakespeare and the material of that particular play. Similarly, an apocalyptic film might incorporate imagery from the Book of Revelation, past apocalyptic cinema, and current warfare and technology, as well as apocalyptic concepts from Christianity, Zoroastrianism, and Islam, and in so doing, it accrues various apocalyptic lenses. In this way, reading or watching apocalypse is like the experience of Shakespeare on film: the audience is always bearing witness to an adaptation and interpretation of a narrative, which by definition possesses a beginning, middle, and end, that nevertheless continually resurrects in new incarnations, repeating the narrative pattern with varying hermeneutic approaches. Like prophets, we know and expect a promised end, for we have seen and heard the story before, but the predictive visions did not reveal all. Ironically, the protean story never ceases evolving and metamorphosing throughout history, changing with the zeitgeist and, phoenix-like, reviving after each cataclysmic end.

Another principal method of approaching the apocalyptic is through its diverse *functions*. Potentially, this also is a more fruitful and less reductive approach than applying a checklist of characteristics or even one particular apocalyptic taxonomy. Although a great many functions have been proposed for apocalyptic, most of these can be synthesized into five general categories: to make sense of the world and to order chaos (Kermode 28–29; Brummett 9–10); to critique the existing social order and respond to social crisis (Berger 7, 34; Brummett 23–26); to serve as a cautionary tale and warn people to change their ways in order to avert an imminent apocalypse (Wittreich 57; Robinson, "Literature" 363); to attempt to work through historical traumas (Berger 19) or to negotiate our way around "human horrors" (Wittreich 125); "[t]o argue that the end is not near [and] to refute or ridicule apocalyptic hysteria" (Robinson, "Literature" 362). Again, these purposes are not mutually exclusive; they often bleed into one another as they appear in texts. Another manifest quality of these five functions is that they allow for and explain the power, fluidity, and specificity of the apocalyptic narrative in its myriad forms and cultural affiliations throughout history. While most scholars discuss the functions of apocalypse, Brummett is one of the few who chooses to define apocalyptic by its function rather than its features, and in so doing, his approach agrees with mine. Brummett's "working definition" of the term is

> a mode of thought and discourse that empowers its audience to live in a time of disorientation and disorder by revealing to them a fundamental plan within the cosmos. Apocalyptic is that discourse that restores order through structures of time or history by revealing the present to be a pivotal moment in time, a moment in which history is reaching a state that will both reveal and fulfill the underlying order and purpose in history [9–10].

As is made clear by the repetition in this quotation, "revelation" and orienting oneself in chaotic times is central to Brummett's conception of apocalyptic. In *The Sense of an Ending*, Kermode repeatedly insists that apocalyptic, which he associates with narrative patterns in general (i.e., beginning, middle, end), is a way of "making sense of the world" (repeated three times, 28–29). He asserts, "For to make sense of our lives from where we are…, stranded in the middle, we need fictions of beginnings and fictions of ends, fictions which unite beginning and end and endow the interval between them with meaning" (190). The array of functions claimed for apocalyptic above lead to the conclusion that these narratives were, are, and will continue to be coping mechanisms and comforters, "equipment for living" for the distressed and disoriented of this world: in a word, everyone (Brummett 19).

Discourses of the Apocalypse

As all the films discussed in this collection are postmodern, the majority of them being post-millennial, postmodern theoretical approaches predominate throughout the volume. Postmodern theory, situated as it is at the end of a millennium, is replete with apocalypticism, and much of postmodern theory is focused on dissolution and destruction. In the wake of the horrors of World War I and II, which seemed to give the lie to "the Enlightenment narrative, in which the hero of knowledge works toward a good ethico-political end — universal peace," Jean-François Lyotard denounced "metanarratives" in his groundbreaking book *The Postmodern Condition*, defining *postmodern* as "incredulity toward metanarratives" (xxiii–xxiv). It had become clear that the early nineteenth century philosopher G. W. F. Hegel's (apocalyptic) notion that history progressed dialectically toward an auspicious and inevitable end, at which point its development (history) ceased and all would be harmonious, was not reflected by reality. Moreover, as Hannah Arendt has established, Marxists and fascists throughout the twentieth century justified their actions by using the Hegelian argument that there are immutable "laws of Nature or of History" that govern historical movement, regardless of moral principles; asserting their reductive ideologies (or metanarratives), Marxists and fascists of various types formed totalitarian regimes and committed unconscionable crimes against humanity, such as Stalin's purges and the Holocaust (159–61). This is the terrifying danger of "self-legitimating" metanarratives. While Lyotard's idea of surpassing grand narratives certainly can be implemented positively (e.g., exploring discourses of feminism, multiculturalism, postcolonialism), it is predicated on the end of ideologies of human virtue, progress, and potential for perfection. It is, therefore, on several levels, post-apocalyptic.[11]

In the middle of the twentieth century, Max Horkheimer and Theodor

Adorno, along with other members of the Frankfurt School, argued that media technology was being used by the economically dominant to pacify and manipulate the masses:

> The individual is entirely nullified in face of the economic powers. These powers are taking society's domination over nature to unimagined heights. While individuals as such are vanishing before the apparatus they serve, they are provided for by that apparatus better than ever before. In the unjust state of society the powerlessness and pliability of the masses increase with the quantity of goods allocated to them [xvii].

The rhetoric in this passage is glaringly and disturbingly apocalyptic (or post-apocalyptic). Perhaps ironically, cinema itself has frequently portrayed the metaphorical and literal "vanishing" or destruction of the individual, or of humanity (both beings and humaneness), due to technology. Several of the films discussed in this volume engage precisely this concept, particularly Almereyda's *Hamlet*, Cox's *Revengers Tragedy*, and Godard's *King Lear*. The latter two films are distinctly post-apocalyptic, set in post-cataclysmic worlds, but Almereyda's *Hamlet* is set in present-day Manhattan and features a "prince" fighting to remain an authentic individual in a world of fleeting images and struggling not to be absorbed by the media conglomerate that is the Denmark Corporation. However, authenticity is another casualty of the postmodern world, according to Jean Baudrillard and Frederic Jameson. Baudrillard argues that we are beyond the end of time: "[T]he acceleration of modernity, of technology, events and media, of all exchanges — economic, political and sexual — has propelled us to 'escape velocity,' with the result that we have flown free of the referential sphere of the real and of history" (*Illusion* 1). Baudrillard believes we "no longer possess a forward-looking, historical, or providential vision, which was the vision of a world of progress or production. The final illusion of history, the final utopia of time no longer exists" (*Vital* 35).[12] What remains, according to Baudrillard, is "simulacra," the "hyperreal," because there are no longer any authentic origins or originals; we are left with only copies, endlessly recycling (*Simulacra* 1–2). Jameson also argues that the late capitalism of postmodernism has led to meaningless copying, "pastiche," and superficial nostalgia, as well as collective and individual fragmentation and "schizophrenia." In summary, all of these prominent postmodern theorists embrace a pessimistic, dystopic apocalypticism, which proposes we may already live in a post-apocalyptic world that is "beyond transformation" and redemption (Sharrett 4–5; Berger 36–38). Consciously and unconsciously, a good deal of apocalyptic film graphically illustrates their philosophies.

It is important, however, to explore the revelatory, utopic side of apocalyptic. Indeed, traditional apocalyptic texts are as much about salvation and renewal, the birth of new worlds, as they are about destruction and judgment: "Ninety-eight verses (of over four hundred) in the Apocalypse of John speak of catastrophe, and 150 refer to joy, consolation, brightness, and hope" (Weber 230). The cataclysm of apocalypse takes place for a purpose, to unveil what is hidden or cannot be acknowledged in histories of every scale, from personal to global. Shakespeare's *King Lear*, perhaps his bleakest and most apocalyptic tragedy, provides poignant examples of this. The violent storm in the center of the play, in which Lear and his companions are caught, forces the bereft king to recognize that he has neglected the poor and suffering during his long reign.

> Poor naked wretches, whereso'er you are,
> That bide the pelting of this pitiless storm,
> How shall your houseless heads and unfed sides,
> Your loop'd and window'd raggedness, defend you
> From seasons such as these? O, I have ta'en
> Too little care of this!   [3.4.28–32]

Lear's spiraling catastrophes — his relinquishing his power to his eldest daughters, his daughters' mistreatment and rejection of him, his dangerous exposure in the tumultuous storm — have unveiled to him the corruption, the insidious solipsism, that has pervaded his life. This epiphany breaks him further, hastening his decline into madness, for the redemptive consequences of revelation are not always immediate. However, Lear's discovery of this truth opens the door to his beautiful reunion with Cordelia, the loving daughter he arrogantly banished. Though the end of *King Lear* is a banquet of death in a blighted world, the newly appointed king, Edgar, has proven himself a fiercely loyal son and subject throughout the hostility and chaos of the play, and this man of integrity will lead the way into a new age. The cataclysm has not only tested and proven his mettle, it also has crowned him king. In his monograph on the apocalyptic in *King Lear*, Joseph Wittreich argues, "Those who survive the crisis [in the play] are not simply saved: they are the saviors of history" (129). Taking a Nietzschean perspective, Wittreich proposes that Shakespeare secularizes apocalypse in *King Lear* by creating a plot in which "the old alliance between God and man" is ruptured, making man "the master of his fate and captain of his destiny" (128). By "disallow[ing] God's intervention in history," Wittreich asserts, Shakespeare "affirm[s] human responsibility," releasing and empowering those in the world of the play to be autonomous agents, free to craft a new heaven and a new earth of their own (128).[13] While many, including Jan Kott and Peter Brook, would disagree with this reading of *King Lear*, the point is that the end of this harrowing, tenebrific play leaves us on the threshold of regeneration and provides a vista of a brave new world.

In the example of *King Lear*, we see that the play's apocalypticism encompasses a great variety of spectacular destruction (bloody war, horrifying bodily torture, murder, a violent storm), but it also displays the positive aspects of revelation, the passing away of a degenerate world and the dawning of a new one. Many, perhaps most, apocalyptic movies made for a mass audience capitalize on all the gory and sensational potentialities in the apocalyptic genre. Nevertheless, in films like *Armageddon, Independence Day*, and *The Day After Tomorrow*, the world survives, even if many perish, and those who remain will go on to forge a new destiny in a renewed landscape. In *Crisis Cinema*, Christopher Sharrett reminds us that "the apocalypse of postmodernity is almost always couched in that very popular misuse of apocalypse not as revelation but doomsday, disaster, the end" (4). In terms of screen time and imagery (and certainly advertisement), Sharrett's point holds true; however, the ends of the vast majority of "popular" apocalyptic films portray survival (salvation), hope, and a glance toward the future, even if only in their very last moments, as in *King Lear*. In his book *The Myth of the Eternal Return*, distinguished philosopher and religious studies scholar Mircea Eliade observes that "there is everywhere a conception of the end and the beginning of a temporal period" and concludes that humans have a universal and profound need for a "periodic regeneration of life," which "presupposes ... a new Creation, that is, a repetition of the cosmogonic act" (52). In humanity's repeated "passage from chaos to cosmos," we are driven to renew and reconstruct our worlds, time and time again (54). Eliade declares that there is hope in the "consciousness of the normality of the cyclical catastrophe, ... the certainty that is has a meaning, and, above all, that it is never final" (88). The end is never the End. The linear narrative pattern of beginning, middle, and end continuously recycles, each conclusion launching a new start and an opportunity for transformation. James Berger writes, "The apocalyptic-historical-traumatic event becomes a crux or pivot that forces a retelling and revaluing of all events that lead up to it and all that follow" (21). In other words, cataclysmic ends are catalysts for redemptive revisions: devastated worlds and shattered worldviews open up the potential for "new — more healthy and more truthful — histories and futures" (Berger 219). Hope is revealed through the cracks of doom.

The Return of the Bard, or
"Shakespeare is dead; long live Shakespeare!"

What does the "Sweet Swan of Avon" have to do with the fearsome four horsemen of the apocalypse? Transformation is the predominant characteristic of the apocalyptic, and just as apocalypticism itself has changed and proliferated over its thousands of years — as our interpretations of crisis, judgment, and salvation have shifted in myriad directions — so have our interpretations and representations of Shakespeare's texts over the past four hundred years. Shakespeare's work is rife with apocalypticism, as was that of his early modern contemporaries. In his time, as in ours, catastrophe was a big seller, always popular with audiences; witnessing the violent ends of others, who may or may not represent ourselves or our neighbors, can be sensational and cathartic. Nevertheless, there were particular factors at play in early modern England that drew writers to focus on the apocalyptic. Throughout the sixteenth and seventeenth centuries, plague continued to be a devastating killer that ravaged England repeatedly, as Carl James Grindley discusses in this volume. In addition, there was social unrest among the masses to the point of large-scale rioting several times due to land enclosure and oppressive grain pricing. From 1585 to 1604, England was engaged in intermittent military conflict with Spain (dubbed the Anglo-Spanish War, though not declared officially), and wars of religion, in which many Englishmen participated, raged on the European continent during Shakespeare's lifetime. Furthermore, Shakespeare lived through an age of intense anxiety regarding who would succeed the magnificent, Protestant Virgin Queen, Elizabeth, on the throne of England. A large number of Shakespeare's plays deal with the perilous problems of the succession of power, including both tetralogies of history plays, *Titus Andronicus, Hamlet, Macbeth, Julius Caesar,* and *King Lear.* The conclusion of a monarch's reign is an extraordinarily vulnerable moment in a nation's history, and it presents the possibility of a cataclysmic end and a chaotic, tragic aftermath, or, perhaps, a promising new beginning. The transition of power from Queen Elizabeth to the Scottish James I in 1603 went fairly smoothly, but his accession to the throne did establish the conditions that would lead to the bloody English Civil War four decades later — which violently suspended the monarchy for over a decade — when James's son, Charles I, was in power. Indeed, Shakespeare and his contemporaries lived in a vibrant time fraught with tensions and fears regarding the realities of catastrophic disease, religiously and politically motivated violence, and even natural disasters (there was a major earthquake in 1580, referred to in *Romeo and Juliet* [1.3.23], and devastating flooding in 1607). In addition, potential threats of power gone awry seemed to loom large over the English, who had recently been through the vicissitudes and vagaries of Henry VIII and then his Catholic daughter, "Bloody" Mary I, to emerge into the reign of Gloriana, Elizabeth I, whose lengthy, stable rule ushered in what is often called the Golden Age of England, a mythically paridisical time of national strength and prosperity accompanied by an unparalleled flourishing of arts and culture; but this time was also haunted by apprehensions arising from the aftermath of the hundred turbulent years leading up to Elizabeth's coronation in 1558, beginning with the brutal, internecine Wars of the Roses (1455–1485). It is no mystery why early modern England turned to the apocalyptic tradition to understand and comment on its own historical circumstances as well as its angst about the future.

With the advent of film in the late nineteenth century, Shakespeare's plays were reborn in a new medium with ever-developing technology and evolving artistic approaches. But *why* do we resurrect Shakespeare on screen? In the silent era, Shakespeare's works were frequently mined for screen material, with the result that "more than four hundred films on Shakespearean subjects" were made during this time (Jackson 2). The fact that Shakespeare's plays were familiar to audiences in many parts of the world, and that filming Shakespeare "conferred respectability" on those involved in the making of the films, made his texts a natural choice for cinematic adaptation (Jackson 2). Since synchronized sound has entered the picture, although the numbers have trended higher and lower throughout the decades, the volume of Shakespeare films being produced has significantly slackened, for which there are many reasons. However, there has been a resurgence in Shakespeare adaptations for the screen since Kenneth Branagh's *Henry V* (1989) and Franco Zeffirelli's *Hamlet* (1990, starring Mel Gibson), both commercially successful, proving that Shakespeare could sell in the postmodern market of late capitalism. Timothy Corrigan has noted that cinematic adaptations of classic literature in general greatly increased in the 1980s and '90s, and that upsurge has not slackened in the new millennium. Corrigan posits three reasons for this "widespread return of the literary classics": (1) it is "a reaction against contemporary filmmaking trends to diminish traditional plot and character"; (2) it is "a conservative or at least therapeutic turn from cultural complexity"; (3) it is a reflection of the contemporary film audiences' "increasing concern with manner over matter" (72). The first two motivations given for turning to classic literature like Shakespeare seem to be responses to the disorientation and overwhelming overload of data constantly streaming in our direction in the postmodern era (see Jameson and Baudrillard). The linear narratives and familiar characters of this literature were created before the technology of perpetual media bombardment dominated people's lives. Films that depict these "simpler" times, stories, and characters could be perceived as comforting, an escape from the frenetic fragmentation demanded by our culture. And, as Frank Kermode declares, Shakespeare is "the greatest creator of confidence" (82), so how could filmmakers resist appropriating the cachet of the immortal Bard to comfort the disturbed? For instance, the makers of Disney's beloved animated classic *The Lion King* used Shakespearean plotlines and characters for precisely this purpose, a subject

Alfredo Modenessi explores in this volume. However, most of the films discussed in *Apocalyptic Shakespeare* take a different approach to the canonical text; these films accentuate the apocalypticism in Shakespeare's plays by creating *mise-en-scènes* and striking visual imagery that create various types of dissonance and disruption — for example, the jarring disjunction between setting and language in Luhrmann's *William Shakespeare's Romeo + Juliet*, Almereyda's *Hamlet*, and Cox's *Revengers Tragedy*; or the cacophonous worlds of "shreds and patches" constructed of the artifacts and detritus of multiple pasts and presents in Taymor's *Titus*, Godard's *King Lear*, and Miroslaw Rogala's "*Macbeth*": *The Witches' Scenes* (1988). These films are more likely to disturb the comfortable than to assuage postmodern malaise. In their disparate apocalyptic approaches, these films avoid reifying the status quo in our culture(s), in Shakespearean hermeneutics, and in cinema. Their apocalypticism functions predominantly as social critique, response to crisis, and cautionary tale. *Titus*, *King Lear*, and "*Macbeth*": *The Witches' Scenes* also vividly, and sometimes grotesquely, attempt to work through historical traumas and negotiate human horrors as well as textual disintegration (both cinematic and literary).

As Corrigan suggests in his third reason for the return to classics, the postmodern audience, in its endless proliferation of media and recycled copies, is often interested in the manner in which something familiar is reproduced. A new film version of a piece of literature always participates in revealing intertextual dialogue with the earlier literary and cinematic renditions. An individual potentially could have seen forty feature film adaptations of Shakespeare's *Hamlet* during his or her lifetime, and such a *Hamlet* devotee could be expected enthusiastically to seek out new *Hamlet* films as they emerge. These filmmakers are crafting Shakespeare's legendary play into their own cinematic expressions, each film exploring a different interpretation. Shakespeare's plays, therefore, are caught up in the rapture of the postmodern and revived in new incarnations. The lover of Shakespeare goes to see multiple film adaptations of the same plays because a new reading of the old text will be unveiled, resulting, perhaps, in revelation. Nonetheless, it would be disingenuous to say that Shakespeare is not the hook that draws the audience to those diverse adaptations of his plays. Indeed, this book is predicated upon the eminence and significance of Shakespeare in our culture. For better or for worse, the "Author" is far from "dead," as Courtney Lehmann emphasizes in her chapter here. Postmodern theorist Roland Barthes famously announced that "the birth of the reader must be at the cost of the death of the Author" (148), proposing that the reader of a text is now the arbiter of his own reading experience, liberated to enter and participate in the "multidimensional space" of the text, "in which a variety of writings, none of them original, blend and clash" (146). This reader-focused, dialogical hermeneutic denies "a single 'theological' meaning (the 'message' of the Author-God)" in any text (146). This concept resonates strongly with Wittreich's argument about the denouement of *King Lear*, that Shakespeare dispenses with God in the tragedy and thereby releases men, hopefully, to create their own destinies. Significantly, adaptation as a practice embraces this logic, as Anthony Guneratne's essay in this volume explores. Barthes's apocalyptic declaration of the "death" of the originary figure (real and symbolic) ushers in a new hermeneutic world for readers, who are now freed to explore their own readings of a given text rather than seek the author's ultimate meaning. This escape from the Law of the Father, the myth of origins, takes place every time a screenwriter and director adapt a piece of literature to the screen. They replace Shakespeare as author, and, in true hermeneutic style, we read and judge their reading (and erasure) of Shakespeare. We bear witness to the new "Shakespeare" film, therefore, to view the demolition and demise of the author alongside the rebirth of the text, celebrating both the vestiges of the dearly departed and his textual transmigration. Shakespeare is dead; long live Shakespeare. Frank Kermode prophesies, "We recreate the horizons we have abolished, the structures that have collapsed; and we do so in terms of the old patterns, adapting them to our new worlds" (58). As with the apocalyptic tradition, and the ever-recycling and metamorphosing apocalyptic narrative, we return to Shakespeare, periodically regenerating the Bard in our own images.

The Ends Justify the Means

> There's a divinity that shapes our ends,
> Rough-hew them how we will.—*Hamlet* 5.2.10–11

In the first essay in this collection, Ramona Wray examines the ways in which postmodern cinema uses Shakespeare's texts to indicate historical continuity, or what endures from the past, while employing apocalyptic themes of disintegration, decline, and destruction to indicate futurity and potential ends. In her study of four divergent films—*"Macbeth": The Witches' Scenes* (dir. Miroslaw Rogala, 1988), *Macbeth* (dir. Michael Bogdanov, 1997), *The Angelic Conversation* (dir. Derek Jarman, 1985), and *The Postman* (dir. Kevin Costner, 1997)—Wray looks at the ways in which these films portray both a pessimistic or dystopic apocalypticism and a redemptive or utopic vision simultaneously, critiquing crises in our historical moment while revealing potential for renewal and hope.

Courtney Lehmann applies systems theory, particularly cybernetics, to her exploration of the ways in which children have been linked to "Renaissance power plays" in contemporary cinema. Starting with the example of the early modern "War of the Theaters" (1599–1602), in which children were used as mediators of cultural conflicts, Lehmann argues that the terms of the current "War" in Shakespearean cinema have been reinvented along the axis of gender. In her investigation of three films—Adrian Noble's *A Midsummer Night's Dream* (1996), Julia Taymor's *Titus* (2000), and Christine Edzard's *The Children's Midsummer Night's Dream* (2001)—Lehmann contends that, through their use of children, the latter two films issue a communal, democratizing corrective to the former, which supports patriarchal, anachronistic visions of authorship that rewrite the Renaissance as the story of great men acting alone.

In the subsequent essay, Kim Fedderson and J. Michael Richardson explore the representation of difference and violence in Julie Taymor's *Titus*. They interrogate Taymor's signature, eclectic postmodern aesthetic (cf. Broadway's *The Lion King*), observing that the plethora of diverse signs used in the film lose their previous cultural specificity and meaning; thus, *Titus* portrays an unrealistic, utopic erasure of difference rather than the legitimate dialogism that could provide a feasible reconciliation and redemption.

In "Post-Apocalyptic Spaces in Baz Luhrmann's *William Shakespeare's Romeo + Juliet*," Richard Vela compares Luhrmann's adaptation to three other prominent *Romeo and Juliet* adaptations—those of George Cukor (1936), Renato Castellani (1954), and Franco Zeffirelli (1968)—examining the telling ways in which Luhrmann uses space and architecture very differently from the earlier directors. Using settings like the ruined Sycamore Grove Theater, a demolished cinema, and a Catholic cathedral teeming with neon crosses, Luhrmann communicates the negative prognostications of postmodernism. Vela goes on to connect *William Shakespeare's Romeo + Juliet* to the significant cinematic patterns and subgenres, such as the "youth apocalypse film" of the 1990s, that clearly influenced Luhrmann in his creation of this remarkable film.

Following Vela's chapter is my contribution to the collection, which explores Michael Almereyda's technology-obsessed *Hamlet* (2000). In the media-saturated Manhattan of this film, we are forced to confront the possibility of the end of human relationships in the face of virtual reality and digital communication. However, unlike Horkheimer and Adorno, Baudrillard, and Jameson, who all make apocalyptic prophecies about the vitiated and meretricious mass-mediatized consumer society and its depthless surfaces, "packed emptiness," and lack of historical consciousness, I argue that Almereyda's film is more expressive of the views of Mikhail Bakhtin regarding the fecundity of intertextuality. A close investigation of Almereyda's splitting of the famous "To be or not to be" soliloquy into three distinct scenes bears this out.

Next, Gretchen E. Minton looks at an intensely post-apocalyptic adaptation of *The Revenger's Tragedy*, a play written by Thomas Middleton, a contemporary of Shakespeare. In the last few years, echoing theorists like Barthes and Baudrillard who have declared that we live in a post–Authorial and post-historical moment, scholars have been putting Shakespeare in a category of post-ness in diverse ways, as evidenced by several published titles: *Shakespeares after Shakespeare: An Encyclopedia of the Bard in Mass Media and Popular Culture* (ed. Richard Burt, 2006), *After Shakespeare: An Anthology* (ed. John Gross, 2003), and *Shakespeare After Theory* (David Scott Kastan, 1999). Alex Cox, well known as an anarchic cult film director, adapts a Jacobean revenge tragedy that is decidedly *not* Shakespeare, thereby rejecting the elite icon of the Bard (while constantly, perhaps anxiously, defining itself by what it is not).[14] Picking up on the inherent post-apocalypticism of all revenge tragedy, Cox situates his adaptation of the play in a punk, post-nuclear *mise-en-scène*, creating a world dominated by homicidal dictators and the menacing all-seeing eye, in the form of satellites, surveillance cameras, and large video screens. This emphasis on the omniscient eye provides a thematic link between the role of god (or lack thereof) in apocalyptic vengeance, meta-theatricality, and postmodern self-awareness.

Carl James Grindley's essay approaches apocalypticism from an early modern perspective, looking at the significant role of the plague in Shakespeare's culture and in his plays, particularly *Romeo and Juliet* and *Twelfth Night*. Grindley argues that plague occupies a pivotal space not only in the plotlines but in the character arcs and settings of these plays; however, when those plays are turned into films, the plague's role turns from that of a societal force, or spectral shape in the landscape, into a personal issue, if it is not erased entirely. This essay proposes various causes for these shifts and disappearances in several film adaptations, including Luhrmann's *William Shakespeare's Romeo + Juliet*, *Shakespeare in Love* (dir. John Madden, 1998), and *She's the Man* (dir. Andy Fickman, 2006).

Adrian Streete juxtaposes the ways in which Michael Radford's *The Merchant of Venice* and Mel Gibson's *The Passion of the Christ*, both released in 2004, problematically negotiate anti–Semitic discourse in a post–Holocaust environment. Streete elucidates the highly exclusionary politics of apocalypticism, asserting that traditional apocalyptic narratives declare the overarching superiority of one group over another, which can and has lead to devastating forms of totalitarianism and intercultural violence.

Like Streete, Alfredo Michel Modenessi examines the ways in which apocalypticism can be used to promote fascism, focusing specifically on Nazi anti–Semitism. In his investigation of the popular and facile association of *Hamlet* with Disney's film *The Lion King* (dir. Roger Allers and Rob Minkoff, 1994), Modenessi offers a critique of commercial, artistic, and academic practices that promote or support such association. He also presents an illuminating comparison of *The Lion King* and another Disney film, *Education for Death*— an anti–Nazi propaganda short made as part of the "war efforts" of the United States and released on DVD at roughly the same time as *The Lion King*. Modenessi argues that *Education for Death* foregrounds and exposes *The Lion King*'s implicit apocalyptic, exclusionary content and political agenda.

Jean-Luc Godard's post-apocalyptic *King Lear* (1987) is the subject of Anthony R. Guneratne's piece, in which he astutely compares the adaptation process to Freud's notion of the Oedipus complex, positing that the son (the director) must kill the father (Shakespeare) to create an artistic production that is truly his own. However, Guneratne complicates this equation by drawing attention to the ways in which Godard grapples with the "death of the Author," which includes within its "sickle's compass" the annihilation of the "Auteur," the theory Godard himself propounded and epitomized. Guneratne explains how each stage of Freud's development resonates with the ideas of auteur theory, with eschatalogical disourse in general, and with the structuring of space and time that Godard follows in a characteristically Freudian manner.

In the final essay in the collection, Carolyn Jess-Cooke returns to some of the key ideas raised in Ramona Wray's opening chapter regarding the ways in which Shakespeare's narratives are used as legitimating cultural texts in films that graphically articulate the shape of impending ends and aftermaths in distinctly postmodern ways. Jess-Cooke discusses Edzard's *The Children's Midsummer Night's Dream* (2001) and Dogme 95's *The King is Alive* (2000)— in which a group of tourists lost in the barren Namibian desert attempts to stage *King Lear*— in terms of their commentary on the "ends" and renewals of artistic and cultural production, particularly in the realm of cinema. Drawing upon the practice of sequelization as a trope of continuation, repetition, and eschatology, Jess-Cooke discusses these films as "sequels" in an otherwise continuous chain of Shakespearean adaptations that draw upon the latent registers of apocalypse, post-ness, and "afterwardness" that inform the dialogues that take place between many film texts based on Shakespeare's works.

The diversity of the essays in this volume reflect the kaleidoscopic nature of apocalypticism in postmodern culture and attest to its pervasive influence. Perhaps, as Frank Kermode insists, we have a "deep need for intelligible Ends" to help us make sense of our pasts, presents, and futures (8). To this *end*, Shakespeare's work offers comprehensibility and continuity in a time of disorientation and dissonance. Mediating our own stories through Shakespeare's, we attempt to negotiate and navigate through times of intense transformation, both positive and negative, enlightening and threatening. In the proposed apocalyptic aftermath of history, authorship, and humanity, we can celebrate the ineluctable regenerative force along with Shakespeare's humble, bemused Shepherd in *The Winter's Tale*: "[T]hou met'st with / things dying, I with things new-born" (3.3.113–14). As what has been passes away, we hopefully behold a new heaven and a new earth, new cinemas and new Shakespeares.

Notes

1. A sizable body of scholarly work has been done on apocalyptic cinema in the last fifteen years, including Michael Sharrett's collection *Crisis Cinema* (1993), Kim Newman's *Apocalypse Movies* (2000), Jerome Shapiro's *Atomic Bomb Cinema* (2001), and Wheeler Winston Dixon's *Visions of the Apocalypse: Spectacles of Destruction in American Cinema* (2003). Other books have approached apocalypse and cinema from diverse angles, such as *The End of Cinema As We Know It: American Film in the Nineties* (ed. Jon Lewis, 2001) and, less academically, Meghann Marco's *Field Guide to the Apocalypse: Movie Survival Skills for the End of the World* (2005), in which she mines apocalyptic films for their wisdom and guidance on such topics as fashion and food in the "false utopia," "how to be a rebel in a post-apocalyptic wasteland," and how to battle "giant insects and other mutant terrors."

2. This is a risibly ironic advertisement slogan for the IndiePlex channel's Memorial Day weekend marathon of movie sequels (aired 14 April 2008).

3. There are obvious echoes in *Metropolis* of the Luddite movement of the early nineteenth century, in which English artisans rebelled against the Industrial Revolution by destroying the machines they believed were replacing them. Eugen Weber compares this movement to the "biocentric millenarian activism" in the 1970s, noting that the 1973 text *Ecodefense: A Field Guide to Monkey-wrenching* "recommended Luddism, or war on machines and tools that destroy life," which included things like "spiking roads with barbed metal stakes" and "sabotaging the instruments used to rape natural surroundings" (202). The subtitle of the third *Terminator* film conveys the same anxiety: *Rise of the Machines* (2003).

4. The X-Men — enduring and beloved Marvel Comics mutant superheroes — have a storyline entitled *The Complete Age of Apocalypse Epic*, which fills four volumes (published in book form in 2006). "Apocalypse" in this series is actually an Anti-Christ character threatening the planet. Three *X-Men* films have been made so far: *X-Men* (2000), *X2* (2003), and *X-Men: The Last Stand* (2006).

5. One could argue that Gibson's much-discussed *The Passion of the Christ* is an apocalyptic film in the same vein, portraying the end of one era (the old covenant with the Judeo-Christian God) and the beginning of another. Some Christians believe that Christ's death ushers in the *eschaton*, or "Last Days." See Adrian Streete's essay in this volume, which discusses the potentially divisive power of apocalypticism in Gibson's *The Passion of the Christ*.

6. The director of *The Road*, John Hillcoat, has been keen to distance *his* post-apocalyptic *mise-en-scène* in the film from that of famous fellow-Australian George Miller in the *Mad Max* series. Hillcoat considers the *Mad Max* world an "anti-model: a fanciful, imaginary version of the end of the world, not the grim, all-too-convincing one that McCarthy had depicted" (McGrath E1).

7. McGinn adamantly and eloquently states his argument in *Visions of the End*: Christian apocalypticism during [the Middle Ages] was not primarily a movement from below, a manifestation of popular religion, a protean enthusiasm forcing its way like molten lava up through the hardened sediment of institutional religious and political forms. It was, for the most part, an attempt by a group of educated religious *literati* to interpret the times, to support their patrons, to console their supporters, and to move men to pursue specified aims at once political and religious in nature. It took its unique power from an ability to locate current events within a schema of universal meaning, to transcendentalize the present by viewing it from the aspect of the End [32].

8. In *Sex, Art, and American Culture*, Camille Paglia, the academic iconoclast, takes joy in pointing out that the emperor of the ivory tower has no clothes:

A serious problem in America is the gap between academe and the mass media, which *is* our culture.... Academic commentary on popular culture is either ghettoized as lackluster "communications," tarted up with semiotics, or loaded down with grim, quasi-Marxist, Frankfurt School censoriousness: the pitifully witless masses are always being brainwashed by the money-grubbing capitalist pigs. But mass media is completely, even servilely commercial. It is a mirror of the popular mind. All the P.R. in the world cannot make a hit movie or sitcom. The people vote with ratings and dollars [ix].

To be fair, Paglia's assessment of the state of popular culture studies in academia is circa 1992, and there has been much development in this area since.

9. See Douglas Robinson (*American* 14; esp. "Literature" 366), Eugen Weber (226–27), and Frank Kermode, who eloquently pays homage to his predecessor: "As St. Augustine observed, anxieties about the end are, in the end, anxieties about one's own end; he was long before me in suggesting that apocalypse, once imaginable as imminent, had the capacity to become immanent instead" (186).

10. Robinson proposes the following classifications:

(1) the *biblical* prediction of an imminent end to history, controlled by God so as to provide a paradisal continuation; (2) the *annihilative* prediction of an imminent end to history controlled by no God at all and followed by oblivion; (3) the *continuative* prediction of no end at all, but of simple secular historical continuity...; (4) the *ethical* internalization of apocalyptic conflict as a figure for personal growth in ongoing history; and (5) the *romantic* or visionary internalization of the fallen world by an act of imaginative incorporation, so that the world is revealed as the paradise it already is [Robinson, "Literature" 373].

11. One of the most poignant and disturbing post-apocalyptic statements on the twentieth century was written by literary and cultural critic Walter Benjamin, a German Jew who allegedly took his own life in 1940 to evade capture by the Nazis. In his brief and tragic revision of St. John's Revelation, Benjamin seems to prophesy a defenseless "angel of history" very unlike the victorious angels in the canonical Apocalypse:

[The angel of history's] face [is] turned toward the past. Where we perceive a chain of events, he sees one single catastrophe which keeps piling wreckage upon wreckage and hurls it in front of his feet. The angel would like to stay, awaken the dead, and make whole what has been smashed. But a storm is blowing from Paradise; it has got caught in his wings with such violence that the angel can no longer close them. The storm irresistibly propels him into the future to which his back is turned, while the pile of debris before him grows skyward. The storm is what we call progress [257–58].

Benjamin's gravely pessimistic treatment of apocalypticism is prescient of the postmodern theorists who would come in the latter half of the century, making him a "touchstone of postmodernity" (Dellamora 1).

12. There are also theorists who put forth optimistic arguments about post-historicity. In his influential essay "The End of History?," neoconservative scholar Francis Fukuyama asserts a positive, perhaps utopic, post-apocalypticism: "What we may be witnessing is not just the end of the Cold War, or the passing of a particular period of postwar history, but the end of history as such: that is, the end point of mankind's ideological

evolution and the universalization of Western liberal democracy as the final form of human government" (4). This position is arguably triumphalist, but it reclaims Hegel's dialectics, presenting a "cheerful vision of history," rather than the doom and gloom of several postmodern theorists discussed here (Pask 182). See also Fukuyama's expanded study on the subject, *The End of History and the Last Man* (New York: Avon, 1992).

13. See Friedrich Nietzsche's "The Parable of the Madman" in *The Gay Science*, ed. Walter Kaufmann (1882,1887; New York: Vintage, 1974) 181–82. Also accessible online at <http://www.fordham.edu/halsall/mod/nietzsche-madman.html>.

14. The *Revengers Tragedy* DVD includes special features in which actor-comedian Eddie Izzard (who plays the evil Lussurioso) insists that Middleton's language is less complex than Shakespeare's and Alex Cox claims that the shift from Elizabethan (e.g., Shakespeare's) to Jacobean (e.g., Middleton's) dramatic rhetoric makes *Revengers Tragedy* easier for modern audiences to comprehend. In "The Don" featurette, Oxford professor John Pitcher asserts,

> Middleton's writing isn't like Shakespeare's, and that's one of the signs of Middleton and his contemporaries separating themselves out and distancing themselves from Shakespeare and that type of ... poetry.... [T]hey'd started to write a plainer language for the stage.... [Middleton's work] is actually much more closely linked to our own idiom and our own syntax than Shakespeare's would have been.

Thus, those involved in making the film self-consciously use Shakespeare as their basis of comparison, a touchstone by which to gauge and defend their use of Middleton instead. It is notable that none of the commentators on the *Revengers Tragedy* DVD mention that Shakespeare also wrote plays during the Jacobean period, including *Macbeth, Anthony and Cleopatra, Coriolanus,* and *Pericles,* during the years surrounding the composition and performance of *The Revenger's Tragedy* (1606–1608).

Works Cited

"Apocalypse." *Oxford English Dictionary.* 2nd ed. 1989.

Arendt, Hannah. *Totalitarianism: Part Three of The Origins of Totalitarianism.* San Diego: Harcourt, 1968.

Barthes, Roland. *Image — Music — Text.* Trans. Stephen Heath. New York: Hill and Wang, 1977.

Baudrillard, Jean. *The Illusion of the End.* Trans. Chris Turner. Stanford: Stanford University Press, 1994.

_____. *Simulacra and Simulation.* Trans. Shelia Faria Glaser. Ann Arbor: University of Michigan Press, 1994.

_____. *The Vital Illusion.* Ed. Julia Witwer. New York: Columbia University Press, 2000.

Benjamin, Walter. *Illuminations: Essays and Reflections.* Ed. and intro. Hannah Arendt. Trans. Harry Zohn. New York: Schocken Books, 1969.

Berger, James. *After the End: Representations of Post-Apocalypse.* Minneapolis: University of Minnesota Press, 1999.

Broderick, Mick. "Heroic Apocalypse: Mad Max, Mythology and the Millennium." *Crisis Cinema: The Apocalyptic Idea in Postmodern Narrative Film.* Ed. Christopher Sharrett. Washington, D.C.: Maisonneuve Press, 1993. 250–72.

Brummett, Barry. *Contemporary Apocalyptic Rhetoric.* New York: Praeger, 1991.

Cohn, Norman. *The Pursuit of the Millenium: Revolutionary Millenarians and Mystical Anarchists of the Middle Ages.* Rev. ed. New York: Oxford University Press, 1970.

Collins, John J. *The Apocalyptic Imagination: An Introduction to the Jewish Matrix of Christianity.* New York: Crossroad, 1984.

Dellamora, Richard, ed. *Postmodern Apocalypse: Theory and Cultural Practice at the End.* Philadelphia: University of Pennsylvania Press, 1995.

Derrida, Jacques. "Of an Apocalyptic Tone Recently Adopted in Philosophy." *Oxford Literary Review* 6.2 (1984): 3–37.

Dixon, Wheeler Winston. *Visions of the Apocalypse: Spectacles of Destruction in American Cinema.* London: Wallflower Press, 2003.

Donne, John. "A Valediction: Forbidding Mourning." *Masters of British Literature: Vol. A.* Ed. David Damrosch and Kevin J. H. Dettmar. New York: Pearson Longman, 2008. 889.

Eliade, Mircea. *The Myth of Eternal Return: Cosmos and History.* Trans. Willard R. Trask. Princeton, NJ: Princeton University Press, 1965.

Fukuyama, Francis. "The End of History?." *National Interest* 16 (Summer 1989): 3–18.

_____. *The End of History and the Last Man.* New York: Avon, 1992.

The Holy Bible. Authorized King James Version. Brussels: Thomas Nelson, 2001.

Horkheimer, Max, and Theodor W. Adorno. *Dialectic of Enlightenment: Philosophical Fragments.* Ed. Gunzelin Schmid Noerr. Trans. Edmund Jephcott. Stanford: Stanford University Press, 2002.

Jackson, Russell, ed. *The Cambridge Companion to Shakespeare on Film.* Cambridge: Cambridge University Press, 2000.

Jameson, Frederic. *Postmodernism, or, The Cultural Logic of Late Capitalism.* Durham, NC: Duke University Press, 1991.

Kermode, Frank. *The Sense of an Ending.* New York and Oxford: Oxford University Press, 2000.

Lewis, Jon, ed. *The End of Cinema As We Know It: American Film in the Nineties.* New York: New York University Press, 2001.

Lyotard, Jean-François. *The Postmodern Condition: A Report on Knowledge.* 1979. Trans. Geoffrey Bennington and Brian Massumi. Minneapolis: University of Minneapolis Press, 1984.

Marco, Meghann. *Field Guide to the Apocalypse: Movie Survival Skills for the End of the World.* Ill. Dominic Bugatto. New York: Simon Spotlight Entertainment, 2005.

McGinn, Bernard. *Visions of the End: Apocalyptic Traditions in the Middle Ages.* New York: Cornell University Press, 1979.

McGrath, Charles. "PDX, The Dreary Backdrop." *The Oregonian* 29 May 2008: E1+.

Newman, Kim. *Apocalypse Movies: End of the World Cinema.* New York: St. Martin's Press, 2000.

Ostwalt, Conrad E., Jr. "Hollywood and Armageddon: Apocalyptic Themes in Recent Cinematic Presentation." *Screening the Sacred: Religion, Myth, and Ideology in Popular American Film.* Boulder, CO: Westview Press, 1995. 55–63.

Paglia, Camille. *Sex, Art, and American Culture: Essays.* London: Penguin, 1993.

Pask, Kevin. "Cyborg Economies: Desire and Labor in the *Terminator* Films." *Postmodern Apocalypse: Theory and Cultural Practice at the End.* Philadelphia: University of Pennsylvania Press, 1995. 182–98.

Revengers Tragedy. Dir. Alex Cox. Screenplay by Frank Cottrell Boyce. 2002. DVD. Fantoma, 2004.

Robinson, Douglas. *American Apocalypses: The Image of the End of the World in American Literature.* Baltimore: Johns Hopkins University Press, 1985.

_____. "Literature and Apocalyptic." *The Encyclopedia of Apocalypticism, Vol. 3: Apocalypticism in the Modern Period and the Contemporary Age.* Ed. Stephen J. Stein. New York: Continuum, 1999. 360–91.

Shakespeare, William. *The Riverside Shakespeare.* Boston: Houghton Mifflin, 1974.

Shapiro, Jerome. *Atomic Bomb Cinema: The Apocalyptic Imagination on Film.* New York and London: Routledge, 2001.

Sharrett, Christopher, ed. *Crisis Cinema: The Apocalyptic Idea in Postmodern Narrative Film.* Washington, D.C.: Maisonneuve Press, 1993.

Sippl, Diane. "Tomorrow Is My Birthday: Placing Apocalypse in Millennial Cinema." *CineAction* 53 (2000): 2–21.

Stone, Jon R. "A Fire in the Sky: 'Apocalyptic' Themes on the Silver Screen." *God in the Details: American Religion in Popular Culture*. Ed. Eric Michael Mazur and Kate McCarthy. New York: Routledge, 2001. 65–82.

Weber, Eugen. *Apocalypses: Prophecies, Cults, and Millennial Beliefs through the Ages*. Cambridge, MA: Harvard University Press, 1999.

Wittreich, Joseph. *"Image of that Horror": History, Prophecy, and Apocalypse in* King Lear. San Marino, CA: Huntington Library, 1984.

1

The "great doom's image": Apocalyptic Trajectories in Contemporary Shakespearean Filmmaking

RAMONA WRAY

Ours is the age of the apocalypse. In the western world, at least, an emphasis upon what has been termed the "eschatological undertow to the war on terrorism" (McLaren 327) has resulted in the growing familiarity of apocalyptic discourse, a darker timbre of public analysis and prognosis, and an increasing sense of imminent disaster. Emerging from the heightened visibility of apocalypticism's political cast is a renewed concentration upon the motifs of the Revelation narrative, which, as commentators never fail to remind us, encompass the arrival of the four horsemen, the ascendancy of the woman clothed with the sun, the coming — and routing — of the beast, Armageddon, and the institution of the heavenly kingdom (Zamora 2, 11). Given these trajectories in the cultural sphere, it is perhaps not surprising that, as much as attention has been directed towards the present and the past, so has it in turn been focused upon the future: versions of millenarian prophecy persist and thrive, as is testified to by those popular attempts to decode signs, extrapolate the bible and attach a definitive date to the end (Chalmers 15). In a variety of ways, and across a range of discursive practices and registers, apocalypse has come to function as a dominant mode of conceptual organization and a major instrument through which the discontinuities and uncertainties of the world might be interpreted.

Arguably, film represents a subsidiary strand of such an interpretive impetus and, in this connection, it is salutary to note, at the end of the twen-

29

tieth and beginning of the twenty-first centuries, the prevalence of apocalyptical or apocalypse-inspired cinematic offerings which, as Felicia Feaster
observes, stand as witness to an unprecedented consumer interest in "destruction ... violence ... [and] catharsis" (Feaster 27). Insofar as his plays are
absorbed in the apocalyptic imaginary, Shakespeare offers a litmus test for
the continuing applications of millennial preoccupations and vocabularies.
Yet, in screen incarnations, what is of interest is the extent to which apocalyptical paradigms are deployed in ways that run counter to, or against the
grain of, the Shakespearean dramatic content. On screen, the Bard and the
apocalypse, this essay argues, often consort as bedfellows over and above an
underlying narrative specificity. Quite why this should be the case is worth
pausing over for a moment. This essay contends that, in postmodernity,
Shakespeare, perennially a guarantor of historical continuity, is a peculiarly
apt repository of meaning to invoke at a time of perceived change, crisis and
temporal rupture. Or, to formulate the point rather differently, if Shakespeare
can connote the past, apocalypse signifies the future, and if apocalypse suggests the end, Shakespeare incarnates what has been enduring. These con-
trarieties interact with each other in a symbiotic relationship in screen
versions of the Bard, as reflection upon four contemporary productions —
The Angelic Conversation (Derek Jarman, 1985), *"Macbeth": The Witches'
Scenes* (Miroslaw Rogala, 1988), *Macbeth* (Michael Bogdanov, 1997) and *The
Postman* (Kevin Costner, 1997) — will demonstrate. Each of these works displays a thematic investment in ruination, decline, despoliation and a shared
sense of ending in order to underline, on the one hand, a dystopian vision
of what is to come and, on the other hand, utopian prospects of recovery.
In this sense, *The Angelic Conversation, "Macbeth": The Witches' Scenes, Macbeth* and *The Postman* follow in their trajectories a dominant conception of
apocalypse, the idea that the end, in Robert Newman's words, heralds either
a redemptive "era of renewal" (2) or "the eternal return of catastrophe" (11).
The rehearsal of a dual construction of apocalypse does not necessarily entail
the institution of either one or the other interpretive reading, however, for,
as this essay goes on to suggest, common to all the Shakespeare films discussed here is a tendency to invert or unmoor any stable point of reference.
Apocalypse, as a recurrent Shakespearean trope, is ultimately indicative of
temporal confusion if not contradiction and of historical processes that, in
the same moment at which they are summoned, founder and fold in upon
themselves. Even as apocalypse is invoked in the filmic Shakespeare, then,
so is it subjected to distortion, manipulation and alteration.

"Macbeth": The Witches' Scenes

"Macbeth": The Witches' Scenes illustrates the point and serves neatly as a platform for a comparative study of its Bardic-apocalyptic screen counterparts. An experimental video and installation artist based in the U.S., Miroslaw Rogala stages in *"Macbeth": The Witches' Scenes* a nightmarish vision of Shakespeare's play which, by prioritizing the speeches of the weird sisters and by elevating the computer into a force of prophesy, teases out what is in the dramatic original merely an apocalyptic subtext. Deploying bravura modalities, the film shows us characters as constructions — Macbeth (Byrne Piven), for instance, is freeze-framed and pixellated — and as fragments dictated to by the witches who use a monitor and keyboard to create and manipulate. "Our masters" (4.1.79) are the technologies that demonic powers enlist to hasten the onset of war and destruction in a world in which, as Bruce Comens observes, apocalypse is primarily communicated via the nuclear "threat of immediate, physical sublimation (vaporization) into the cloud" (Comens 8). But, to adopt a formulation of Jacques Derrida, the "telephone lines or the terminal of this endless computer" (Derrida 27) do not necessarily constitute a flawlessly functioning mechanism: the effects of technology notwithstanding, there is also underscored in *"Macbeth": The Witches' Scenes* an impression of damage and dysfunction. The newsreel displayed is scratched; the witches are pictured using cables as ropes; and jump-leads serve as substitutes for the cauldron's "entrails" (4.1.5). In this sense, in the same moment as the narrative contemplates an apocalypse still to ensue, so does it locate itself in an apocalyptical "afterwards" where systems of communication, and modes of transport, have been grotesquely transformed.

Such a sense of temporal uncertainty also informs the film's engagement with history. At one level, *"Macbeth": The Witches' Scenes* makes a virtue of an imagery that is firmly early modern in orientation. The motif of the skeleton on horseback, for example, which operates so as to announce the arrival of the protagonist, codes Macbeth in terms of the fourth horseman of the apocalypse — in the words of the Geneva Bible, the figure of "Death" who enters "to kill with his sworde, and with ho[n]ger" (Berry 116v). Here, the murderous proclivities of the titular hero are translated into a signifier which expresses specifically anterior associations. Yet, in keeping with its representation of the disruption of time, *"Macbeth": The Witches' Scenes* simultaneously privileges postmodern visual accoutrements that encompass toxic waste, industrial debris, a soldier in a gas mask, flames and the spectacle of an exploding globe. Thanks to productions such as Rogala's, these have become the staple of apocalyptical consciousness, but they also work to place in a contemporary register the concerns of Shakespeare's play:

the cauldron becomes the computer; plague is imagined as virus; and the "fog" and "filthy air" (1.1.11) take on the properties of undesirable pollutants. Competing historical co-ordinates converse with each other in a film that rehearses and merges the apocalypse across a spectrum of historical discontinuity.

Above all, *"Macbeth": The Witches' Scenes* images a postmodern incarnation of the apocalypse in terms of sterility. That concern in *Macbeth* with reproductive failure and the eradication of future generations — which is arguably reflected in the first witch's description of the detumescence of the shipman who will "dwindle, peak and pine" (1.3.22) — is rephrased in *"Macbeth": The Witches' Scenes* in an inset of a child who is glimpsed falling from a climbing frame: in this sequence, a stark realization of crushed opportunity, and the potential for the cessation of life, is afforded. Rita Felski equates the "end of sex" with "discourses of the end of history" (Felski 225) and, certainly, in Rogala's end-charged utterance, there is a connection between the technical engineering of catastrophe and the gradual revelation of the witches who, scarred and half-bearded, appear as both the victims and the perpetrators of cataclysm. Hence, when the film captures the male-dressed witches undressing to display multiple breasts (a phantasmagoric reading of "the best of [their] delights" [4.1.144]), additional ideas, centered upon doubleness, duplication and mutation, are communicated. This, too, is a popular apocalyptic scenario, for, as one critic writes, noting "the symbolic affinity of gender confusion and historical exhaustion," the "destabilization of the male/female divide ... bring[s] with it a waning of temporality, teleology and grand narrative" (Felski 226). Hybridized and paradoxically formulated, the witches in *"Macbeth": The Witches' Scenes* are at one and the same time technologically generative and physically afflicted by the destructive practices for which they themselves are partly responsible.

As befits a production that collapses the junctures between apocalypses, and that unravels the dividing-lines between the sexes, *"Macbeth": The Witches' Scenes* is further characterized by a representative strategy that places the spectator in a state of limbo. Images disintegrate and reassemble, reassemble and disintegrate, with no firm sense either of a stable frame of reference or a linear trajectory. As a result, the film is at its most powerful in promoting a destabilizing, and disorienting, imperative. Hence, with words purposefully failing to match the movement of lips, an illusion of a lack of synchronicity, or a lapse in connection, is created: in this version of Shakespeare, at least, speech and language are no longer the prime origins of meaning or the main routes to interpretation. The key concept here is surely "confusion" (3.5.29) and, because the second witch (Amy Galper) is made up to resemble the perennial image of Shakespeare, further disorientation is encouraged, with the boundary being unhinged between the character and the author, the artist and his creation. Part of the effect of the promotion of an apocalyptic agenda in *"Macbeth": The Witches' Scenes* is to rob the Bard of a traditional sense of possession: no longer can the work be called his own. Authority and text, fiction and reality, all disappear, in Jean Baudrillard's words, behind a computer "screen" of millennial "information [and] ... alienation" (213).

To such a periodically charged utilization of apocalyptic landscapes several implications are attached. Emerging from the film's preoccupation with the collapse of civil society is the suggestion that whatever language has survived from Shakespeare's "original" is tainted: blood is seen emanating from a robot's mouth, pointing up an unsettling equation between words and violence, while the fact that images are scored across with bars of red implies both the imprisoning hold of technology and the possibility of physical assault. And, given the passing over if not the death of the author, the recipient of the implied brutality, as this is engineered in the film's *mise-en-scène*, would seem to be the corpus of the play, *Macbeth*, which, amputated and expurgated, survives only as a remnant of a more familiar manifestation. In the place of Shakespeare is the figure of Macbeth who is represented as endeavouring to overcome his computer-determined status: the end of the film shows him looming towards the camera to deliver the desperately turned realization that he is "accursèd in the calendar" (4.1.150). As Damian Thompson points out, the term "calendar" derives "from the Latin verb *calendare*, meaning to call out" (Thompson 5) to the extent that, in *"Macbeth": The Witches' Scenes*, the protagonist's address to the audience appears a cry for help or, at least, release from an insufferable temporal disjointedness. Yet, as Macbeth's face self-implodes, recalling an earlier montage of a globe discandying, there seems no alternative mode for the character or the world other than the perpetual replay of immolation and disaster.

Apocalyptical Notes

In its recasting of *Macbeth* as a fully-fledged apocalyptic narrative, *"Macbeth": The Witches' Scenes* sets the scene for related transformation strategies as they are undertaken in other Shakespearean filmic undertakings. For example, in *The Angelic Conversation*, *Macbeth* and *The Postman*, apocalyptical subtexts are also magnified into major components for specific thematic purposes. This is nowhere more evident than in the made-for-television production, financed by Channel 4 and the English Shakespeare Company, of *Macbeth*: an apocalyptic frame of reference dominates, the implication being that the characters inhabit a condition of ending. At once in this production, a sense of exhaustion and abandonment is to the fore, as is reflected in the deployment of a used-up quarry (the heath), a former mine (which substitutes for Duncan's [Philip Madoc] headquarters) and empty industrial buildings (serving as Macbeth's [Sean Pertwee] castle). This is an environment, then, which bears upon it the ravages of internecine conflict, which displays in its very constitution apocalyptic markers of depopulation, upset and dereliction. Mark Thornton Burnett notes the predilection for red in *Macbeth*, including the "blood-red spots ... upon Macbeth's white shirt, Lady Macbeth's [Greta Scacchi] ... red dress" and the "bloody hues" with which Duncan is "laced" (Burnett 195), yet neglects to mention the apocalyptic resonances of the property and color. For instance, a bloody redness is inseparable in the film's *mise-en-scène* from the emphasis upon fire, and nowhere more obviously than in the scenes in which Macbeth and Lady Macbeth meet on a fire-escape to plan their intrigue: here, the impression is of a imminent escape from conflagration, of an urgent need to flee an approaching consummation. Elsewhere in *Macbeth*, shots of the castle's courtyard, which reveal a burning brazier, smoke emanating from extractors, oil drums and an abandoned car, function as powerful analogues to metaphors of earthly disturbance and the "great doom's image" (2.3.75). Even before the murder of Duncan has taken place, Macbeth's seat, with its broken windows and bare interiors, appears a "building" from which the "life" (2.3.65) has gone. Working in this way, and building upon suggestions in the play, the production favours an anti–Christian interpretation of the apocalypse, and it is entirely in keeping with this view that the royal residence into which Macbeth moves should be a disused church in which fallen masonry testifies to religious institutions forsaken and affirmative spirituality eclipsed. We are in that moment, it is implied, before the second coming during which the Antichrist reigns. *Macbeth* takes place both inside the end and yet not at the end; it derives its effect from the representation of battles that have not yet been fully won; and it conjures an apocalypse that is as terrifying as it is unfolding.

By contrast, if apocalypse in *Macbeth* is part of a process, in *The Postman*, it has come to a conclusion. In this "spin-off" film, a drifter by the name of "Shakespeare" tours the American midwest putting on performances of the Bard—*Macbeth* is a particular favourite—to eke out a living. Crucially, "Shakespeare" belongs to a not-too-distant futurity (the year is 2013) during which a conflict of apocalyptical proportions has, as the voiceover states, destroyed "the last of the great cities.... ['Shakespeare'] told stories of the three-year winter, and how the dirty snow never stopped falling ... he saw the ocean barren, poisoned." Clearly, this is a vision of apocalypse that owes its inspiration to global warming rather than biblical lore, yet even here there is an echo of the second angel of Revelation pouring a "vial vpon the sea ... and euerie liuing thing dyed in the sea" (Berry 119v). By association, "Shakespeare" and the corpus of work he enacts are what are stable and unchanging in a world of dislocation and collapse. The Bard's works, the film has it, survive because of the natural truths they incarnate — as opposed to the unnaturalness of the circumstances in which they are now acted out. *The Postman* trades upon a humanist essentialism that sees Shakespeare as timeless and, in developing this construction, it underscores the time-afflicted characteristics of the America that is its subject.

Less obviously apocalyptic, at least at first sight, is the art-house reading of Shakespeare's sonnets, *The Angelic Conversation*. The general imagery animating the film has been linked by critics to the "occult beliefs of ... Dr John Dee ... the leading English intellectual of the Elizabethan period whose involvement with the sciences and the cabala was renowned in Europe" (O'Pray 100), yet a closer look at specific motifs demonstrates, in the director's own words, "apocalyptic visions of fire, with ... people lost in eternity" (Jarman 222). Illuminating, then, are the sequences involving a journey assisted by flaming torches, an anonymous man dazzling the camera with a sun-shaped mirror, another anonymous grouping cradling a golden orb and a third figure blowing a trumpet. Innocuous in and of themselves, these moments take on a charged appositeness in the context of the stress in Revelation upon "the heat of fyre," fanfares of trumpets, a "golden censer" and a "woman clothed with the sunne" (Berry 115r, 116r, 117r, 119v), all salient indicators either of the final battle between good and evil or the ascendancy of the heavenly kingdom. Judged against this imagistic investment, the sonnets that *The Angelic Conversation* selects for attention appear less as representations of a free-flowing psychic state and more as utterances concerned with beginning, ending and judgment. The particular visual machinery of the film is instrumental, in this connection, in highlighting those themes centered upon the movement and eventual cessation of time. We hear, for instance, of "the world-without-end" (Sonnet 57.5), of the "sickle-hour" (Sonnet 126.2) and of a lover who will "shine ... bright in these contents" (Sonnet 55.3). Because apocalypse involves a linear progress — from confrontation to irresolution to resolution — so do the sonnets, which have traditionally been slighted for their seeming lack of a definite trajectory, take on the proportions of a more recognizable narrative clarity. If only implicitly, the suggestion is that the lover of the sonnets will be called to account, and will undergo a period of trial, so as to be presented with the possibility of entering a transfigured state of final erotic union.

Dystopian Visions

On the one hand, all three films would seem to prioritize apocalypse so as to support a dystopian reading of the end's meanings and applications. Via periodically charged utilizations of wasted landscapes, and through the deployment of intensely realized framing techniques, the salient features of apocalypses seemingly without redemptive possibility are underscored. Mary Wilson Carpenter asserts that "the words of Revelation ... write a paranoia about the persecution of males by another male (or males)" (Carpenter 110): certainly, in *The Angelic Conversation*, a preoccupation with exploitation and repression is abundantly apparent. The image of a man bearing an oil drum upon his shoulders implies suffering if not slavery, while the rocky and fog-bound territory he traverses points both to a profitless enterprise and to a social system that is repressive, unyielding and hostile. At the same time, the sequence involving a burning car and a man strapped to a stake evokes a climate of pain and exile (industry has made martyrs of its workers), with the recurring motif of the radar serving only to reinforce these suggestions: surveillance, the film would appear to argue, is the sign of a culture anxious about retaliation, aggression and attack. At one level, Revelation is the key here, not least in the film's equation of a smoky netherworld with the "bottomless pit" (Berry 117r) of the end of days. On another level, because the essential subject of *The Angelic Conversation* is love between men, these apocalyptic realizations take on a critical — and contemporary — resonance. Inside such a framework, the shot of a fenced-off area of land comes to function as an indicator of a brutalizing society's policing of its sexual borders and mores. (The radar, in this regard, symbolizes the seeking out of local as well as international examples of perceived infraction). Understood as indicative of an apocalyptical culture's ghettoization of same-sex desire, the sonnets in the film thus speak for if not to a queer agenda: "They that have power to hurt" (Sonnet 94.1) refers to those structures of authority that institute normative notions of sexuality, while "My outcast state" (Sonnet 29.2) alludes to the isolation of a gay subjectivity.

A conservative elaboration of homoeroticism is nowhere more apparent in *The Angelic Conversation* than in the scene in which an emperor is washed and worshipped. Surrounded by black-suited acolytes, and given a cup, crown and pearls, the emperor operates most immediately as a modern cinematic rendering of the Whore of Babylon figure in Revelation who, similarly, is "guilded with ... pearles" and holds "a cup of golde in her hand, ful of abominations, and filthines of her fornication" (Berry 120r). Moreover, in that the emperor is tattooed, a further apocalyptical dimension — centered upon the "mark"— comes into view; as Peter Levi states, "There was a real custom in late antiquity ... to carry the mark of one's private god tattooed on one's body" (*Revelation* 7). Combined with its cabbalistic associations, the sequence purposefully casts a negative judgment upon male same-sex practice through its invocation of the sexually licentious Whore of Babylon figure: the emperor is effeminized, and problematized, by being linked to femaleness and excess. Because the tattoo displayed is a death's head — a skull with horns — one might also suggest that the emperor is cast as a type of Antichrist: Jarman advertises a socially reprehensible image of same-sex desire, a reactionary construction that sees as synonymous male-male sexuality and satanism. These are the assumptions and dominant stereotypes that must be rejected and superseded, the film implies, if homosexuality is to be properly honored and prioritized.

Macbeth, too, articulates apocalypse in a dystopian fashion: it is not so much the specifics of Revelation that are conjured, however, as a world lacking in authenticity. Thus, when he encounters the witches for the second time, Macbeth is greeted with a vision in which dolls and shop dummies substitute for the show of kings: what is apocalyptic about this procession that stretches to the "crack of doom" (4.1.133) is the implication that the future is robotic and lacking in human agency or intervention: all that is revealed is a demonstration of plastic casings without substance. We are, then, in that phantasmagoric universe which Jean Baudrillard defines as operating according to "a principle of simulation" and "not of reality" (120). The idea is extended into the opening scene in which the witches, surrounded by rubbish, glimpse Macbeth riding on a motorbike on a television monitor: favouring, in Gabriel Weimann's words, a "reconstructed image of war" (280), the production makes clear that any conflict is meaningless in so far as it has already taken place. Apocalypse, in this sense, is to be bewailed rather than celebrated: the fight for godly ascendancy falters, it is suggested, in a welter of mediated representations and images. If the dummies are unsettlingly hollow, so too is the victory achieved by Malcolm (Jack Davenport) and his troops. The concluding montage reveals a triumphal entry on a Land Rover to the tinny rendition of the hymn "Jerusalem" on a portable loudspeaker. The music, second-hand and pre-recorded, is available only as an afterthought of an untenable history: neither live nor present, it fails to form part of an affirmative simultaneity. Moreover, the hymn's aspiration towards the attainment of heaven — the promised end — is ironically undercut by a montage that establishes that we are still in the world of "dark satanic mills" (Blake 480–81), even if that world is phrased in postmodern terms. Apocalypse is dystopian in *Macbeth* in that it appears so radically divorced from any redemptive alternative.

Such a dystopian phase of apocalypse is also at work in *The Postman* —

and in such a way as to recall the twentieth century's most far-reaching manifestation of millenarianism. Following a successful performance, "Shakespeare" is forced into labor in the quarries by the Holnists, a tyrannical organization presided over by Bethlehem (Will Patton), a general opposed to multicultural reproduction and a democratic futurity. Terming himself as a "father" to his "clan," Bethlehem refuses ethnic diversity in his ranks and presides over a camp whose harsh regime is modelled upon militaristic lines. This, then, is nothing less than a fantasy of a secular millennial kingdom, a neo-fascist projection that elevates the "*führer*" into a type of deity and that, by espousing white supremacy, gives credence to a monomaniacal version of the future in which the singular ruler is paramount. It is here that the connections binding fascism and the apocalypse come into their own. As Andrew Hewitt states: "fascism seems to have become the privileged modality of the apocalypse, functioning both spatially as a totalitarian model of society's destructive self-completion, and temporally through a rhetoric of 'final' solutions, of ends and thousand-year regimes without end" (Hewitt 18). To promote his agenda, Bethlehem uses Shakespeare, with inspiration being taken, crucially, from the Roman and history plays. Yet Bethlehem rarely uses Shakespeare transparently; rather, the Bard is parodied and manipulated to serve a self-aggrandizing purpose. For example, when Bethlehem cites *Julius Caesar*'s line, "Cry 'havoc' and let slip the dogs of war" (3.1.276), he passes over the fact that the speech originates with Anthony, not Caesar: the former merely ventriloquizes the latter's spirit so that the evil of his murder may be popularly revenged. Concerned with shoring up his own kudos, Bethlehem is centred only upon the enactment of Caesar as a face-value imperialist. In a later citation, Bethlehem quotes from *Henry V* and the "We few, we happy few, we band of brothers" (4.3.60) address: once again, parody enters the fray, for here a specious summoning of camaraderie is the excuse for the idea of a master-race — and a master — to be disseminated. The dystopian dimensions of apocalypse show themselves in *The Postman* in the cinematic rendering of modern history; they are also revealed in the extent to which Shakespeare is disallowed from speaking for a sacralizing purpose and robbed of his communal relevance.

Utopian Prospects

On the other hand, this grouping of films endeavours to counter a dystopian tendency by simultaneously rehearsing a utopian construction of apocalypse. "Ideas of renewal and revivification," as Carolyn Jess-Cooke puts it in her chapter, are equally inscribed into the fabric of the apocalyptical Shakespeare film, and in such a way as to pinpoint a vision of inspired vin-

In *The Postman* (1997), "Shakespeare," played by Kevin Costner, leads a struggling remnant back to freedom in a post-apocalyptic world (Photofest).

dication, judicious reconstruction and psychic repair. *The Postman* is no exception to this rule. At first, "Shakespeare" owes the success of his trade to the skill with which he parodies the Bard: hence, in a performance of *Macbeth* for villagers, he delivers the prophetic parts of the play (5.5.42–43) in a mocking manner, and in this he is ably assisted by his mule. The man-animal double-act has the effect of generating laughter and uniting the community: the demonality of the play is undercut with comedy, tyranny and absolutism are banished via the transformation of the instruments of their representation, and the present is privileged through the reduction of an anticipation of what is to come. Notably, "Tomorrow, and tomorrow" (5.5.18) is rendered in a vernacular idiom ("till the day after that" replaces "tomorrow"), which works to strip the soliloquy of its alarming implications and to palliate the prospect of a meaningless future. On the whole, "Shakespeare" denudes Shakespeare and executes a therapeutic function by robbing the plays of their worse apocalyptical imaginings.

In a different context, however, this approach to Shakespeare takes on a more openly political cast. Installed in the quarries, "Shakespeare" replies to Bethlehem's citations with his own Bardic extracts, delivering snippets from Hamlet's soliloquy ("To be or not to be, that is the question" [3.1.58]) and Richard III's solitary reflection ("Now is the winter of our discontent / Made glorious summer by this son of York" [1.1.1–2]). Within the purview of a neo-fascist environment these quotations serve both to promote a debate about a political dictatorship and to spotlight the condition of the oppressed and the marginalized. Shakespeare thus becomes, at one level, a force with which to deal with adversity and even, as the film continues, a locus of democratic instincts implicitly placed against an imperialist hegemony. Such a collision of ideologies is realized when, later still, "Shakespeare" prepares for his final confrontation with Bethlehem by intoning to himself Henry V's "Once more unto the breach" (3.1.1) peroration. Crucially, the disappearance of parody in the voiceover points to a more transfiguring cultural deployment of Shakespeare, to an internalization of the Bard's resistant potential, and to a new agenda of action. No longer is "Shakespeare" equated with philosophy or rejection; instead, he is indissoluble from an assertive masculinity. With this development comes a further connection: on his way to challenge the character who is a version of Macbeth (Bethlehem), "Shakespeare" incarnates Macduff or, at least, an Anthony, an underdog and a spirit of fruitful change.

Thanks in part to his use of Shakespeare, "Shakespeare" is able to reinstitute the U.S. Postal Service. This development, it is suggested, grows out of the exchanges of conversation that accompany positivist Shakespearean applications. The words of letters are the figurative expression of the ways in which "Shakespeare" inaugurates social transfiguration through Bardic reinvention. And it is salutary here that it is children who send and receive letters, with *The Postman* making clear that a shared future resides in just such generation-specific acts of contact and communication. Once again, if only implicitly, "Shakespeare" emerges as an anti–Macbethian figure and a spokesperson for historical continuity. According to Derrida, apocalypse is constituted by acts of "sending" and "dispatch," and this is in part because John of Patmos, the assumed author of Revelation, is "the one who ... receives mail" and subsequently "transmits a message" (Derrida 26). Hence, in apocalypse, "everything speculates on messengers and postmen ... the announcement of the news" (Derrida 31). Judged in this light, "Shakespeare" operates most significantly both as an agent of restitution and as a herald for a condition of apocalyptical improvement.

In this process, "Shakespeare" is represented as gradually shedding the properties of the characters and taking on the mantle of his namesake. Like Shakespeare, "Shakespeare" is hailed as a "saviour, a godsend," as the "greatest man who ever lived." The elaboration of the trajectory that shows "Shakespeare" transformed from drifter to hero mimes, in certain respects, the narratives of bardolatry that, through history, have helped to elevate Shakespeare into a continuing repository of universal humanism and essentialism. It is entirely in keeping with this logic, then, that, at the end of *The Postman*, the symbolic importance of "Shakespeare" should be naturalized: he finds his life partner in a verdant community entitled "Pineview," and he becomes father to a daughter named "Hope." There is a telling implication of resurrection and new life here; there is also an apocalyptical prognosis of redemption.

The closer one looks at Shakespeare film the more vividly a utopian construction of apocalypse comes into view. Thus, in *Macbeth*, the prospect of a universal descent into the worse millennial manifestations can be countered, as in *The Postman*, by a reification of nature as an affirmative living property. Exchanges among the rank and file take place in a stable, suggesting a still applicable relation between human and non-human worlds, while the "testing" of Macduff (Lorcan Cranitch) unfolds in the grounds of an English country house: the greenery on display and the sounds of peacocks both bring to mind the absence of references to birds in the scenes involving Macbeth's castle and hint at a replacement for the urban apocalyptical blight of elsewhere. But it is in *The Angelic Conversation* that a redemptive notion of apocalypse receives its most sustained statement. Interestingly, this initially takes the form of a visually erotic rather than a strictly theological interpretation of the end of days. For instance, shots of juxtaposed male bodies indicate that the film is concerned less, in Peter Levi's phrase, with "John of Patmos' conversations with angels" (*Revelation* 3), still less, to adopt a formulation of William Pencak, with John Dee's "fortune-telling tools for conversing with angels" (Pencak 89), and far more with dialogues and exchanges among men that have a transformative social and cultural effect. The ethos of the film is purposefully demythologizing (one musical theme is entitled "How to destroy angels"), and this is reinforced in the female voiceover by Judi Dench which lends an anti-patriarchal air to the Bardic proceedings.

Yet, popular theological elements are not entirely lacking in *The Angelic Conversation*, not least in the scene in which an anonymous man, against a background of apocalyptical flames, and to the sound of gunfire, wrestles with his own shadow. Matching the questioning of the sonnets, the sequence activates an impression of a questioning of inner demons as much as it analogizes institutional conflict and persecution: this is a figure obliged to fight with himself and his world. It is here that the anti-hegemonic tendencies of *The Angelic Conversation* are articulated with a particular force, for, in the context of a battle with powers within and without, the film announces itself as an exercise in nothing less than what Mary Wilson Carpenter has termed a "gay apocalyptic" or an "apocalyptic of the closet" that hinges upon a "pervasive concern with issues of secrecy/disclosure, knowledge/ignorance, private/public" (Carpenter 109, 119–20). Brought vividly to mind here, I think, is the biblical story of Jacob wrestling the angel of God (perhaps God himself) in Genesis 32.24–28. In this archetypal myth, in which Jacob only stops fighting when he is blessed by the "Man" (who also renames him Israel), a powerful equation of inner and outer, and new and old (arguably sexual) identities, is suggested. Not surprisingly, then, *The Angelic Conversation* invests in a series of events of movement and "coming out": thanks to his battles, one subject, at least, can achieve sexual and psychic progress. This is underscored in a sequence in which a man, illuminating a cave-like interior with a flare, finally emerges into the day: the idea is both of a lover who will "shine ... bright in these contents" (Sonnet 55.3) and of an approach to enlightenment. The recurring deployment of the motif of water makes a similar point. Shots of a young man in water, coupled with images of flowers, illustrate an arrival at a pastoral-idyllic destination or a journey whose sexual orientation is naturally legitimated. Such is the film's conception of a condition of perfection, one which, recalling the lives of "kings" (Sonnet 29.14), facilitates a state of calm between men and a "Return of love" (Sonnet 56.12). Apocalypse deferred, the film implies, allows for apocalypse realized, a state of affairs in which the eroticisation of the male form finally — and paradoxically — comes to assume a quasi-religious intensity.

Millennial Blurrings

To suggest that the Shakespearean apocalyptic film rests secure in its utopian aspirations, however, would be a mistake. For, even as *The Angelic Conversation*, *Macbeth* and *The Postman* yearn for an escape-route from apocalyptical despair, so do they fall into ideological impasses that would seem to mitigate against and even decommission positivist resolution. Indeed, more generally in the films, one is left in a state of limbo or indecision that, refracting one definition of apocalypse, confounds neat distinctions between dystopian and redemptive scenarios. *The Angelic Conversation* is typical. The ending may suggest a paradise regained (a glorious future), but it simultaneously points to a utopia lost (a past never to be recovered): revealing is the final sequence in which an anonymous figure looks through a mullioned window as the voiceover recalls "beauty's summer dead" (Sonnet 104.14). Implied is the impossibility of a restorative time, and figuratively actualized is a mixed condition constituted by forward and backward projection, dream and "reality," retrospection and anticipation. *Macbeth* is no less ambivalent in focus. Hence, a compromised Malcolm celebrates victory in the same moment as the body of Macbeth is tipped onto the debris of the heath by a dumper: the film's alternating between the figures creates a third space between two dominant constructions of apocalypse in which the arch-criminal and the supposed redeemer are each allowed critical attention.

In themselves, such blurrings between apocalyptical paradigms are only to be expected. Damian Thompson writes that the "juxtaposition" and "coexistence" of discordant "features" defines "visions" (Thompson 58) of the end, while Frank Kermode comments that apocalypse defies easy categorizations because it transports our "usual apprehension" of things into "another order of time" (84). If these are films that appear unable to decide between which modality of apocalypse to prioritize, then this is realized with a peculiar immediacy in *The Postman*, a work in which the central conflict between Bethlehem and "Shakespeare" appears less diagrammatic as the narrative progresses. One difficulty is that, in the place of Bethlehem's imperialism, "Shakespeare" develops a fledgling postal service that brings to mind an unreflective manifestation of American patriotism. Richard Burt notes that the film's elaboration of "democracy" is "contradictory" and that its "wannabe progressive politics" are continually "compromised" (155, 156): a potent illustration of the thesis can be found, I suggest, in the ways in which the "Shakespearean" enterprise is modelled along the lines of a now commodified and brand-name U.S. institution, the "Pony Express." Both the young horse riders fictionalized in the film, and the speed and efficiency with which they expand horizons of knowledge and geography, suggest a cultural commemoration of the mailmen who, from 1860 to 1861, sought the fastest postal routes across the western states in the interests of securing a million dollar government contract. In the literature on the subject, the "Pony Express" is invariably extolled as an incarnation of empire-building, as an example of the frontier spirit, and as a seminal element in the systems of communication that enabled the Union to win the Civil War (Benson). That represented endeavour by "Shakespeare" to go beyond an apocalyptical version of tyranny and absolutism is, in fact, called into question by the contextual underpinnings of his proposed alternative. "Shakespeare" fails in countering imperialism, for what he represents is not sufficiently different in its essential contours and outlines. An apocalyptical future America may be challenged in *The Postman*, but it is not altogether rejected: the forces that come in Bethlehem's wake are themselves constituted by the very nationalist ideology that they would ostensibly resist.

Conclusions

In Shakespearean studies in recent years much has been made of the new turn towards spirituality. Critics influenced by a "presentist" orientation argue that the works are important — and even enduring — in that they sacralize salient religious truths; such truths, moreover, rather than being resistant to theoretical applications, are enriched and highlighted when juxtaposed with ideological and/or political critique. One wonders if the interest in Shakespeare and apocalypse on film — and arguably this book — belongs with such a critical imperative. Do Shakespeare films, in line with some interpretations of deconstruction, offer us salvific or fideistic approaches to ending? Do they incarnate the apocalypse according to a logic of "promise" and "democracy"? This essay has suggested that, such is the conflicted movement of Shakespeare-apocalypse films and their representation of Revelation, answers to these sorts of questions can never confidently be in the affirmative; and here it may be helpful to remember that Derrida, for all his reification of "enlightenment," may be seen as a materialist-pragmatist critic who, in the same moment as he writes, "I shall come," qualifies such an assertion with the formulation, "the coming is always to come" (25).

If constructions of the Shakespearean apocalypse on film do not underscore faith — or, if they do, this occurs only in a piecemeal fashion — what agenda do they subscribe to? Perhaps Fredric Jameson's concept of a "crisis in historicity" (22) might come to our assistance here. The "great doom's image" in Shakespeare films is responsive to the particularities and contexts of its moment of production. That moment is determined by perceived crises of various kinds, from global warming and technological breakdown to sexual repression and the rise of political tyranny. In airing these preoccupations, works such as *The Angelic Conversation*, *"Macbeth": The Witches' Scenes*, *Macbeth* and *The Postman* are acutely politically freighted: they rehearse mediated images and ideas in order to intervene in prognosis and prophecy, and they canvass multiple apocalypses (which can be identified at the level of beginning, process, termination and limbo) as part of a passing of judgment upon present and future social and cultural circumstances. Too, the films discussed in this essay make a virtue of the Shakespeare and apocalypse connection. Both categories with a global reach, Shakespeare and apocalypse function most sublimely as vehicles of explanation, measures of meaning, and repositories of wisdom and lore. Both entrenched as interpretive paradigms, the two have been forced into dialogue by the needs and requirements of postmodernity. Hence, what lasts (Shakespeare) enters into dialogue with what might change (apocalypse), with the Bard and the millennium themselves altering in composition and appearance in the wake of their continuing partnership. Apocalypse as a technological phenomenon takes energy from the recreation of early modern theater in the sphere of television, cinema and mass media, and notions of the end consort with the symbolic capital of Shakespeare so as to pursue commentary on the concerns of a crucial juncture in history. Apocalypses revisited reshape Shakespeare for postmodernity, and Shakespeares revived allow the apocalypse to play itself out in ever more pertinent combinations and employments.

Works Cited

The Angelic Conversation. Dir. Derek Jarman. 1985. DVD. Dolmen, 2004.

Baudrillard, Jean. *Jean Baudrillard: Selected Writings.* Ed. Mark Poster. Cambridge: Polity, 1988.

Bensen, Joe. *The Traveler's Guide to the Pony Express Trail.* Helena, Montana: Falcon, 1995.

Berry, Lloyd E., ed. *The Geneva Bible: A Facsimile of the 1560 Edition.* Madison: University of Wisconsin Press, 1969.

Blake, William. *Complete Writings.* Ed. Geoffrey Keynes. Oxford: Oxford University Press, 1976.

Burnett, Mark Thornton. "Local *Macbeth*/global Shakespeare: Scotland's screen destiny." *Shakespeare and Scotland.* Ed. Willy Maley and Andrew Murphy. Manchester: Manchester University Press, 2004. 189–206.

Burt, Richard. *Unspeakable ShaXXXspeares: Queer Theory and American Kiddie Culture.* 2nd ed. New York: Palgrave, 1998.

Carpenter, Mary Wilson. "Representing Apocalypse: Sexual Politics and the Violence of Revelation." *Postmodern Apocalypse: Theory and Cultural Practice at the End.* Ed. Richard Dellamora. Philadelphia: University of Pennsylvania Press, 1995. 107–135.

Chalmers, Sarah. "Armageddon 2012." *Daily Mail* 26 Feb. 2007: 15.

Comens, Bruce. *Apocalypse and After: Modern Strategy and Postmodern Tactics in Pound, Williams, and Zukofsky.* Tuscaloosa: University of Alabama Press, 1995.

Derrida, Jacques. "Of an Apocalyptic Tone Recently Adopted in Philosophy." *The Oxford Literary Review* 6.2 (1984): 3–37.

Feaster, Felicia. "Living in Oblivion: Apocalypse Cinema at the End of the Millennium." *Art Papers* 23.6 (1999): 20–27.

Felski, Rita. "*Fin de Siècle, Fin de Sexe*: Transsexuality, Postmodernism, and the Death of History." *Centuries' Ends/Narrative Means.* Ed. Robert Newman. Stanford: Stanford University Press, 1996. 225–37.

Hewitt, Andrew. "Coitus Interruptus: Fascism and the Deaths of History." *Postmodern Apocalypse: Theory and Cultural Practice at the End.* Ed. Richard Dellamora. Philadelphia: University of Pennsylvania Press, 1995. 17–40.

Jameson, Fredric. *Postmodernism, or, the Cultural Logic of Late Capitalism.* London and New York: Verso, 1991.

Jarman, Derek. *Dancing Ledge.* London: Quartet, 1984.

Kermode, Frank. *The Sense of an Ending: Studies in the Theory of Fiction.* New York: Oxford University Press, 1967.

"Macbeth": The Witches' Scenes. Dir. Miroslaw Rogala. Facets, 1988.

Macbeth. Dir. Michael Bogdanov. Videocassette. Channel Four, 1997.

McLaren, Peter. "George Bush, Apocalypse Sometime Soon, and the American Imperium." *Cultural Studies/Critical Methodologies* 2.3 (2002): 327–33.

Newman, Robert. Introduction. *Centuries' Ends/Narrative Means.* Ed. Robert Newman. Stanford: Stanford University Press, 1996. 1–12.

O'Pray, Michael. *Derek Jarman: Dreams of England.* London: BFI, 1996.

Pencak, William. *The Films of Derek Jarman.* Jefferson, NC: McFarland, 2002.

The Postman. Dir. Kevin Costner. 1997. DVD. Warner Brothers, 1998.

The Revelation of John. Introd. by Peter Levi. London: Kyle Cathie, 1992.

Shakespeare, William. *The Norton Shakespeare.* Ed. Stephen Greenblatt, Walter Cohen, Jean E. Howard, and Katharine Eisaman Maus. New York: W. W. Norton, 1997.

Thompson, Damian. *The End of Time: Faith and Fear in the Shadow of the Millennium.* London: Sinclair-Stevenson, 1996.

Weimann, Gabriel. *Communicating Unreality: Modern Media and the Reconstruction of Reality.* London: Sage, 2000.

Zamora, Lois Parkinson. *Writing the Apocalypse: Historical Vision in Contemporary U.S. and Latin American Fiction.* Cambridge: Cambridge University Press, 1989.

2

Apocalyptic Paternalism, Family Values, and the War of the Cinemas; or, How Shakespeare Became Posthuman

Courtney Lehmann

Four hundred years after the curious skirmish known as the "War of the Theaters," a markedly similar phenomenon has taken hold of the cinema, emerging in films that purport to represent the Renaissance and, particularly, its bankside beacon, Shakespeare. Revolving around a fundamental division, as Richard Helgerson has persuasively argued, between a "players' theater" and an "authors' theater," the War was really a bid for social preferment and economic survival in a culture making an uneven transition from patronage to market forces.[1] On one side, the proponents of the "authors' theater" strove to distinguish the singularity of their poetry from its debased embodiment on stage, catering to a privileged clientele through learned plays performed by elite children's companies, whose combined objective was to disparage the unsophisticated audiences and common players associated with the public amphitheaters. On the other side, the so-called "players' theater" remained the "caviar" of "the general."[2] Refusing the lure of more privatized venues such as Blackfriars and St. Paul's, as well as the social division of labor between players and "authors" which, for figures like Shakespeare, proved a paradox, advocates of the "players' theater" continued to rely on collaborative authorship, adult actors, and popular themes for their plays — but not without leaving scathing rejoinders in their wake.[3] Nevertheless, what distinguished the War as a bizarre interlude in the English theater's ongoing struggle for respectability was the way in which *children* came to mediate this debate. As the most "impressionable" members of society (a fact that Renaissance child-rearing manuals anxiously certify), children were used and, often, abused by both sides as mouthpieces for cultural changes they were poised to inherit but not benefit from — since, with any luck, they would live to become the adults who were the very subject of their spite.[4] Although the War of the Theaters was a small-scale, short-lived contest of wits enacted on both page and stage, it had a lasting impact on the repertories, venues, and reputation through which Renaissance theater culture was understood and experienced.

What I wish to explore here are the ways in which children are currently being linked to Renaissance power plays in the *cinema*, wherein, I will argue, the terms of the War have been reinvented along the axis of gender. Whether present as implied audiences, conspicuous absences, or actual performers, children have emerged in recent years as an unlikely hermeneutic for articulating the rival claims of the "authors' cinema" and what I will call the "cybercinema." Representing the "authors' cinema," films such as *Shakespeare in Love* (dir. John Madden, 1998), *Dangerous Beauty* (dir. Marshall Herscovitz, 1998), and Adrian Noble's *A Midsummer Night's Dream* (1996) offer highly-romantic and unabashedly anachronistic takes on the Renaissance by recreating it as an author's paradise. Literalizing the Renaissance trope that conflates supple writing surfaces with the female body, these films represent authorship as an erotic and, ultimately, male prerogative, often performed for the prurient gaze of young boys eager to learn how to become men.[5] By contrast, films from *Shakespeare: The Animated Tales*[6] series, as well as Julie Taymor's *Titus* (2000) and Christine Edzard's *The Children's A Midsummer Night's Dream* (2001) adapt Shakespeare's cautionary tales of political tyranny and patriarchal absolutism as allegories of authorship which, provocatively, employ children in ways that return us to the contested terrain of female authorship in the Renaissance. Indeed, children figured centrally in the complex nexus of filiation, encryption, and self-abnegation that precipitated Renaissance women's entry into print — a precarious process that Wendy Wall describes, appropriately, as "dancing in a net" (*Imprint of Gender* 279). In keeping with this precedent, contemporary Shakespeare films by the feminist vanguard resist situating children as the offspring of a unilateral and frequently violent process of "impressment," locating them instead within a *systems* environment that privileges flows across and between boundaries. In light of important recent work focusing on plural authorship and textual economies in which women function only as metaphors for collateral and, often, homoerotic exchanges between men,[7] these films invite us to imagine both early modern and postmodern authorship in a more dynamic, cybernetic context in which optimization supplants eroticization and collaboration is understood not as reciprocity but as complex circuitry, born of fluid combinations of "the organic, the technical, and the textual" (Haraway, *Simians* 212).

Although systems theory is a relatively recent invention of the computer age, systems themselves are as old as the universe, accounting for how complex biological, mechanical, and conceptual "organisms" become self-regulating. Cybernetics, which is a critical sub-field of systems theory, is concerned with how mechanisms of communications and control — foremost among them, feedback — use information to produce homeostasis or, alternatively, entropy. Cybernetic theory offers a particularly useful bridge between the early modern and postmodern concerns of this essay because it explores the gap that separates a potentially democratizing implementation of communication technology from what Donna Haraway calls the "informatics of domination," or, the militaristic deployment of C^3I (command-control-communication-intelligence). Akin to Haraway's socialist-feminist objective of "recoding communication and intelligence to subvert command and control" (*Simians* 175),[8] I will consider how the *cinematics* of domination may be subverted by an oppositional approach to authorship — one that derives from the communication technology of Renaissance child-rearing practices.

In social systems such as families, children play a central role as channels through which information passes and is fed back into the system as a means of achieving equilibrium. Within the sex-gender system of the English Renaissance, however, children were considered to be dangerously capable of altering the feedback loop, particularly during the formative years in which boys and girls were in the care of women. As critical sites for the inculcation of authority, children also became the locus of competing ideas of authorship. Aspiring women writers, for example, used children to subvert gender protocols against female speech while communicating legacies that were legally denied to them by their culture. As Wall explains of the emergent discourse of the maternal legacy, pregnant women leveraged the presumption of their death in childbirth against the stigma of print, publishing advice to their unborn children and, in so doing, achieving immortality for themselves. What is fascinating about this authorial dynamic is not only the way in which children come to be positioned, paradoxically, as "midwives" but also the fact that, long before the advent of poststructuralism, Renaissance women acknowledged the "death of the author" as constitutive of the birth of the text.

Remarkably, the work of the feminist filmmaking vanguard that I will discuss here reproduces this dynamic by employing children as the birthing agents of their cinematic narratives and, more importantly, as the repository of subversive codes of conduct in a system which, like cinema itself, cannot function without such collaboration. By contrast, the films of the authors' cinema appear bent on decoupling their portraits of authorship from the contingencies of collaboration and, to this end, either eliminate children altogether or position them as guardians of a resolutely patriarchal status quo. A variation on the Renaissance theme of primogeniture, children in the authors' cinema are charged with maintaining system equilibrium at all costs. To import the terms of cybernetics into what I am calling the "war of the cinemas," then, whereas the authors' cinema situates children as mechanisms of *control* operating in a "closed" or autonomous system, the cybercinema positions children as mechanisms of *communication* within an "open" system, which depends on interaction with its surrounding environment to evolve. In what follows, I will focus on the point at which children become the site of convergence between cultural assumptions about gender and authorship, and what happens to the equation — indeed, the system — when these terms do not comply with each other.

* * *

It is a striking coincidence that Adrian Noble's 1996 version of *A Midsummer Night's Dream* and Julie Taymor's 1999 film, *Titus*, position a child at the threshold of entry into their respective cinemascapes. Noble's addition of an anonymous boy observer and Taymor's considerable augmentation of the role of Young Lucius lead to uncanny similarities between these two very different films: both situate the boy as a semi-interactive witness linking the filmic frame to the play; both employ a "rabbit hole" effect through which the boy falls from the frame into the world of the film-proper; and both contain a somewhat ominous, leather-clad, goggles-sporting motorcyclist who transports the boy at a critical juncture in each film. Yet what is even more remarkable is that the role of the child is played by the *same* actor: Osheen Jones. Whether or not Taymor consciously intended *Titus* to be a re-make of Noble's *Dream*, Jones's presence in both films produces a *mise-en-abyme* effect that leads to an unexpected feedback loop between them, particularly when we realize that Jones plays a character whose age, in terms of Renaissance child-rearing practices, would place him at the threshold of passage from maternal to paternal care. Hence, although in Noble's film the boy's ultimate rejection of the mother appears to seal his education in and perpetuation of patriarchal tyranny, we cannot help but recognize this same boy as the slightly older and wiser young Lucius who, in Taymor's *Titus*, actually becomes a mother himself. As we shall see, in his later incarnation as Young Lucius, Jones causes an unbearable surge of entropy in the otherwise self-contained system that characterizes Adrian Noble's *A Midsummer Night's Dream*.

Fears about the adverse effects of prolonged exposure to female nurture were particularly high in late sixteenth- and early seventeenth-century England, which witnessed a Puritanical revival of the doctrine of original sin. The ensuing cultural hysteria surrounding children and their "proper" education was based on the "deadly fear of the liability of children to corruption and sin, particularly those cardinal sins of pride and disobedience," to which women were considered exceptionally prone (Stone 125). Consequently, Puritan ex-patriot John Robinson warns in his 1628 treatise on education that although "children, in their first days, have the greater benefit of good mothers, not only because they suck their milk, but in a sort, their manners also, by being continually with them, and receiving their first impressions from them," when "they come to their riper years, good fathers are more behoveful for their forming in virtue and good manners, by their greater wisdom and authority: and oftentimes also, by *correcting the fruits of their mother's indulgence, by their severity*" (11, my emphasis). Robinson's invocation of a gender-segregated system of child rearing, presided over by biological mother and father, respectively, is an extremely efficient rendering of the elaborate network of surrogate parenting to which children in the Renaissance were subject. This bifurcated system of nurture began with wet nurses, serving women, and sundry other female domestics who, in the case of male pre-adolescents, were abruptly replaced by all-male "households," constituted by the authoritarian environment of schools, apprenticeships, and universities. A boy's first encounter with these more "severe" sites of nurture would likely be the Latin classroom, which, as Wall explains, "was designed to correct the faults inculcated in the female and vernacular world of early childhood. Hyperdetermined against a gender- and class-based commonality, Latin enabled the production of the 'closed male environment' of academia, as well as the professional and courtly institutions it fed" ("'Household Stuff'" 5). Yet the violence of this learning process, which often entailed beatings with a rod, ferula, or other suitably phallic objects, betrays the extent to which gender education in the Renaissance was not the product of a "closed male environment" but, rather, a dangerously open system wherein biological sex and gender did not always agree with each other. Under such circumstances, then, might the male child be prone toward emulating *either* end of the spectrum of parental surrogation to which he had been exposed?[9] In other words, in a cultural milieu wherein gender is an ongoing performance rather than a fixed destination, *could* the maternal legacy exert a pull beyond the household — or, indeed, the grave — coaxing the male child back into the more fluid "social alliances" and "common" citational practices he enjoyed while still in the company of women?[10]

By framing his adaptation of Shakespeare's play with a preadolescent boy who becomes a site of the competing gender impressions that Robinson anxiously invokes, Noble's version of *Dream* implicitly begs this question. The film begins in the boy's bedroom, which, significantly, is not marked as distinctly feminine or masculine. In fact, the only prevailing sign of the child's interests is the puppet theater that the camera momentarily lingers over, suggesting the performative, provisional relationship between identity-formation and play production that the boy — if he is to become a man, let alone an author — must come to reject. Nevertheless, the fear that the boy has not yet made the necessary transition from maternal nurture to paternal emulation and, therefore, is susceptible to "corruption" by the twin sins of pride and disobedience born of bad (female) example is broached in the very first scene; here, the boy is represented as a sympathetic witness to Hermia's defiance of her father's will and to Hippolyta's decision to slap Theseus as she exits the room, an interpolated expression of her disgust with his threat to subject Hermia to the strict Athenian law that polices female sexuality with death. That the plight of these women has made an impression on the boy is implied by his ensuing fascination with Helena, whose plan to pursue Demetrius into the woods causes the boy to run after her and, in his excitement, accidentally propel himself out of a second-story window. The clash of child-rearing systems thus begins when he falls down a distinctly uterine-shaped shoot out of the comforts of his home and into the film-proper, shrieking "Mummy!" only to find himself deposited in the all-male "household" of Oberon and Puck's fairy kingdom. And, as in the Athenian world he left behind, the boy soon learns that the specter of female insubordination also haunts the green world, for Titania is denying Oberon's bed and refusing to hand over the Indian child (also played by Osheen Jones), who is the subject of their custodial dispute. In representing Jones's boy as an outsider looking into Titania's system, while presenting his alter ego as a figure trapped within this system, Noble cleverly materializes the crisis of the male child's riven subjectivity at the "breeching" age, that is, the point at which a boy must abandon the company of women and, quite literally, learn to "wear the pants."[11] But Noble goes one step further to dramatize the rejection of *all* bonds — including those between men — that might corrupt the feedback loop that perpetuates the dynastic chain between fathers and sons.

Accordingly, although we might expect the film to valorize Oberon and Puck's surrogate parenting of the boy as an alternative to the "common" and "indulgent" system of maternal nurture to which he has evidently grown accustomed, Noble proceeds to render the relationship between Oberon and Puck as one that revolves around deviance and, even, sodomy. For example, the first time the boy encounters Oberon and Puck, he sees them engage in a passionate kiss after a series of flirtatious verbal and physical exchanges.

Later, when Oberon discovers that his script has miscarried due to Puck's improvisations, Noble glosses this moment of textual deviation as evidence of Puck's sexual aberration; begging Oberon's forgiveness on all fours, Puck pulls down his pants and invites Oberon to spank him — a form of punishment that both parties clearly enjoy. By presenting the commerce between Puck and Oberon through the lens of nonprocreative sexual relations and, therefore, as a threat to the autonomous reproduction of the system, Noble's film unwittingly recapitulates the editorial tradition that considers collaboration to be synonymous with "corruption."[12] And what could be more corrupt than Noble's implication that the perfect complement to Oberon's sodometrical relationship with Puck would be the boy's entry into this perverse partnership as an apt pupil for pederasty? It is little wonder that the boy appears to be utterly terrified of Oberon, whose authority he must nevertheless learn to emulate. Thus, it is Noble who, as an extension of Oberon, takes it upon himself to break the boy to the rod, by demonstrating its proper function in the realm of "normative," that is, reproductive sexual and textual relations, wherein the boy will come to recognize that learning how to become a man involves schooling *women*.

* * *

Look what kinde of words or behaviour thou wouldst
dislike from thy servant or childe, those must thou
not give to thine husband, for thou art equally
commanded to be subject.
— William Whately, *A Bride-Bush: or a
direction for married persons* (1619)[13]

If the fundamental goal of cybernetic systems is to maximize the capacity to communicate and, therefore, replicate, then the greatest threat to this self-sustaining equilibrium is the potential for "noise" or disorganization that increases with the repeated transmission of information, raising the level of entropy to potentially unsustainable levels. As Lisa Trahair explains, entropy is defined "algorithmically" as "the maximum amount of disorganization permitted before what is perceived as a system is transformed into another system" (198). In an effort to prevent such transformation, systems develop an "algorithm for redundancy," a built-in maintenance program that that 1) detects external influences; 2) monitors corresponding internal changes; and 3) performs adjustments to regulate operations. This maintenance function is precisely the role assigned to the boy in Noble's film, for in the context of the patriarchal sex-gender system at stake in *Dream*, children are critical components of this cultural hardware as literal repositories of the code for system redundancy. Our first indication that Jones's boy is aiding rather than aggravating system maintenance is the fact that, like Shakespeare's Oberon, he becomes increasingly associated with an omnipotent, "god's eye" perspective, looking down on the drama from the oculus of his puppet theater. Even more striking is the boy's shift from observer to participant, when Noble suddenly reveals him to be literally pulling Oberon and Puck's strings, lifting them out of the playing space to set the stage for Titania's roll in the hay with Bottom. Unlike Shakespeare's play, as well as other cinematic adaptations of *Dream*, in Noble's film, the boy actually accompanies Bottom and Titania on their tryst, as Bottom takes his diminutive dominatrix and the boy on an *E. T.*-style (motorcycle) ride across the moon to the fairy queen's bower.[14] Yet not even this striking allusion to the topos of children's cinema can bridge the gap between Bottom's grotesque appearance and the boy's apparent innocence. Indeed, against the cinematic tradition of rendering Bottom as a sympathetic and essentially likable figure, Noble envisions Bottom as hairy and obese, replete with filthy, protruding teeth and, we are led to believe, a donkey-sized "rod."[15] Since this is the point at which Titania must learn to revere the rod and, in keeping with Puritanical pedagogy, have her child-like "stubbornness, and stoutness of mind ... broken and beaten down" (Robinson 13), it is perhaps not surprising to find that phallic objects dominate the *mise-en-scène*. What *is* troubling, however, is that the most prominent of them is an obscenely long, strapped-on carrot nose worn by a member of Titania's fairy train — an unmistakable allusion to Stanley Kubrick's *A Clockwork Orange*— which, in turn, casts the ensuing "love scene" in terms of rape. Worse, in positioning the boy as the surrogate puppeteer of Oberon's production, Noble begs the question as to who the author of this perverse sexual encounter really is.

After the boy and Titania's fairy train wish the odd couple good night, the camera steadily retreats from his anxious gaze, suddenly cutting away to a close-up of Oberon, who exclaims, "This falls out better than I could devise." As Oberon nods over his shoulder to reveal Puck by his side, our attention is drawn to the off-screen space where, even before the camera lights on Bottom and Titania, we hear hard, rhythmic pounding followed by groans that suggest more pain than pleasure. Clinging to her inverted umbrella as though it were a stripper's pole, Titania arches her back and braces for the impact as Bottom stands and thrusts violently into her, emitting a crude "hee-haw" with each effort. Noble's decision to represent this potentially subversive exchange between Bottom and Titania as an encounter more akin to rape is disturbing on multiple levels. In the context of cybernetic communications, wherein boundaries are constantly traversed and strange bedfellows are born of unexpected acts of interfacing, Bottom's aggressive violation of boundaries suggests a brutal burlesque of Titania's open system. For unlike Theseus and Oberon, Titania is a character who continually shifts the investment strategies around which her system is configured, first by moving away from Oberon to "gossi[p] by [the] side" of the Indian votress (2.1.125) — an image evocative of the "female and vernacular world of early childhood" (Wall, "'Household Stuff'" 5) — and later, by building her system around the child who proved mortal to this configuration. But Bottom's violent subjugation of Titania turns her capacity for embracing entropy against her; for this scene is intended to teach Titania a lesson by placing her on the same level as the child she nurtures — a particularly sinister application of the Puritanical commonplace that a child must be made as "serviceable" as a horse, "being never to be left to his own government, but always to have his rider on his back, and the bit in his mouth" (Robinson 14). Yet what is most troubling about the bridling of Titania's will is the possibility that the boy *himself* devised this misogynistic spectacle. Although Noble is careful not to position Jones's character as a direct observer of Bottom and Titania's "violent delights," it is his gaze that marks the vanishing point from which this scene springs. And what better way to get back at "mummy" for refusing his cry for help than to imagine having his way with a mother-substitute? Ultimately, though, whether the boy is a bystander in or an instigator of this fantasy, the upshot remains the same. For if the goal of the closed patriarchal system toward which Shakespeare's play and Noble's film slouches is to control the investment strategies of its component parts and, in so doing, maximize its capacity for reproduction, then this mission is accomplished when Titania relinquishes control of both her body *and* her Indian boy to Oberon — a clear indication that opportunistic domination has replaced her ethos of radical connection.

But in Noble's film, there is still one child to be accounted for in order to insure that system autonomy has been achieved. The sign that Oberon's system no longer requires the boy's monitoring and maintenance is the emergence of the unidentifiable hand that suddenly takes over for the boy's puppetry. As an extension of Oberon or, perhaps, Noble himself, this mysterious force that now pulls the strings alludes to the invisible hand that polices the closed system of the authors' cinema. All that is required to complete this vision of order restored, then, is the sought-after "algorithm for redundancy" that perpetuates system homeostasis, healing the breach in Oberon's authority once and for all. This algorithm is, of course, the heterosexual imperative of marriage, which, as in Shakespeare's play, is articulated by Puck as follows: "And the country proverb known / Every man should take his own." Spoken in voiceover to accentuate its disembodied ubiquity, this algorithm is reinforced by a visual gloss from the boy, who spins giddily in circles as the scenery is lifted high over his head, becoming an emblem of the restoration of the unimpeded feedback loop between father and son. Fittingly, at this threshold moment, Puck repeats the algorithm in the form of an easily memorized nursery rhyme: "Jack shall have Jill; / Nought shall go ill; / The man shall have his mare again, and all shall be well." In keeping with the self-determining logic of the authors' cinema, the boy now willingly takes hold of Puck's hand and walks with him into a larger-than-life moonrise, smiling for the first time without hesitation because, we are led to believe, his place in the system is at last secure. After a final dance in which he is lifted high into the air and spun around by the fairy cohort beneath him, the boy is carefully placed between Oberon and Titania, as the film ends, appropriately, with a tableau of a family portrait.

* * *

Perhaps it is just a coincidence that Julie Taymor's *Titus* culminates in a vision that inverts this image of the ideal nuclear family, picturing a solitary Osheen Jones cradling a mixed-race infant in his arms as he walks toward an imposing, artificial sunrise. But it would be hard not to notice the other aspects of Taymor's tragedy that suggest parallels with Noble's comedy. Indeed, Taymor's film similarly opens with establishing shots that take us into the boy's world, beginning not in his bedroom but in the kitchen. This time, however, rather than venturing down the hallway and peering through a keyhole onto a play that will eventually be performed in his puppet theater, the boy peers out from the eye holes of a crude paper bag mask, as the camera pulls back to reveal that he has converted his kitchen table into a stage for a dramatic clash of action figures. Uncannily, the boy's "fall" from this filmic frame into the world of Shakespeare's play is brought about by a gruff-appearing man who sports motorcycle goggles but no motorcycle — a figure who looks so out of place that it is hard not to recall the only slightly less bizarre figure of Bottom in Noble's film. Finally, in a shot that dovetails with the end of *Dream*, *Titus* begins officially when the boy is raised up over the head of his rescuer/abductor, a gesture of triumph that results in cheers from a crowd that is, rather disturbingly, nowhere to be found. *Titus* thus takes shape as a film which, like Noble's, positions the audience as an observer of an observer; that the latter observer is Osheen Jones is significant because his presence ruptures the homeostasis achieved by Noble's *Dream*, prying open this closed system as if to retroactively inject entropy — and transformation — into it.

Although Jones's boy is central to the monitoring, maintenance, and marring of the feedback loop in *Titus*, Taymor creates a complex observational dynamic that implicates the audience in this process as early as the film's opening frames. In the very first scene, for example, our attention is skewed between Young Lucius's perspective and a menacing off-screen space that derives from an unseen television, which bathes Lucius's drama of toy carnage in an eerie blue glow. As the noise and flicker of light subsumes the room, it becomes increasingly difficult to determine whether the boy is watching TV or the TV is watching *him*. This unsettling observational milieu sets the stage for the ensuing collapse of boundaries between the boy and his toys, for the more he mimics the unguided rage of battery-operated, remote-control machines, the more his plastic action figures assume human qualities, appearing to writhe in agony under his unrelenting blows. And when the disturbingly real, escalating violence of the boy's mock battle transports the viewer into the Roman coliseum, the audience experiences yet another reversal of terms, suddenly confronted by an entourage of stiff-legged gladiators marching in mechanistic unison toward the boy — like so many toy soldiers seeking revenge against his child's play. Posing stark contrast to these robotic warriors, nimble Roman "chariots" comprised of high-tech combinations of hummers, horses, and humans amble across the coliseum floor, linking the military prowess of ancient Rome to the cyborg technology of postmodern warfare, wherein remote-control, "smart" weaponry demonstrates the extent to which "our machines are disturbingly lively, and we ourselves frighteningly inert" (Haraway, *Simians* 152). But in the midst of this otherworldly, anachronistic space-time, Taymor's decision to feature two shooting locations in particular — the remains of Mussolini's government center and a Roman coliseum in Croatia — unmistakably grounds the audience in the twentieth-century traumas of Fascism and genocide; moreover, as the architectural structure through which the audience enters and exits the film, the coliseum — which Taymor describes as "the archetypal theatre of cruelty" (178) — serves as an insidious reminder of the inexorable feedback loop between violence and entertainment that sustains such apocalyptic spectacles. Hence, by dispersing our gaze across a spectrum of real and virtual points of identification that originate in the seemingly innocent world of child's play, Taymor cleverly seduces us into entering a far more sinister space, wherein we have the sneaking suspicion that the fun and games are over — and the toys are *us*.[16]

In his complex assessment of *Titus*'s allusions to Fascism and the Holocaust, Richard Burt contends that Taymor's film actually becomes complicit in the violence it sets out to critique by relentlessly "romanticizing" the figure of the "innocent child" who, "dead or alive, ... often legitimates violence against the Other in German and Italian Fascist cinema" (95). Such a claim, while highly provocative, ignores the fact that Young Lucius is patently *not* innocent, a point that is underscored from the very beginning of *Titus*, as well as throughout the film. Moreover, in contending that Taymor's "attempt to critique violence via Fascism and the Holocaust are inevitably in tension with her reinscription of the horror genre" (Burt 92), Burt does not acknowledge Taymor's revisionary approach to horror as yet another genre that employs the topos of child development (or lack thereof) as its preferred mode of legitimating violence against the Other — in this case, the female body. While Fascist cinema positions the child as an agent that mediates or incites violence between men, horror — particularly the slasher subgenre often associated with *Titus*— revolves around a male character who, still in the throes of boyhood, brutally inscribes his psychosexual confusion on the bodies of women only to be vanquished by a female survivor, or, the so-called "Final Girl."[17] Taymor's *Titus* presents us with a series of disturbing variations on these combined themes. Despite the powerful lead played by Anthony Hopkins, the focus of Taymor's film is the violence that women perpetrate against other women, reflected not only in the elaborate, highly sophisticated production values Taymor employs to represent Tamora and Lavinia, but also in the comments revealing her directorial fascination with Tamora and her barely concealed disdain for Lavinia as "Daddy's little girl, all ready for defilement" (181). If this shift of emphasis suggests a reversal of the gendered violence of Fascist cinema, then it also has a transformative impact on the perverse child psychology adumbrated by the horror film. Rather than representing childhood as inherently pathological, while depicting the female adolescent survivor as the boyish, Final Girl left to negotiate an uncertain future, *Titus* represents childhood as the locus of a potentially progressive reversion in the form of a male adolescent who becomes — in cybernetic fashion — at once Other, mother, and "Final *Boy*."

If we are to view *Titus* through the combined lens of Fascist cinema and the horror genre, then we cannot ignore the ways in which this structure of allusion retroactively glosses *A Midsummer Night's Dream*, as Jones's presence in Taymor's film strikes a blow in the war of the cinemas by injecting "noise" into Noble's vision of patriarchal closure. "Noise," as Michael Serres observes in his sci-fi novel *The Parasite*, "destroys and horrifies.... Noise nourishes a new order" (127). But which of these entropic effects — the purely destructive or the potentially transformative — will prevail in the feedback loop between *Dream* and *Titus*? On the one hand, as Titus's grandson, Young Lucius clearly contains the code for perpetuating the phallocratic tyranny featured in Noble's *Dream*, a point that is underscored by the film's ongoing flirtation with the specter of Fascism that inheres in Roman military orthodoxy. Indeed, the potential for system redundancy is implied not only by Young Lucius's initial kitchen table brutality but also by his dinner table "murder" of a fly which, he explains to Titus, he mistook for "a coal black moor." In assigning this role to Young Lucius rather than, as in Shakespeare's play, to the boy's granduncle, Marcus (see 3.2.50–80), Taymor does in fact draw attention to the function of the child in Fascist cinema as an excuse for and, in this case, an agent of, racist violence against the Other. On the other hand, Young Lucius's encounters with the castrating specter of Lavinia's raped and mutilated body do *not* precipitate the "dread of difference" that is the *raison d'être* of violence against women in the horror film but, rather, lead to a profound assertion of kinship with her.[18] In an interpolated scene, Young Lucius confronts Lavinia with a pair of wooden hands from a nearby doll shop, a gesture that recalls his destructive role in the film's opening frames as an agent of inter-animation between people and playthings alike, as girls and dolls — like boys and their toys — merge unexpectedly and, indeed, horrifically. Yet Lavinia's prosthetic hands, while evincing a sense of revulsion at the absence they cannot ultimately conceal, also suggest a subversion of horror, for as Lisa Trahair asserts, "Horror opens the door ... to a history of philosophy whose basic method is to differentiate and distinguish, to attribute value to, to set parameters and boundaries so as to make inclusion and exclusion, truth and fiction, subject and object — all the polarities that make meaning — possible" (205). Hence, as Young Lucius presents Lavinia with a pair of wooden hands that elide the gap between the animate and the inanimate, organic and synthetic, Taymor opens the door to a semantic system governed by a distinctly cybernetic ethos whereby, as Donna Haraway might conclude, "our bodies and our tools" are not sacrosanct but, rather, mutually imbricated in a system of potentially subversive conjuncture, wherein authorship — like maternity — offers a liberating *escape* from certainty (Haraway, *Simians* 181).

The *Osheen-en-abyme* effect that renders *Titus* an unlikely remake of *Dream* thus ruptures the self-identity of both films, leaving in its wake a series of virtual films that are ultimately left for the spectator to imagine.[19] In so doing, Taymor radicalizes the act of observation as a form of filmmaking in its own right — an act which, at the end of *Titus*, is assigned not to Jones's boy but to the spectators who now occupy the coliseum. As Taymor explains, in contrast to the image of the empty coliseum with which the film begins, "[t]his time the bleachers are filled with spectators. Watching. They are silent. They are we" (185). *Titus* concludes with a vision of Young Lucius's back to the camera, as he walks out of the film bearing Aaron and Tamora's mulatto child in his arms. Whether the boy will kill the child as he did the fly or nurture it as he has Lavinia remains to be seen and, perhaps, screened. Nevertheless, in deliberately *exiting* the theater of cruelty featured in *Titus*, Jones's character avenges his earlier role in Noble's film. For in representing Young Lucius as simultaneously mother, other, and "Final Boy," this tableau scrambles the vision of the discrete nuclear family with which Noble's *Dream* ends, replacing the algorithm of redundancy with entropy, born of "the interpenetration of boundaries between problematic selves and unexpected others" (Haraway, "The Actors" 24). Unlike the spectators whose silence encircles and, in effect, protects the genocidal violence of the film's conclusion, Young Lucius now recognizes that our machines and our screens *are* us: their codes reflect our drives, their programs our processes, their networks our destinies. Neither vanquisher nor victim, he stands at the threshold of a cybernetic system wherein violence and healing are privileges that are actuated through observation — and feedback — and, in turning his back on us, it is only *our* gaze that can lead toward, or away from, the sequel.

* * *

In her recent book, *How We Became Posthuman: Virtual Bodies in Cybernetics, Literature, and Informatics*, N. Katherine Hayles explores the perils and possibilities of a systems-based approach to subjectivity, taking for her point of departure cybernetic theory and its originary act of severing information from embodiment. During its early articulation in the nineteen forties, cybernetics was concerned, as Hayles notes of Norbert Weiner's work in particular, with "extend[ing] liberal humanism, not subvert[ing] it" (7).[20] "[S]educed by fantasies of unlimited power and disembodied immortality," first-wave cybernetics was concerned "less to show that man was a machine than to demonstrate that a machine could function like a man" and, in the process, learn the tactics of domination and oppression (5, 7). Apropos of *Titus*'s vaguely World War II setting, cybernetics emerged from Weiner's war-time discovery of the feedback loop as a regulatory mechanism for insuring communication and control across a system's constituent subsystems — a discovery that endowed anti-aircraft guns with the capacity to "think," that is, to continuously adjust their trajectories to strike moving targets. This encounter between the Enlightenment subject and cybernetics led to the notion that humans are not merely information-processing entities but also self-regulating — if not self-creating — mechanisms, an assumption that has been hypostatized as an exclusively male prerogative within the authors' cinema. Second-wave cybernetic theory, which reached its zenith in 1980 in conjunction with the work of figures like Niklas Luhmann, dealt a resounding blow to this logic of self-determinism by focusing on the *reflexivity* of systems, recognizing that systems are comprised of mutually-constitutive components in a continuous feedback loop.[21] As we have seen, Julie Taymor's *Titus* goes one step further to demonstrate how new systems, born of differential replication, can be generated by extending the feedback loop from the observed to the observer. Christine Edzard's *The Children Midsummer Night's Dream* offers a coda to *Titus* by aligning her filmmaking enterprise with third-wave cybernetic theory — the intent of which, in the age of virtual reality and artificial life, is "to evolve the capacity to evolve" by recasting replication as "the springboard to emergence" (Hayles 11).

* * *

What, are they children? Who maintains 'em?
How are they escoted? Will they pursue the quality
no longer than they can sing? Will they not say
afterwards, if they should grow themselves to common
players—as it is like most will, if their means are not
better—their writers do them wrong to make them
exclaim against their own succession?
                    — Shakespeare, Hamlet 2.2.345–51

In the original War of the Theaters, much was made of the fact that children were being employed as puppets of the so-called authors' theater playwrights, who, as Thomas Heywood lamented in his *Apology for Actors*, took advantage of the children's "juniority," supposing it "to be a privilege for any rayling" against their adult rivals in the bankside theaters.[22] But in so doing, the children were dealing a preemptive strike to their own future; they were, as Hamlet observes, being made to "exclaim against their own succession." Four-hundred years later, Christine Edzard revised this scenario for the war of the cinemas, releasing a film version of *Dream* in which the adults are puppets and the children follow their own cues. Beginning with a vision of schoolchildren gathered in a small theater, the film opens onto a life-size, puppet-show version of Shakespeare's *Dream* in which the parts of the principal players, Theseus and Hippolyta, are spoken by Derek Jacobi and Samantha Bond, respectively—two paragons of the British theatrical tradition whose voices instantly command reverence. The children auditors, however, are not so easily impressed, taking exception not only to the puppets' stiff appearance and stuffy delivery but also to Theseus and Egeus's abuse of Hermia. Hence, in a moment of childlike spontaneity, a girl springs up from the audience and usurps the puppet-Hermia's line: "I would my father looked with my eyes"—and a complete *coup de théâtre* ensues. As the children proceed to displace their adult counterparts by taking over the performance, the rarified milieu of the small theater is replaced with the more naturalistic settings associated with cinematic realism. Significantly, this change of venue is represented by Edzard as a kind of rebirth, as the children's gradual shedding of their school uniforms enables them to negotiate a new relationship to their identities and bodies, having escaped from British educational orthodoxy and their "wooden" adult mentors.

When explored from the perspective of the war of the cinemas, this sequence encapsulates the challenge that third-wave cybernetics poses to the concepts of homeostasis and redundancy adumbrated by the authors' cinema. For example, in recreating the adult authority figures in Shakespeare's play as puppets, Edzard implies the crisis of accountability incited by "the leap from embodied reality to abstract information," as Theseus and Egeus wield their power with machine-like compulsion, unable to accommodate any deviation from their phallocratic program (Hayles 12). Here Theseus's notorious rebuke of Hermia — "To you your father should be as a God ... / To whom you are but as a form in wax / By him imprinted, and within his power, / To leave the figure or disfigure it" — sounds uncannily similar to the warning issued to the "mechas" in Spielberg's *AI* and the replicants in Ridley Scott's *Bladerunner*, who are informed that any malfunction or deviation will lead to their destruction. Like these intentionally futuristic films, Edzard's *Dream* dramatizes what happens when replicants prove to be more human than their creators. Consequently, in their rush to enforce homeostasis through Athenian law, Theseus and Egeus neglect the tension building within the recursive loop between programmer and progeny until, "like a spring compressed and suddenly released," the children "break out of the pattern of circular self-organization and leap outward into the new" (Hayles 222). Indeed, in seeking to *embody* rather than merely succumb to their prosthetic extensions on stage, the children attempt to establish a new, more interactive relationship between identity-formation and information. Insisting on the ways in which the technology of performance can forge meaningful connections between the simulated and real bodies and, therefore, "evolve spontaneously in directions the programmer may not have anticipated," the children of Edzard's film succeed — at least temporarily — in replacing patriarchal structures of succession with skeumorphs of emergence (Hayles 11).

Central to the history of cybernetics, skeumorphs demarcate the path of seriation, indicating how systems develop their capacity to evolve from a continual feedback loop between replication and innovation. With one eye fixed on the past and one eye focused on the future, skeumorphs, as Hayles points out, are "threshold devices" that simultaneously undermine both temporalities (17).[23] Children are, in a sense, the ultimate skeumorphs, selectively reflecting "their parents and original" (*Dream* 2.1.117) in the very act of displacing them with their own performance of adulthood. In Edzard's film, the children's status as threshold figures is underscored by their ages, for Edzard chooses to feature 360 eight- to thirteen-year-olds from London-area schools — boys and girls poised not only on the brink of adulthood but also of gender definition.[24] Critics have taken great exception to Edzard's casting of amateurs, describing the film as "some horribly over-extended school play, in which you know none of the children" (Tookey 7). Another typical objection is aimed at the performers' often-awkward pronunciation which, uttered in their native Southwark dialects, sounds to some like a "search and destroy work on Shakespeare's poetry" (Andrews 12), suggesting the extent to which the Renaissance disdain for the local or "female" vernacular remains a powerful code for perpetuating dominant views of social entitlement today. Such criticisms imply an ongoing concern with paternity in a culture that places a pathological premium on individuality. For to "know" the children — based on their bankable faces or well-trained accents — is to recognize them as products of a biological, institutional, or national pedigree that halts the sliding of the faceless, raceless signifiers that mingle promiscuously amid Edzard's stunningly multiracial cast which, in and of itself, generates a visual pun that equates the children's undisciplined language with the specter of loose-tongued and, therefore, sexually available mothers. That the children's relative anonymity, unpolished accents, and racial diversity also reflect the environs of Edzard's own production company, Sands Films, is particularly significant. Located in two abandoned warehouses with views of the dilapidated Rotherhithe dockyards — signifiers of the post-industrial fall-out from Thatcherite neglect — Sands Films is itself a kind of skeumorph, indeed, a graveyard of unfulfilled promises. Hence, Edzard's film is positioned similarly to the unborn children whom Renaissance women writers charged with the future performance of their will. With one foot in the neglected past of their parents and one foot in the prospect of a more just future, the children of Edzard's *Dream* embody the democratizing dream of what I will call the feminist filmmaking "vernacular" which, hard-wired with the code for emergence rather than succession, leads to the literal renaissance of "an alternative idea of community and nation" (Wall, "Household Stuff" 29).

But according to the logic of this film, once their midsummer night's dream meets the morning after, these same children will be subject to a counter-education which, if the opening scene is any indication, will take shape as an oppressive hardening process that converts them into adults and, therefore, "puppets" of the dominant social order. When, at the end of the film, the child performers of the roles of Hermia, Helena, Demetrius, and Lysander are replaced on stage by their puppet counterparts, it is hard not to read this act of disembodiment as the victory of precisely this order. Yet I would argue that what the children have arrived at is something more powerful than what their bodies alone could achieve — something that Renaissance women writers imagined long ago as an *embodied* virtuality.[25] Having abandoned the limits of their given identities, the "real" Hermia, Helena, Demetrius, and Lysander have, by the end of the performance, not only morphed into the puppets on stage but also remain, at least in spirit, with the anonymous children now viewing the play, who evince the feistiness of their precursors by reprimanding the "adults" for interrupting the rude mechanicals. In this final incarnation, the child protagonists of Edzard's film signal their intervention in the war of the cinemas by replacing the concept of the authorial holograph — so essential to the eponymous replication of the authors' cinema — with a *hologram* of the interactive performances that had to be suppressed in order for Shakespeare to lose his body to a fantasy of male parthenogenesis in the first place, credited with the supreme authorial honor of "inventing the human" before he even became one.[26]

In positioning children as a veritable seriation chart of the ways in which Shakespeare has emerged as the "original" unruly replicant, the adaptations by the feminist filmmaking vanguard I have examined here forge a provocative kinship between Shakespeare's posthuman status as the signifier of disembodied information *par excellence* and the pre-human status of women writers in the Renaissance. Hence, if "the posthuman view thinks of the body as the original prosthesis we all learn to manipulate" (Hayles 3), then we might think of "embodied virtuality" as the sequel to the ways in which Renaissance women converted their own bodies into microcosmic versions of cybernetic systems, according to the subjective technology of the "matrix." In Renaissance midwifery and medical manuals, the womb was commonly called the matrix, and its constituent parts were thought to function or "agree" with each other by entering into relationships of empathy in the act of exchanging information.[27] In a culture wherein authors are pronounced virtually dead but are, in reality, alive and well in the apocalyptic paternalism of U.S.-led preemptive strikes and the disembodied promptings of terrorist leaders, might we consider a model of communication more akin to this early modern one, which can teach us how to handle the very prospect of the future — indeed, of virtual life — with care, so we do not all wind up exclaiming against our own succession? If, as Bruno Latour claims, "we were never modern" and, as Hayles replies, "we have always been posthuman" (291), then does it follow that we might yet become *early* modern?[28] Renaissance women past and present suggest that this could be a step in the right direction. For in a global culture whose authorities increasingly value acting alone, the cybercinema's vision of a system wherein "individuality," in Donna Haraway's memorable phrasing, is "a strategic defense problem," may suggest nothing less than the code for our collective survival (Haraway, *Simians* 212). We might call it the matrix: reloaded.

Notes

1. For an elaborate treatment of this subject, see Richard Helgerson's *Forms of Nationhood: The Elizabethan Writing of England*, esp. "Staging Exclusion," 193–245.

2. I appropriate this phrase from Shakespeare's *Hamlet* (2.2.438–39) in *The Oxford Shakespeare: Tragedies*, ed. Stanley Wells, et al. Subsequent references to *Hamlet* are from this edition, hereafter cited in the text.

3. I am oversimplifying the relations between the playwrights involved in the War of the Theaters. For a more thorough exploration of this phenomenon, see Rosalyn Knut-

son's "Falconer to the Little Eyases: A New Date and Commercial Agenda for the 'Little Eyases' Passage in *Hamlet*"; James P. Bednarz's "Marston's Subversion of Shakespeare and Jonson: *Histriomastix* and the War of the Theaters"; and Andrew Gurr's *Playgoing in Shakespeare's London.*

4. Particularly in the wake of Puritanism, children became a literal and literary source of impression-making activities — through physical, sexual, and/or rhetorical violence. I will be exploring the anxiety incited by children in the context of the Puritanical thinking that shaped the grammar school experience of seventeenth-century English boys in particular. For primary materials from this era, see *Educational Documents: 800–1816*, D. W. Sylvester (London: Methuen 1970), esp. 156–62 on "The Puritan Revolution and Education." See also John Robinson's 1628 treatise "Of Children and Their Education" in *Child-Rearing Concepts, 1628–1861: Historical Sources*, ed. Philip J. Greven, Jr. (Itaska, Illinois: F.E. Peacock, 1973), 9–18. For extremely useful secondary readings, see Lawrence Stone's *The Family, Sex and Marriage in England: 1500–1800* (New York: Harper and Row, 1979) and Wendy Wall's "'Household Stuff': The Sexual Politics of Domesticity and the Advent of English Comedy," *ELH* 65.1 (1998): 1–45.

5. *Shakespeare in Love*, Dir. John Madden (Miramax Films/Universal Pictures/The Bedford Falls Company, 1998); *Dangerous Beauty*, Dir. Michael Herskovitz (Warner/Regency/Bedford Falls, 1998); and *A Midsummer Night's Dream*, Dir. Adrian Noble (Paul Arnott, 1996). The trope equating the female body with impressionable parchment or wax is a commonplace in the Renaissance. For a concise exploration of this act of appropriation, see the introduction to Wendy Wall's *The Imprint of Gender: Authorship and Publication in the Renaissance* (Ithaca: Cornell University Press, 1993), titled "To be 'A Man in Print,'" 1–22. For an account of a slightly different phenomenon, whereby the male poet appropriates womb imagery as an example of "pregnancy without impregnation," see Katherine Eisaman Maus, "A Womb of His Own: Male Poets in the Female Body" in *Sexuality and Gender in Early Modern Europe: Institutions, Texts, Images*, ed. James Grantham Turner (Cambridge: Cambridge University Press, 1993), 266–88 (275).

6. In the longer version of this essay, I focus on Mariya Muyat's *Twelfth Night* (Shakespeare Animated Films Limited, Christmas Films, and Soyuzmultifilm, 1992); Aida Ziablikova's *Taming of the Shrew* (Christmas Films with S4C, 1996); and Natalya Orlova's *Hamlet* (Shakespeare Animated Films Limited, Christmas Films, and Soyuzmultifilm 1992) and *Richard III* (Christmas Films with S4C, 1996). See also *Titus*, Dir. Julie Taymor (Clear Blue Sky Productions, 2000) and *The Children's Midsummer Night's Dream*, Dir. Christine Edzard (Sands Films, 2001).

7. I am thinking particularly of Jeffrey Masten's pathbreaking work on plural authorship, especially *Textual Intercourse: Collaboration, Authorship, and Sexualities in Renaissance Drama.*

8. In employing cybernetic discourse, I mean to invoke its socialist-feminist application in works such as Haraway's *Simians, Cyborgs, and Women* and N. Katherine Hayles's *How We Became Posthuman: Virtual Bodies in Cybernetics, Literature, and Informatics* (Chicago: University of Chicago Press, 1999). Both appropriate the terminology and technology of cybernetics to explore various means of handling the information age, the environment, and the human subject with greater care, calling for situated knowledges, vulnerable bodies and, above all, the recognition that subjectivity is not given but, rather, the product of strategic assemblages.

9. By describing Renaissance child-rearing as a system conceived around "surrogation," I mean to invoke W. B. Worthen's coining of the term to describe cultural practices that derive their meaning from citation, repetition and, most critically, performance. See Worthen's essay on "Drama, Performance, Performativity," *PMLA* 113 (1998): 1093–1107.

10. As Jeffrey Masten observes, wills are, above all, not legal but social practices that "seek to preserve affiliations beyond the grave" and, in so doing, "reproduce social alliances" (4). In this context, then, the maternal legacy not only suggests a powerful attempt to leave an impression on the unborn child but also a preemptive strike against the other forces that will inevitably stake a claim to its moral upbringing. In fact, I would suggest that the paradoxical status of the mother's will, which demands "the erasure of the subject at the very moment of powerful self-assertion" (Wall, *The Imprint of Gender* 286), resonates with the "riven subjectivity" of the male child in particular, whose own passage to adulthood is contingent upon killing off the remnants of female influence for fear of a gender "relapse." For analyses of this cultural fear of lapsing from male to female, see Wall's "'Household Stuff'" and Stephen Orgel's essay "Nobody's Perfect: Or Why Did the English Stage Take Boys for Women?"

11. See Stephen Orgel's discussion of the Renaissance practice of breeching in "Nobody's Perfect."

12. Masten offers a rigorous exploration of negative attitudes toward collaboration in *Textual Intercourse.*

13. The excerpt from William Whately's *A Bride-Bush: or a direction for married persons* (1619) is quoted from Lisa Jardine's *Still Harping on Daughters: Women and Drama in the Age of Shakespeare* (New York: Columbia University Press, 1989), 106.

14. Stephen Spielberg's *E. T. Extra Terrestrial* (Universal, 1982) contains the famous image of the boy and E. T. riding a bicycle across an enormous moonscape. Noble's most obvious allusions to other children's/family films include *Mary Poppins*, Dir. Robert Stevenson (Walt Disney, 1964) and *Home Alone*, Dir. Chris Columbus (TCF/John Hughes, 1990).

15. Consider, among the most popular versions of *Dream*, James Cagney's lovable impersonation of Bottom in Max Reinhardt and William Dieterle's version (Warner Bros., 1935) and Kevin Kline's more pathetic Bottom in Michael Hoffman's *William Shakespeare's A Midsummer Night's Dream* (Fox Searchlight Pictures/Regency Enterprises, 1999).

16. An extensive analysis of the dynamics of spectatorship in *Titus* may be found by consulting Lehmann, Bryan Reynolds, and Lisa S. Starks's essay, "'For such a sight will blind a father's eye': The Spectacle of Suffering in Taymor's *Titus.*"

17. For a discussion of *Titus* and the slasher subgenre of horror film see Lisa S. Starks's essay "Cinema of Cruelty: Powers of Horror in Julie Taymor's *Titus*" in *The Reel Shakespeare*, ed. Lisa S. Starks and Courtney Lehmann (Madison: Fairleigh Dickinson University Press, 2002), 121–42. See also Carol J. Clover's foundational essay on horror and the Final Girl phenomenon in "Her Body, Himself: Gender in the Slasher Film," in *The Dread of Difference: Gender and the Horror Film*, ed. Barry Keith Grant (Austin: University of Texas Press, 1996), 66–113.

18. I invoke Barry Keith Grant's collection of essays on the sexual politics of the horror genre, titled *The Dread of Difference: Gender and the Horror Film.* More specifically, as the essays throughout this collection demonstrate, it is the encounter with the female body's disturbing "lack" that gives rise to the "dread of difference" and instigates male violence against women.

19. Lisa Trahair explores the capacity of the re-make genre to generate "virtual films" in "For the Noise of a Fly" in *The Illusion of Life: Essays on Animation*, ed. Alan Cholodenko (Sidney: Power Publications, 1991), 183–208.

20. Hayles provides an excellent introduction to cybernetic theory in her first chapter, "Toward Embodied Virtuality," 1–24. Likewise, Haraway's *Simians, Cyborgs, and Women* contains a brilliant chapter on cybernetics titled "The Biological Enterprise: Sex, Mind, and Profit from Human Engineering to Sociobiology," 43–70. For examples of Weiner's work, see *Cybernetics: or, Control and Communication in the Animal and the Machine* and *The Human Use of Human Beings: Cybernetics and Society.*

21. For a collection of Niklas Luhmann's reflections on reflexivity, see Luhmann's *Essays on Self-Reference.*

22. The exact date of Heywood's pamphlet is unknown, though is conjectured to have been written in 1607–8. This excerpt is quoted from Gurr's *Playgoing in Shakespeare's London,* 155.

23. Hayles observes that a skeumorph is akin to a Janus figure, for it is "a design feature that is no longer functional in and of itself" but that is, nevertheless, retained in the form of "a gesture or an allusion used to authenticate new elements in the emerging constellation of reflexivity" (17). In her introductory chapter of *How We Became Posthuman,* Hayles presents an extremely useful seriation chart documenting the history of cybernetic theory (16).

24. As if updating the Renaissance practice of clothing girls and unbreeched boys in dresses, Edzard employs an age-group in her film that is particularly prone to gender ambiguity, since the boys' high-pitched voices are virtually indistinguishable from the girls' and, if anything, the girls' bodies are taller and stronger than the boys' physiques. Accentuating the anxiety that Shakespeare's play seeks to dispel, namely, that female dominance may spread from throne to household, Edzard highlights the disproportionate maturity of the girls. In the exchanges between Oberon and Titania, for example, the camera consistently looks down on Oberon, emphasizing his height disadvantage and subtly entering into league with the defiant Titania. But it is Edzard's vision of Titania's beloved Indian "boy"—with his hair mounted in two high ponytails and his body clad in a sari-like combination of pants and dress — that most powerfully engages Renaissance anxieties about emerging from the "common gender" of childhood and excessive exposure to female nurture.

25. I borrow the concept of "embodied virtuality" from Hayles, who uses this phrase in her introductory chapter in an effort to intervene in the crisis of subjectivity posed by posthuman disembodiment. While Hayles explains that she does not "mourn the passing" of the liberal humanist subject into the posthuman subject, she explains that she is wary of the prospect of disembodiment "being, rewritten, once again, into prevailing concepts of subjectivity." Nevertheless, Hayles is equally interested in determining how "certain characteristics, especially agency and choice, *can* be articulated within a posthuman context" (5, emphasis mine). Hence, her project is to "show what had to be elided, suppressed, and forgotten to make information lose its body" (13).

26. I am invoking Harold Bloom's ambitious tome *Shakespeare: The Invention of the Human.*

27. See Elaine Hobby's "Note on Humoral Theory" in her edition of Jane Sharp's *The Midwives Book,* xxxiii-xxxv (xxxiii).

28. In the first half of this "if/then" clause, I am playing on the title of a book by Bruno Latour, *We Have Never Been Modern,* and, of course, Hayles's work.

Works Cited

AI. Dir. Steven Spielberg. Dreamworks, 2001.

Andrews, Nigel. Rev. of *The Children's Midsummer Night's Dream. The Financial Times* 21 June 2001: 12.

Bednarz, James. "Marston's Subversion of Shakespeare and Jonson: *Histriomastix* and the War of the Theaters." *Medieval and Renaissance Drama in England: An Annual Gathering of Research, Criticism and Reviews* 6 (1993): 103-128.

Bladerunner. Dir. Ridley Scott. Warner/Ladd/Bladerunner Partnership, 1982.

Bloom, Harold. *Shakespeare: The Invention of the Human.* New York: Riverhead Books, 1998.

Burt, Richard. "Shakespeare and the Holocaust: Julie Taymor's *Titus* is Beautiful, or Shakesploi Meets (the) Camp." *Colby Quarterly* 37.1 (2001): 78-106.

A Clockwork Orange. Dir. Stanley Kubrick. Warner Bros./Polaris, 1971.

Clover, Carol J. "Her Body, Himself: Gender in the Slasher Film." *The Dread of Difference: Gender and the Horror Film.* Ed. Barry Keith Grant. Austin: University of Texas Press, 1996. 66-113.

Dangerous Beauty. Dir. Michael Herskovitz. Warner/Regency/Bedford Falls, 1998.

Gurr, Andrew. *Playgoing in Shakespeare's London.* Cambridge: Cambridge University Press, 1987.

Haraway, Donna. "The Actors Are Cyborg, Nature Is Coyote, and the Geography Is Elsewhere: Postscript to 'Cyborgs at Large.'" *Technoculture.* Ed. Constance Penley and Andrew Ross. Minneapolis: University of Minnesota Press, 1991. 21-26.

_____. *Simians, Cyborgs, and Women: The Reinvention of Nature.* London and New York: Routledge, 1991.

Helgerson, Richard. *Forms of Nationhood: The Elizabethan Writing of England.* Chicago: University of Chicago Press, 1992.

Jardine, Lisa. *Still Harping on Daughters: Women and Drama in the Age of Shakespeare.* New York: Columbia University Press, 1989.

Knutson, Rosalyn. "Falconer to the Little Eyases: A New Date and Commercial Agenda for the 'Little Eyases' Passage in *Hamlet*." *Shakespeare Quarterly* 46.1 (1995): 1-31.

Latour, Bruno. *We Have Never Been Modern.* Trans. Catherine Porter. Cambridge: Harvard University Press, 1993.

Lehmann, Courtney. "Dancing in a (Cyber)net: 'Renaissance Women,' Systems Theory, and the War of the Cinemas." *Renaissance Drama: New Series* 34 (2005): 121-161.

_____, Bryan Reynolds, and Lisa S. Starks. "'For such a sight will blind a father's eye': The Spectacle of Suffering in Taymor's Titus." *Performing Transversally: Reimagining Shakespeare and the Critical Future.* By Bryan Reynolds. London and New York: Palgrave Macmillan, 2003. 215-43.

Luhmann, Niklas. *Essays on Self-Reference.* New York: Columbia University Press, 1990.

Masten, Jeffrey. *Textual Intercourse: Collaboration, Authorship, and Sexualities in Renaissance Drama.* Cambridge: Cambridge University Press, 1997.

Maus, Katherine Eisaman. "A Womb of His Own: Male Poets in the Female Body." *Sexuality and Gender in Early Modern Europe: Institutions, Texts, Images.* Ed. James GranthamTurner. Cambridge: Cambridge University Press, 1993. 266-88.

A Midsummer Night's Dream, Dir. Adrian Noble. Prod. Paul Arnott. Capitol, 1996.

Orgel, Stephen. "Nobody's Perfect: Or Why Did the English Stage Take Boys for Women?" *Displacing Homophobia: Gay Male Perspectives in Literature and Culture.* Ed. Ronald R. Butters, et al. Durham, NC: Duke University Press, 1989. 7-29.

Robinson, John. "Of Children and Their Education (1628)." *Child-Rearing Concepts, 1628-1861: Historical Sources.* Ed. Philip J. Greven, Jr. Itaska, Illinois: F.E. Peacock, 1973.

Serres, Michael. "The Parasite." Trans. Laurence R. Schehr. Baltimore: Johns Hopkins University Press, 1982.

Shakespeare in Love. Dir. John Madden. Miramax Films/Universal Pictures/The Bedford Falls Company, 1998.

Shakespeare, William. *Hamlet. The Oxford Shakespeare: Tragedies.* Ed. Stanley Wells, et al. 4 vols. Oxford: Oxford University Press, 1987. Vol. 3: 1123-1163.

Starks, Lisa S. "Cinema of Cruelty: Powers of Horror in Julie Taymor's *Titus*." *The Reel Shakespeare.* Ed. Lisa S. Starks and Courtney Lehmann. Madison, NJ: Fairleigh Dickinson University Press, 2002. 121-42.

Stone, Lawrence. *The Family, Sex and Marriage In England: 1500-1800.* New York: Harper and Row, 1979.

Sylvester, D. W., ed. *Educational Documents: 800-1816.* London: Methuen, 1970.

Taymor, Julie. "Director's Notes." *Titus: The Illustrated Screenplay.* New York: Newmarket Press, 2000. 172-185.

Titus. Dir. Julie Taymor. Perf. Anthony Hopkins, Jessica Lange, and Harry Lennix. 2000. DVD Special Edition (2 Discs). Twentieth Century Fox, 2006.

Trahair, Lisa. "For the Noise of a Fly." *The Illusion of Life: Essays on Animation.* Ed. Alan Cholodenko. Sydney: Power Publications, 1991. 183-208.

Wall, Wendy. "'Household Stuff': The Sexual Politics of Domesticity and the Advent of English Comedy." *ELH* 65.1 (1998): 1-45.

_____. *The Imprint of Gender: Authorship and Publication in the Renaissance.* Ithaca: Cornell University Press, 1993.

Weiner, Norbert. *Cybernetics: or, Control and Communication in the Animal and the Machine.* Cambridge: MIT Press, 1948.

_____. *The Human Use of Human Beings: Cybernetics and Society.* 2nd ed. New York: Doubleday, 1954.

Whately, William. *A Bride-Bush: or a direction for married persons* (1619).

Worthen, W.B. "Drama, Performance, Performativity." *PMLA* 113 (1998): 1093-1107.

3

Liberty's Taken, or How "captive women may be cleansed and used": Julie Taymor's *Titus* and 9/11

KIM FEDDERSON AND J. MICHAEL RICHARDSON

> 10. When thou goest forth to war against thine enemies, and the LORD thy God hath delivered them into thine hands, and thou hast taken them captive,
> 11. And seest among the captives a beautiful woman, and hast a desire unto her, that thou wouldest have her to thy wife;
> 12. Then thou shalt bring her home to thine house, and she shall shave her head, and pare her nails;
> 13. And she shall put the raiment of her captivity from off her, and shall remain in thine house, and bewail her father and her mother a full month: and after that thou shalt go in unto her, and be her husband, and she shall be thy wife.
> — Deuteronomy 21.10–13 (King James Version)

Eight days after the attack on the World Trade Center, Bill Moyers asked Julie Taymor, the director and designer of the spectacular musical *The Lion King* and the film *Titus*, "what [can] artists say to us about the tragedy of September 11th?" (Taymor and Moyers). Perhaps her adaptation of *Titus Andronicus*—the bloodiest and, not coincidentally, the most popular of Shakespeare's plays among Elizabethans—had something to tell us about apocalyptic violence: what causes it, how it might be prevented, and how we can recover from the traumas it inflicts.

Taymor's *Titus* (2000) differs markedly from Shakespeare's play in that it offers a guardedly optimistic answer to the play's concern with the tragic consequences of failing to recognize and reconcile cultural differences. Stand-

70

ing amidst dismembered and mutilated bodies at the conclusion of the play, Marcus Andronicus, tribune of the people and brother of the now dead Titus, seeks to learn

> ... how to knit again
> This scattered corn into one mutual sheaf,
> These broken limbs again into one body [5.3.70–72].

Taymor's film offers an answer. While the play is capable of receiving various treatments in interpretation and production, the prevailing tonality of its conclusion is unrelentingly grim. There are few assurances that a newer, more stable order is going to emerge out of the tragedy we have witnessed. Taymor, however, closes her film of the play with a scene which she herself admits is "sentimental,"[1] and which others have called "romantic," "schlocky" and "straight out of *E.T.*" (Burt 300). The young boy whom we met playing with action figures at the outset of the film, who is subsequently dragged down its cinematic rabbit hole to become young Lucius (played by Osheen Jones), Titus Andronicus's grandson, leaves the coliseum — the theater of cruelty which frames the film's version of the play — and carries Aaron the Moor's baby into a new dawn. In Taymor's version, there is the promise of an easy recovery from apocalypse. The sun will come out tomorrow. If, like Disney, we put our trust in the latent uncorrupted goodness of children, as the lyrics of the song in *The Lion King* suggest, all will be well: *Hakuna Matata*.[2] Taymor, most would agree, has a voracious aesthetic appetite. Yet, she frequently fails to respect the ontological boundaries that separate events and their representations. This indifference enables her to mistake a reconciliation of differences in the imaginary (on stage, on screen) for their reconciliation in the real (off stage, off screen), and thus she is able to "graft" a happy ending worthy of Walt Disney onto a brutal revenge tragedy worthy of Quentin Tarantino (McCandless 511).[3]

The Treatment of the Other in *Titus Andronicus*

Shakespeare's *Titus Andronicus* reveals much about the failure of accommodating difference and how that failure incites apocalyptic violence, the kind of violence that threatens to bring civilizations to an end. Its lessons are particularly timely, given our current difficulties in reconciling competing ethnic, religious, cultural, and political claims in an increasingly interconnected world. How do we provide a space for others which does not require them to relinquish the differences that constitute their identity? Recognizing the other entails attending both to the surface features of otherness (e.g., visible marks of cultural difference) and to the significance of these markers in their particular cultural and historical contexts. Our failing to recognize the other typically results in appropriation or assimilation rather than in accommodation. This failure, if taken to the extreme, as it is in ethnic cleansing, results in an apocalyptic effacement of the other's identity. The others cease to exist or continue to exist in a mutilated form. So reduced, the others are faced with the choice of capitulating or retaliating; in either event the result is tragic.

The space within which both self and other negotiate their respective identities is "a space of questions" (Taylor 34). This interrogative space establishes the ideological frame in which identity is formed. It is within this space that the self is provided with an historically and socially specific set of cultural norms — norms which establish its place and orientation in the world. It is within this space that the self acquires, or fails to acquire, the tools that allow it to negotiate, or to fail to negotiate, those norms it has inherited. It is within this space that the self develops whatever provisional answers it deems necessary to address epistemological, aesthetic, and ethical questions about the nature of truth, beauty, and goodness. Over the course of human history, this space of questions has been conceptualized in various, often divergent and incompatible, ways: as natural or conventional, as eternal or historical, as necessary or contingent, as certain or indeterminate, as teleological or interminable, as essential or adventitious, as dialectical or dialogical.

One line of thought beginning with Hegel through Kojeve and then Fanon and others regards the dynamic within this space dialectically. So conceived, the subject's struggle for recognition is an all or nothing affair taking place within a hegemonic space that is dominated monologically. In such a space — and this is very much the space of *Titus Andronicus*— there is only the ongoing oscillation of winners or losers, masters or slaves, colonizers or colonized, Romans or Goths. At any given moment, those with the power to do so establish the norms which provide the prevailing answers to the questions of the true, the beautiful, and the good. These answers then create the context within which, and the criteria whereby, decisions are made about who will be regarded as a subject, and about how those regarded as subjects will be valued. Thus a playing field within which the subject's struggles for recognition take place is established — a playing field, which, as the genocides of the Holocaust, Cambodia, and more recently Rwanda and Croatia, demonstrate, can be readily transformed into a killing field.

Another line of thought emerging in the work of Bahktin, Taylor, Kymlicka and others explores the possibilities for creating and sustaining different kinds of interrogative spaces — ones in which the dialectical death struggle for recognition is replaced by an accommodation of others. In these dialogical spaces, the terms upon which the struggle for recognition takes place are themselves open for negotiation; thus the rules of the game can be altered and the accommodation of those formerly excluded or marginalized becomes possible. In these negotiable spaces, minorities — e.g., indigenous peoples, the Quebecois in Canada, the Basques in Spain, the Tibetans in China, gays and lesbians, etc.— may be able to maintain their identities without having to separate from the dominant culture and without having to compromise these identities through some form of assimilation. Here self and other struggle to create a space in which different identities can live together peaceably (i.e., share general agreements about borders, property laws, human rights, criminal and civil codes) without risking their own distinctive identities. This dialogical space is not as prone to genocide as its dialectical cousin because it attempts to negotiate the terms upon which self and other can be reconciled.

Unlike Shakespeare's *Titus Andronicus*, which anatomizes, but provides no way of escape from, the theater of cruelty that emerges from the either/or logic of a dialectical history, Taymor's *Titus* posits a way out. In the cross-cultural bricolage of her art, Taymor believes she has found the means with which to reconcile alien elements. Yet, it is one thing to reconcile disparate

Titus (Anthony Hopkins) and Saturninus (Alan Cumming) backed by toy-like Roman soldiers in Julie Taymor's aesthetically eclectic *Titus* (2000) (Photofest).

cultural forms, genres, and media within aesthetic borders and quite another to reconcile disparate peoples within geo-political ones. Presenting an image of lions and lambs (or Roman boys and Goth-Moor babies) happily co-existing is not the same thing as enabling them get along in real life. Dialogical appearances and dialogical realities are different. Shakespeare understands the difference between politics and art. It is only by failing to recognize the difference that Taymor is able to present a facile and improbable solution to the problem of genocide. *Titus*'s wishful thinking may console us, but it may also interfere with the practical and political work of creating historical, as opposed to merely aesthetic, interrogative spaces in which self and other can be reconciled.

Titus Andronicus is explicitly concerned with how we interact with others and how to avoid apocalyptic cycles of violence. The play is a chronicle of horrors that could come from any 21st-century newspaper: politically and racially motivated murders, ritual sacrifice, kidnapping, rape, torture, dismemberment, honor-killings, and cannibalism. These horrors result from various failures in the recognition of otherness. *Titus Andronicus* centralizes the numerous kinds of difference that can separate people and peoples:

1. the political rupture in the Roman state with which the play opens — i.e., is the new emperor to be selected on the basis of primogeniture (Saturninus's position), merit as judged by the citizenry (Bassianus's stance), or nomination by the tribunes (who choose Titus)?

2. the cultural gaps dividing the Moors, Goths, and Romans, not to mention those dividing the older conservative Romans like Titus from the younger libertine Romans like Saturninus;

3. the generational and gender differences within the Andronicus family.

Titus, by sacrificing Alarbus, the eldest son of Tamora, Queen of the Goths, to Roman gods and by nominating the corrupt Saturninus as emperor, simply because he is the eldest son of the late emperor, sets in motion a series of actions that leads to the fracturing of the Roman state and the destruction, almost complete annihilation, of his own family. For Rome, the play is apocalyptic. The Romans fail to properly sort out their internal differences and are unwilling or unable to handle the conquered Goth culture with the recognition and accommodation required to guarantee both the safety of Rome and the integrity of the Goths. *Titus Andronicus* focuses on the end of Rome not its restoration.

At the close of the play, there are those, like Marcus, standing in an imperial Roman killing field, who hope for restoration:

You sad faced men, people and sons of Rome
By uproars severed like a flight of fowls,
Scattered by the winds and high tempestuous gusts:
O let me teach you how to knit again
This scattered corn into one mutual sheaf,
These broken limbs again into one body [5.3.67–72].

There is little in the play to suggest that Marcus, or anyone else, could do either the requisite knitting or teaching. For example, it is not clear at the end that Marcus has learned the play's lessons: his images of a flight of fowls (one species per flock), scattered corn (not corn mixed with barley, for example), and broken limbs (from the same body) all presume that in the beginning was a primary unity that has been somehow ruptured. But Shakespeare takes great pains to suggest that such an originary unity was never really there and does nothing to suggest that Marcus possesses a vision of difference sufficiently comprehensive upon which to ground his instruction. Moreover, given that Rome at the end is ruled by Titus's son, the ruthless, peremptory, and ferocious Lucius, backed by a Goth army of undetermined loyalties, Marcus's offer of instruction seems more like a question: how can the numerous differences in the world of the play be resolved or reconciled? How can so many disparate things be unified, knit together into one "mutual sheaf"? Titus's tragedy, and that of Rome, is that these questions were not responsibly dealt with from the outset. The play throughout examines and interrogates these very failures. It does not, however, provide a solution to them.

Shakespeare frames his examination of our interactions with others, not in the vocabulary of recognition and accommodation of difference, but rather in that of *piety* and its etymological sibling, *pity*. These terms have the Latin *pietas* as a common ancestor, and both arise from a deep awareness that human beings are social animals, that they must live with others and make adjustments in order to do so. Both piety and pity require that one lay aside, at least for a while, the claims that self-interest lays upon us, and instead to focus, in the case of piety, on codified obligations beyond the self to parents, family, ancestors, the state, the gods, etc., and in the case of pity, on the legitimate and commanding, if less codified, claims of others to some form of protection or relief from potential or actual suffering and distress. For example, in times of war or cultural conflict, victors must refrain from imposing peace conditions that involve the complete humiliation of the defeated and the seething resentment such treatment breeds. Similarly, they must allow defeated nations to retain a decent amount of their lands and incomes so that their citizenry will not starve, and to retain their languages, religions, and at least some of their political, cultural, and social structures. True piety thus entails the recognition of difference and embraces pity, the feeling of and acting on genuine empathy with others. At its most basic, these are the obligations owed to others because of the common humanity of all.

Piety ensures continuity from generation to generation and is essential to the continuation of states and cultures, which, like individuals, must live with others and hence make accommodations with them. A "pious" present constructs a future that grows out of its past, including its interactions with others, and does so by incorporating aspects of that past into the present. It cannot succeed by deploying a fascistic elision of the difference between past and present in an attempt to perpetuate or re-impose the practices of the past upon a resistant present. Piety, including its secular and cultural manifestations, is by its very nature "religious" in the etymological sense of joining together or, to use Marcus's term, "knitting" things together again. In *Titus Andronicus*, the descent into chaos begins with the Andronici performing an act of brutal cultural imperialism: they sacrifice Alarbus in order to "appease the shadows" (1.1.103) of Titus's slain sons. Alarbus is sacrificed to gods not his own; his family is not granted any funeral rites; there is no concern for the fate of his soul. Tamora aptly labels this "cruel, irreligious piety" (1.1.133). Titus, "surnamed Pius" (1.1.23), is carrying out what he perceives as a codified obligation to his sons and his gods. It is "cruel" in that it is pitiless to Tamora's maternal pleas. It is "irreligious" in that it severs ties with then current Roman practices, which did not include human sacrifice, and in that it refuses to provide due recognition of the Goths and their culture. The Romans simply assume that they can do whatever they like to a conquered people and expect Tamora willingly to bow to Roman "superiority." Shortly thereafter, oblivious to the implications of this humiliation of the defeated Goths, the new emperor, Saturninus, takes Tamora, the "captive woman" (Deuteronomy 21.11), as his bride and empress. Anyone lacking the blind arrogance of these Romans can readily see that making Tamora "incorporate" in Rome (1.1.467) introduces a deadly virus into the body politic. Tamora confirms this in an aside, vowing to massacre them all (1.1.455). The lesson she has learned from Titus, is to be "pitiless" (2.3.162).[4] Despite marrying a Roman, assuming Roman garb, and outwardly conforming to Roman practices, Tamora remains, underneath it all, a Goth, a queen, and a deeply aggrieved mother. And, of course, Titus and Rome pay dearly for Titus's fervent, but woefully incomplete, understanding of piety.

At the opposite extreme from irreligious piety, which insists on sameness and hence excludes the pity required for the accommodation of difference, lies complete impiety, a disregard for piety in which a narcissistic present attempts to expunge the past by destroying or ignoring the traditions, rituals, and practices upon which the present and the future are founded and directed. This revolutionary impiety is every bit as "irreligious" and potentially destructive as its fascistic cousin,[5] and is thematized in *Titus Andronicus* by Saturninus and Aaron the Moor. Saturninus treats his emperorship as his personal toy rather than as a sacred obligation that "knits" him together with Rome. He rules by his own will and whim, heedless of tradition, history, law, and even reason. His ill judgment in marrying Tamora is really an expression of his impiety — his assumption that he can use anything he wishes for his own selfish ends without a sense of obligation to anything beyond himself. He welcomes her difference, but only superficially. Indifferent to Tamora's history and context, Saturninus chooses her as "a goodly lady ... of the hue / That I would choose, were I to choose anew" (1.1.261–262), not for her own sake. He assumes that he can take this captive woman, this exoticized other, and overwrite her at his will. In not really apprehending the radical otherness of Tamora, nor the effects of the Roman humiliation of her as monarch and mother, Saturninus becomes easy prey for her machinations.

Saturninus's impiety is a form of immature narcissism and ignorance, though it is corrigible in principle. The play does not in any way suggest that such reconciliations between others, though necessary to strive for, are easy to attain or likely to be completely successful in the long run. Certain differences, however, are presented as being irreconcilable in principle. Aaron is the case in point here. He knows enough about others to be able to maliciously manipulate them to serve his own ends, but has absolutely no respect for them and is notoriously incapable of either piety or pity. He revels in the evils he has perpetrated, wishes he could have performed ten thousand worse deeds (5.3.186–187), and if he ever did one good deed, repents it from his very soul (5.3.188–189). The core of his evil is the outright denial that he has any meaningful obligations to others. It is the self-centredness of Saturninus matured, become self-conscious, and taken to such an extreme that everyone else becomes either an instrument to be used or an obstacle to be overcome. In effect, Aaron's behavior signifies a complete removal from participation in humanity. His own son, whom he may seem to love, is nothing but a version of himself (4.2.109–113), whom Aaron wishes to raise to be a tool, a weapon, an extension of his malicious will rather than an autonomous person in his own right. Aaron is irreconcilable in principle to the Roman polity, or indeed to any polity at all, and thus must be denied accommodation, must be excluded. Tamora, on the other hand, is made irreconcilable to the Roman polity because of the Andronici's fanatical commitment to one conception of piety, a conception that deliberately excludes the tempering pity that is necessary to make piety truly religious.

Titus Andronicus teaches by negative example. Through it, we are expected to learn that it is only through piety, properly understood as embracing pity, that apocalypse can be avoided. The play's bloodbath was preventable. But preventing it would have required the recognition of others; that is an apprehension of difference and a willingness to accommodate it. The gap between Roman and Goth cannot be as unbridgeable as Titus perceives it to be, since Lucius is able to negotiate a common, if temporary and dodgy, space in which Goth and Roman can unite. However, Lucius at the end explicitly denies pity towards Aaron and Tamora (5.3.180, 198–199). He also excludes any form of piety as he denies them appropriate burial rites. He is sufficiently Romano-centric as to presume that the ghosts of Goths and Moors do not need to be appeased as Roman ones do. The lessons about piety and pity that we learn in *Titus Andronicus* cannot repair the damage that irreligious piety and impiety have done to Rome: nothing can restore Alarbus, Mutius, Lavinia, Tamora, Titus, and the rest. Rome has been taken over by a Lucius, who, denying pity and piety, and pronouncing peremptory judgment and sentence upon Aaron and Tamora as an act of personal revenge, is every bit as arbitrary and whimsical as was Saturninus. And that cannot bode well for Rome.

Hope would be in the offing only if those within the play could learn from the obscene violence they witness to recognize difference, to choose pity and to reject the vengeance demanded by "irreligious piety" or narcissistic impiety. The play demonstrates that they do not learn this. We have noted that Titus's mercilessness teaches Tamora to be equally relentless in seeking vengeance. The play also shows how Titus teaches his grandson, young Lucius, to observe Andronican piety and to reject pity. Titus's education of young Lucius begins in 3.2. The boy is overcome with pity for the woes of Lavinia and asks Titus to make her "merry with some pleasing tale" (3.2.47). Titus rejects this suggestion along with the pity that motivated it: "Peace, tender sapling, thou art made of tears, / And tears will quickly melt thy life away" (3.2.50–51). The scene ends with Titus telling Lavinia that he will instead read her "sad stories, chanced in times of old" and that the boy will assume the task of reading to her when Titus's eyesight tires (3.2.82–86). Later, after Lavinia has revealed the identity of her tormentors, Titus says to the boy, "And where's our lesson then? Boy, what say you?," to which young Lucius replies that, if he were a man, their mother's bedchamber would not be safe for "these base bondmen to the yoke of Rome." Marcus chimes in with "Ay, that's my boy!" (4.1.106–110).

At the end of the play, young Lucius does weep, as do all the Andronici, for their own dead, but we have no reason to assume that this implies any sense of a common humanity that would lead him to repudiate Titus's sacrifice of Alarbus or any of the acts of retaliation that that sacrifice inaugurated. Indeed in his final speech, young Lucius says, "e'en with all my heart / Would *I* were dead, so you did live again" (5.3.171–172, emphasis added), an expression of the old republican virtues that "pius Titus" was praised for at the beginning. What young Lucius has learned from his grandfather, his father, his uncle, his reading, and all the events he has witnessed or participated in, is — in the interests of the Andronican reading of piety — to kill pitilessly.

Shakespeare's purpose in presenting this tragedy is to offer the audience outside the play a teaching decidedly at odds with the scenes of education within it. The audience is expected to reject the failures of piety depicted in the play. It is expected to see "irreligious piety" and impiety, to know their fatal consequences, and to abstain, thus learning the lesson the participants within the play do not. There is no real hope for Rome in the play, but there is a glimmer of hope in the lesson that the audience might learn from this theater of cruelty — i.e., to avoid apocalypse, we must be very serious about all of the obligations that piety and pity demand. But the play also suggests that, in the real world off the stage, negotiating the demands and limits implicit in the recognition of difference is extraordinarily difficult and the results uncertain.

The Treatment of the Other in *Titus*

As we have seen, the problem of accommodating others is at the core of *Titus Andronicus*. The action of the play stems from a failure of recognition. Tamora is, literally, a captive woman taken in battle, who is by Saturninus "cleansed and used."[6] Divested of the primitive clothes of the savage animalistic Goths, Tamora becomes the resplendent Empress of Rome. Though, despite her claim to be "incorporate" in Rome, her rehabilitation is only skin deep. Tamora becomes the unassimilatable other. What makes the reconciliation of difference so difficult in *Titus Andronicus* is the resistance of others to "rehabilitation" and assimilation. The pious obligations one has to one's own identity, culture and history, one's family, one's nation are not easily cleansed way. Recognizing the inveterate nature of otherness, readers of *Titus Andronicus* are instructed to be dubious about comic endings, or a return to political and social harmony.

The revelations about cultural conflict in *Titus Andronicus* have much current relevance. As we learn from the North American occupation of Iraq, the United Nations's intervention in Afghanistan, ethnic tensions throughout the European Union, racial division in the United States and elsewhere, separatist longings in Quebec, and ongoing protests among indigenous peoples throughout the world, the various selves and others negotiating across a landscape fissured with generational, political, ethnic and gendered divides are not easily reconciled. The "rehabilitation" of others, their assimilation into a foreign culture is, as Tamora's Gothic persistence attests, not easily accomplished. Piety cuts both ways. The bonds that selves and others have to what they have been taught to regard as their own are not easily loosened, and the complex dynamic of over-esteeming and under-esteeming these bonds complicates any easy reconciliation of individuals and communities.

In *Titus Andronicus,* we learn, contra the biblical teaching in Deuteronomy 21.10–14, that captive women taken in battle are not easily cleansed and used. During Shakespeare's time, this biblical commonplace had both a strong literal and figurative resonance. Understood literally, it provided an occasion to examine the limits of piety and pity that the conquering self had to the conquered other. Figuratively, it was read, especially by Elizabethan Puritans, as providing direction on how the plain language that they had mandated as the preferred style of their sermons could incorporate its problematic other — the duplicitous tropes and schemes of rhetoric. For them, the rehabilitation of rhetoric was as difficult as it was necessary. If the plain truth of scripture was to be made compelling, it required the persuasive force of rhetorical ornament. Yet, these very same ornaments might seduce the audience, diverting its attention away from the truths of scripture. For Puritans, rhetorical language was, as Thomas Cartwright put it, "warily to be used" (165). John King, preaching on the book of Jonah, compared rhetorical language to "a captive woman taken in battle, she may be cleansed and used" (sig. M). Like Tamora, rhetorical ornament was the alluring exotic other. The challenge for the Puritans was Saturninus's challenge: how can this other be made "incorporate"? How may this other be "cleansed and used" and thus accommodated to a new context.

In her treatment of *Titus Andronicus,* a play about accommodating the other, how does Taymor treat the other? Accommodating the other is at the core of her aesthetics and her ethics. She hopes through a representation of otherness and a representation of the horrific violence done to the other — her "theater of cruelty" — that viewers may be jarred out of their complacency and forced to recognize their own voyeuristic complicity in violence. *Titus* estranges the film audience from its customary perspective on the other — i.e., regarding the other as the pleasurable object of a sadistic gaze — and thus is designed to shock the viewers, thereby motivating them to "stop demonizing the other and refrain from the violence that so often accompanies demonization" (Vaughan 78).

Taymor tells us that "it's very important that we constantly look at the other" (Taymor and Moyers), and otherness abounds in her *Titus.* The film draws from numerous cultural traditions (e.g., African, Indonesian, Japanese, and Western), mixes high and popular culture (e.g., Shakespearean tragedy, slasher films, classical theater and television), and blurs temporal and spatial distinctions between ancient Rome, Mussolini's Rome, suburban America and contemporary Croatia. *Titus*—frequently characterized as "eclectic," as a "pastiche"—embraces a postmodern aesthetic which privileges heterogeneity, pluralism, and discontinuity.

Yet, Taymor's apprehension of cultural difference is largely aesthetic, which is evident in her elevated concern with the signifier over its customary signifieds. Focusing her own and our attention on the commutable signifier—a dazzling spectacle of shapes, colors, patterns, and gestures drawn from all over the globe—she draws attention away from the historically-saturated meanings that have accrued to them in the very specific historical and geographical contexts from which they are derived. Thus, images of Africa that constitute the landscape of *The Lion King*—a lion, a lioness, a cub, giraffes, hyenas, a warthog—enter that landscape with meanings that accrued to them prior to their being inserted into the dramatic space in which she will "use" them. There, they are over-written as western archetypes and pressed into the service of narratives which are foreign to them, such as the Disneyfied version of the Oedipus/Hamlet story of *The Lion King.* In ahistorical, theatrical spaces such as these, differences can be reconciled that would be impossible to reconcile in historical spaces outside the text. In imaginary, utopian spaces such as these, lions can lie down with lambs, and a mermaid, as Disney's *The Little Mermaid* tells us, yearns to leave her origins behind and hopes for the transformation—in this instance, dismemberment and rememberment, no less transfiguring, though decidedly less horrific in its representation, than Lavinia's—that will allow her to become "part of that world." On the surface, the union of Taymor's *avant garde* aesthetic, often read as elitist, and the Disney corporation's industrial approach to the production of popular cultural objects seems counter-intuitive. Yet, the two are allied in their belief in the core values of a globalized American capitalism which is incapable of interrogating the problematic particularity of its own claims to universalism. At the level of design, Taymor's art challenges the evolving populist schlock of Mickey, Goofy, Ariel, Aladdin, Beauty and the Beast *et al.*, but ideologically, they share the same cultural logic. Her work is entirely at home and finds meaning within the same fantastic space outside of history that Disney has created. Disneyland is the place where all signs can happily co-exist, where lions and lambs, penguins and polar bears, lie down together; where African safari land, Tomorrowland, and Frontierland flow seamlessly into each other. All of these imaginary constructions borrow from images which exist in real space and time, and it is these signs, these "captive women" that are taken, cleansed and used. Appropriated and deployed anew, they constitute an anamorphic space in history that simultaneously points to itself and points to a space beyond history: a fictive space situated in the real historical space of early twenty-first century global capitalism. It is not only in Taymor's and Disney's dramatic spaces that signs can be "cleansed" (i.e., divested of their traditional significations) and "used" (i.e., transformed to serve new ends). This is also the underlying logic of a global capitalist marketplace, which by transforming use-value into exchange-value turns all objects and relations into commodities which can be endlessly exchanged. The place of the signs in Taymor's art is not unlike that of all the goods — clothes, pottery, artwork, weapons, ceremonial artifacts, relics — made available to North American consumers in ethnic-themed stores such as Pier One, Global Experience, and Ten Thousand Villages. Here the goods of the world in all their unharmonious incongruity are all conveniently found and happily offer themselves up for sale.

The text Taymor appropriates is, as we have already seen, internally dissonant, but Taymor amplifies and adds to those differences, ramping up their complexity. Despite this intensification of otherness, which would seem to make reconciliation more challenging than it is in the less intentionally heterogeneous *Titus Andronicus,* she remains optimistic that the differences within can be reconciled.

What is the source of this optimism? Virginia Mason Vaughan, in her "Looking at the Other in Julie Taymor's *Titus,*" claims that Taymor's art "presages an embrace of difference that ignores difference" (78). Taymor, she concludes in her reading of the film's close, points "to an unknown destination outside of human history and far from the religious, political and military practices that have shaped that history"; it is "only outside human history [that] we can stop demonizing the other and refrain from the violence that so often accompanies demonization" (78).

Where is this utopian space "outside" where reconciliation is possible and where all the differences that divide can be accommodated? It does not exist in the real; it only exists in the imaginary space of her film and in the historically specific space of the same American imagination that gives us Disneyland.

Silly talk "about an embrace of difference that ignores difference" is only possible if one has, like Saturninus, an egocentric acknowledgement of difference that portends no real recognition of otherness, or if one's apprehension of the other acknowledges only the most superficial of differences. Despite a well-intentioned regard for otherness, Taymor's sense of it is finally only aesthetic. Taymor talks much of *Playing with Fire,* the title of her book with Eileen Blumenthal, though it is the "word," not the element that she loves, an archetypal symbol, not something that literally burns.[7] *Titus* does not give us otherness; it offers representations of otherness, and the visual signs that constitute these representations do not necessarily correspond to their material referents. As signs appropriated for use within the film, they are, like those captive women taken in battle, cleansed and used; that is, shorn of their previous range of signification within a particular time and space. According to Eileen Blumenthal,

> Taymor's work — in theatre, opera and film — is not so much eclectic as it is cross bred. She draws on an enormous pool of forms, genres, and traditions. She grasps the centre of each form, how it works in its home context, and how it might resonate somewhere else. She conceives new theatrical organisms, combining traits from the most disparate sources to bring original hybrids to life [7].

Although, tellingly, she adds, "Usually [Taymor] assimilates disparate elements rather than leaving them in native dress" (7). Signs of otherness enter the film *Titus* largely as emblems ("a cruel temptress") or symbols ("revenge") wrenched from the historical contexts in which they circulated and from which they derived a particularized range of meanings. Thus appropriated and hollowed out, they are relocated into a new context in which they carry only the generalized and abstract significance of myth and ritual. Though it is not the myth and ritual of their own cultures that acts as the code through which they are apprehended, but that of the new context into which they have been inserted. Reduced to types, they are seized upon as other, appropriated and relocated into foreign narratives which typically read them in some exoticized fashion. We have seen this form of misrecognition before in Saturninus's deciding to make Tamora the object of a colonizing gaze that constructs her as "a goodly lady" with an alluring Gothic "hue" (1.1.261). Similarly, the use of Africa in *The Lion King* does not point outside the film to Africa, only to an orientalist conception of Africa circulating within the Western imagination. Incorporated and overwritten, these rehabilitated signs of cultural difference populate both Taymor's *Titus* and Disney's *The Lion King*, which is inspired by her aesthetic. It is these impoverished and appropriated others that prove so easy to reconcile, and the reconciliation takes place entirely and only within the text of the film and at the level of decoration and interior design.

This facile reconciliation of otherness is not only accomplished in "unknown destination[s] outside of human history"; it can also, as the preface to *Julie Taymor: Playing with Fire* shows, be realized in the equally fantastical, though decidedly material, world of Taymor's New York apartment:

> Her cheeks and breast distressed as if from years of sea winds, a giant figurehead labeled "The Havoc" greets visitors to Julie Taymor's New York apartment. Past this veteran of *Liberty's Taken*, Taymor's musical about the American revolution, a dozen white doors line a living room wall like the setting for a

Meyerhold farce. Indonesian batik and Itak weavings cover a sofa. Nearby two-foot-high Javanese peasants, which Taymor carved for *Way of Snow*, peer out between philodendron leaves, and tiny masked totems adorned with chicken feathers, from the same show, rest on the window sill. A ten-foot long bas relief Brazilian Indian from Taymor's design for *Savages*, nurses her baby in a jute hammock overhead. A sharp-lined alabaster bust from *Juan Darien* casts a critical eye around the room from his perch atop a stool. And somehow it all blends to evoke a sense of elegance and home [7].

At home and abroad, Taymor offers aesthetic solutions to political problems, seemingly unaware of the often intractable historical realities that trouble these imaginary reconciliations. It is only within aestheticized spaces — such as her apartment, the theatre and the screen — that the radical otherness of the deliberately intensified differences that she incorporates into her art can be made to happily co-exist. It is only by superficially apprehending difference that it can be so easily accommodated. Despite a continuing interest in other cultures and an aesthetic heavily indebted to their artistic traditions, she shows a Saturninus-like indifference to the otherness of the other. As Goesta Struve-Dencher notes, "while Julie Taymor was having a mystical experience on a Balinese volcano, the Indonesian government was bloodily annexing East Timor, with the tacit complicity of the United States. Except for (or despite?) a brush with authorities over the content of *Way of Snow*, Indonesian politics seem to have affected Taymor very little" (11–12). It is only her own lack of piety towards the other that allows her to appropriate it and assimilate it to her art.

This blindness is also evident in her appropriation of Shakespeare's play. Disregarding its skeptical attitude to the complex problems of familial, cultural and political reconciliation, Taymor recasts the play as a comic *bildungsroman*. The boy we meet at the beginning of *Titus* is largely an innocent spectator to the very real violence going on all around him, but gradually becomes a participant in the action. This boy's part is not only significantly greater than the corresponding part in the play, but Taymor ultimately uses him for quite contrary purposes. She eliminates young Lucius's pious farewell to Titus at the end of the play, approving those antiquated values that set in motion the cycle of revenge. This scene in the playtext suggests the cycle of violence is likely to continue. Young Lucius, schooled in the "irreligious piety" of his grandfather, has learned first-hand why and how to seek revenge. Instead, in the final scene, Taymor has young Lucius carry Aaron's son out of the coliseum, implying that he has assumed responsibility for his upbringing and that a happy reconciliation of a fragmented and mutilated Rome is on the horizon:

So with Lucius opening that cage and taking the boy out of the coliseum, this child, now of his own free will, takes the baby and exits out of the coliseum, this theatre of violence, of cruelty, and into the bleak but open landscape that has water, which means there's a possibility for fruition, of cleansing, of forgiveness. It's also a movement towards the sunrise, which is the next generation or the next one hundred years or the next millennium. But it freezes on that image, just that slice of the sun coming up. It's not a full sunrise. It's about possibility and hope but it's not about solution [qtd. in DeLuca and Lindroth 29].

Taymor would have us believe that the incredible violence the boy has witnessed and participated in has been therapeutic, purging violence out of the boy's system and allowing him, and the society in which he will eventually assume a leadership role, to heal. Taymor tells us that she decided to use the child's experience as "bookends" because "the development of the child from innocence through knowledge to compassion is, to [her], the essentially most important theme" (qtd. in Johnson-Haddad 35). The cure she proposes is essentially homeopathic: it proposes to cure by introducing into the body the very pathogen responsible for the illness. The problem here is that Taymor has not shown how this therapy could possibly work and how it might prevent the very disease it seeks to cure from spreading.

In fact, the way Taymor recasts one of the most important scenes of young Lucius's education, home-schooled among the Andronici, implies the exact opposite of her intended theme. This is the banquet scene in which Marcus kills a black fly that had the temerity to disrupt the feast. Tellingly, Taymor transfers the fly-killing and the associated dialogue from Marcus to young Lucius. She has young Lucius enthusiastically cheer old Titus along as he madly stabs at the table as though it were the Moor and Tamora; and Marcus, instead of uttering the Shakespearean observation that Titus is mistaking "false shadows for true substances" (3.2. 79–80), laughs along at the feckless stabbing. The main effect of Taymor's revision of the scene is to let us see young Lucius learning even more directly than in Shakespeare to absorb his grandfather's hatred, violence, and desire for revenge. In her commentary on the scene, Taymor notes that although Shakespeare had assigned the fly-killing to Marcus, that seemed wrong to her, so she gave it to young Lucius, noting that the child innocently shows hatred for the blackamoor and is "starting to learn his lessons as children will" (commentary on DVD). Ironically, by this recasting of the play, she actually reinforces its main thematic of "irreligious piety," and shows young Lucius learning exactly what the play implies he learns. The optimistic ending Taymor then imposes on the narrative is unfounded. There is nothing in the scenes of instruction underwriting young Lucius's renunciation of violence except

Taymor's romantic faith in the persistence of childhood innocence despite the predations of experience, a faith which Richard Burt has somewhat less generously characterized as "fascist" (300).

Unlike Shakespeare, Taymor has the boy serve as a proxy for the audience. She expects that, like the boy, we will leave the theater rejecting violence. However, the audience sees a mere mimesis of violence, its representation, whereas the boy has seen and participated in the real thing. Eliding the distinction between acts of violence and their representation, Taymor's homeopathic cure asks us to believe that the "false shadows" and "true substance" of violence can have the same effect.

Conclusion

Taymor, in believing that the reconciliation of differences in the imaginary is equivalent to their reconciliation in the real, is unwittingly complicit with the very problem she seeks to resolve. She can accommodate otherness by allowing only easily assimilated and superficial differences to cross the borders which separate the aesthetic worlds of stage and screen from those we actually have to live in. In the closed aesthetic spaces of her art, the most heterogeneous ideas can be harmoniously yoked together. To the delight of some and the dismay of others, Taymor feels equally at home with William Shakespeare and with Walt Disney. Canonical culture, with its implications of elitism and inaccessibility, fuses with mass culture, with its implications of democracy and ease of absorption. Out of the union emerges a miraculous and/or monstrous hybrid, steadfast in its faith in the truth and goodness of the American Dream. Such dreams may simply be ideological covers distancing us from disconcerting realities. Taymor is also equally at home with the National Museum of Women in the Arts and with their sponsors of a retrospective of her work, America's largest defense contractor, General Dynamics. Strange bedfellows. Taymor's ability to negotiate the worlds of art, commerce, and war bespeaks a disturbing and dilettantish eclecticism. We need to be wary of a "tamed menagerie of fetishized otherness" (Croteau) in which disconcerting material realities can "somehow ... all blend to a sense of elegance and home" (Taymor and Blumenthal 7). Taymor is right when she says we need to "constantly look at the other." However, when we look at the other with a Saturninian eye — only as an object with a desirable "hue," hoping to assimilate it while ensuring that it retains only those differences that serve to exoticize it — we are not really looking at the other at all, but only at ourselves.

Notes

1. Moyers interviews Taymor on *America Responds: Moyers in Conversation* (aired on PBS 20 Sept. 2001):

BM: *Titus* ends not with an American happy ending. We do not know whether the killing is going to continue or whether there is hope for the future.

JT: No, I changed *Titus*. Many people think I was **sentimental** about this [emphasis added]. At the end everybody dies practically. There is the child of the enemy, Aaron the Moor, has a baby [*sic*]. Normally I think in any normal culture, that baby would have been confined or killed. Because, of course, as these children, if their parents are slaughtered they're going to grow up and avenge their parents and their culture. But I had a different ending. This is the ending that I would hope for, which is I took my 12-year-old boy because the whole sequence is told through the eyes of Titus's grandson, the whole movie I set through these eyes. At the end of the film on his own after he's seen all the slaughter, after he's been complicit. He was also part of the vengeance act, he took this child, this black child, out of a cage — because I had it in a cage. They wouldn't kill the child but keep it in a cage, his parents, the young boy's father. But he himself on his own will took the child out and held his enemy and moved out of the coliseum. And the book ends with this coliseum, the theater of vengeance and cruelty. We didn't talk about the entertainment value of violence as well. And he exited. Now he's going to a bleak landscape. There's water. There's the beginning of a sunrise, but he's taking that enemy out of the coliseum. When we opened on Christmas Day 1999, that's what I hoped for. I hoped that when we went to the next millennium that there would be that, that the children.... And I believe there has to be the children.... The children have to start to question because they're inculcated [Taymor and Moyers].

2. The popular song from *The Lion King*, "Hakuna Matata," expresses Disney's and Taymor's shared faith that cultural and political differences can be resolved if all believe in the same "problem-free philosophy."

3. A number of recent studies of the film (and by extension, the play) have placed it in the context of various manifestations of human brutality and unspeakable atrocities. R. A. Foakes, for example, tells us that *Titus* "ambitiously seeks to merge ancient and modern, and to comment on the appalling acceptance of, and insensibility to, violence in our own time" ("Torture, Rape, and Cannibalism: *Titus Andronicus*," in his *Shakespeare and Violence*, Cambridge: Cambridge University Press, 2003, 57). Richard Burt puts the film in the context of the Holocaust ("Shakespeare and the Holocaust: Julie Taymor's *Titus* is Beautiful, or Shaksploi Meets (the) Camp," in Richard Burt, ed., *Shakespeare After Mass Media*, New York: Palgrave, 2002, 295–329); Judith Buchanan puts it in the context of the conflicts in the Balkans ("Leaves of Brass and Gads of Steel: Cinema as Subject in Shakespeare Films, 1991–2000," in her *Shakespeare on Film*. London: Pearson Education Limited, 2004, 242–260); and David F. McCandless situates it in the events of and following 9/11 ("A Tale of Two *Titus*es: Julie Taymor's Vision on Stage and Screen," *Shakespeare Quarterly* 53.4 [2002], 487–511). McCandless notes that "America's response to terrorist incursion is the same one as Titus's: emotionally charged, exterminatory vengeance" (489) and argues that Taymor's project in *Titus* is to produce a reading of the play that would counter the mindset that produces such traumatized rushes to vengeance, a project that he sees as being carried out much more effectively in Taymor's 1994 stage version of the play:

> In attempting to extend her vision of *Titus Andronicus* to potential millions in the American moviegoing public, Taymor, despite her explicit intentions, offers Shakespeare's play as a cultural prosthetic, a tool with which to conquer contemporary traumas, even including, two years later, the 9/11 catastrophe. By grafting a happy ending onto a brutal revenge movie, Taymor lets her spectators have it both ways, sanctioning both retaliation

against and redemption of the enemy, in either case disavowing lack by imposing it on a mystified, marginalized other. In Taymor's *Titus*, trauma is largely evaded through the agencies of figures unseen in the stage production but relatively indispensable to movies: the vengeful antihero, the scapegoated villain, the fetishized woman, and the incorruptible child who will lead us into the new millennium [510–511].

4. In her instructions to her sons, Chiron and Demetrius, on how to conduct the rape and mutilation of Lavinia, Tamora claims that she has learned to be pitiless from Titus:

> TAMORA. Hadst thou in person ne'er offended me,
> Even for his sake am I pitiless.
> Remember, boys, I pour'd forth tears in vain
> To save your brother from the sacrifice,
> But fierce Andronicus would not relent.
> Therefore away with her, and use her as you will;
> The worse to her, the better lov'd of me [2.3.161–7].

5. Elsewhere (K. Fedderson and J. M. Richardson, "*Titus*: Shakespeare in Pieces." *SRASP [Shakespeare and Renaissance Association Selected Papers]*, 25 [2002], 70–80), we have argued that

> [i]n its extreme form, piety turns into fascism, the condition in which the present form of the state elides the distinction between past and present, claiming that the present is a restoration of the past in its purest form. Invoking this myth of palingenesis, Mussolini, for instance, claims that the new Rome that will rise from the ashes of the current Rome, following the expurgation of accreted alien elements, is the old Rome purified and born again (GK *palin* again + *genesis* born). Its opposite, an "impious" and, therefore revolutionary, present expunges its past, razing the monuments upon which the present and future are founded. Thus, the former Soviet Union pulls down the statues of Lenin, and, in a similar iconoclastic gesture, the Taliban Republic sets its tanks loose on the Buddhas within its borders [71].

6. John King, "Lectures upon Ionas delivered at Yorke in the yeare of our Lorde 1594," Oxford 1597, sig. M.

7. "Fire is a transformative element," Taymor says. "I love the word 'fire.' Think about the first shadows on the cave wall, the shadow puppets that are the oldest art form in Indonesia. All of this happens with the element of fire. In my work I'm always seeking the elemental essence of that subject matter, of that idea" (qtd. in Pender).

Works Cited

Bakhtin, Mikhail. *The Dialogic Imagination: Four Essays*. Ed. C. Emerson and M. Holquist. Austin: University of Texas Press, 1981

Burt, Richard. "Shakespeare and the Holocaust: Julie Taymor's *Titus* is Beautiful, or Shakesploi Meets (the) Camp." *Shakespeare After Mass Media*. Ed. Richard Burt. New York: Palgrave, 2002. 295–329.

Cartwright, Thomas. *A Commentary upon the epistle of Sainte Paule written to the Colossians. Preached by Thomas Cartwright, and now published for the further use of the Church of God*. London: George Norton, 1612.

Croteau, Melissa. E-mail to the authors. 14 Oct. 2007.

DeLuca, Maria, and Mary Lindroth. "Mayhem, Madness, Method: An Interview with Julie Taymor." *Cineaste* 25.3 (2000): 28–31.

Fanon, Frantz. *Black Skin, White Masks*. New York: Grove Press, 1967.

_____. *The Wretched of the Earth*. New York: Grove Press, 1965.

Johnson-Haddad, Miranda. "A Time for *Titus*: An Interview with Julie Taymor." *Shakespeare Bulletin* 18.4 (2000): 34–36.

King, John. "Lectures upon Ionas delivered at Yorke in the yeare of our Lorde 1594." Oxford, 1597.

Kojeve, Alexandre. *Introduction to the Reading of Hegel*. Ed. Allan Bloom. Trans. James H. Nichols Jr. Ithaca: Cornell University Press, 1986.

Kymlicka, Will. *Multicultural Citizenship: A Liberal Theory of Minority Rights*. Oxford: Oxford University Press, 1995.

McCandless, David F. "A Tale of Two *Titus*es: Julie Taymor's Vision on Stage and Screen," *Shakespeare Quarterly* 53.4 (2002): 487–511.

Pender, Rick. "Hurricane Julie." *CityBeat: Cincinnati* 23–29 Sept. 1999 <http://citybeat.com/1999–09–23/printable/art3.html>.

Shakespeare, William. *Titus Andronicus. The Riverside Shakespeare: The Complete Works.* 2nd ed. Ed. G. Blakemore Evans, et al. Boston and New York: Houghton Mifflin Company, 1997.

Struve-Dencher, Goesta. "'Theatre is my Skin': Tracing Julie Taymor's Creative Ethos." 25 April 2008 <http://goesta.net/files/ideas/misc/taymor.pdf>.

Taylor, Charles. *Sources of the Self.* Cambridge: Cambridge University Press, 1989.

Taymor, Julie. "Commentary" on *Titus*. Disc 1. Dir. Julie Taymor. 2000. DVD Special edition (2 Discs). Twentieth Century–Fox, 2006.

_____. Interview with Bill Moyers. *America Responds: Moyers in Conversation*. PBS. Washington, DC. 20 Sept. 2001. PBS.org. 6 February 2005 <http://www.pbs.org/americaresponds/moyers920.html>.

_____, with Eileen Blumenthal. *Julie Taymor: Playing with Fire.* Updated and expanded ed. 1995. New York: Harry N. Abrams, 1999.

Titus. Dir. Julie Taymor. Perf. Anthony Hopkins, Jessica Lange, and Harry Lennix. 2000. DVD Special Edition (2 Discs). Twentieth Century–Fox, 2006.

Vaughan, Virginia Mason. "Looking at the 'Other' in Julie Taymor's *Titus*." *Shakespeare Bulletin* 21.3 (2003): 71–80.

4

Post-Apocalyptic Spaces in Baz Luhrmann's *William Shakespeare's Romeo + Juliet*

RICHARD VELA

Film versions of *Romeo and Juliet* have always been attracted to the implied imagery of the houses, which Mercutio famously cursed (3.1.92).[1] While identification seems particularly true of Baz Luhrmann's film, where the two houses are presented in the opening credits as actual skyscrapers, one on each side of a digitally imposed Christ statue, in fact, each of the three most significant previous film versions develops a *mise-en-scène* that uses spatial metaphors to articulate and embody its adaptive approach. George Cukor plans his 1936 literary prestige version around the elegant and elaborate sets on his Hollywood back lot Verona. Renato Castellani in 1954 uses neo-realism and emphasizes authentic medieval buildings, music and paintings. Franco Zeffirelli's 1968 version uses *cinéma vérité* techniques as he contrasts the lush garden and the barren city square to dramatize the late 1960s conflict between youth and age.[2] Baz Luhrmann in his 1996 film rejects any attempt to explore Italian or Early Modern worlds and instead develops an entirely artificial world, taking images from both Mexico City and the coastal city of Vera Cruz together with superimposed computer generated images and then borrowing from a wide range of films and film genres to reveal a post-apocalyptic landscape in what he describes as his attempt "to find modern day images and equivalents that could de-code the language of Shakespeare" for today's audience (Luhrmann). To achieve this effect, as Peter Donaldson argues, Luhrmann links his film to media rather than history, "Old-time TV, not Elizabethan London, is the point of origin" ("'In Fair Verona'" 63), and, through his perhaps overactive camera, Luhrmann seems to dissolve space and make it a function of the media, in short, to "undermine the sense of realistic location" (Donaldson, "'All Which It Inherit'" 198). Specifically, through his invocation of other films and genres, Luhrmann reminds the audience that they are watching images that seem intended to evoke other somewhat familiar images.[3]

This essay will argue that Luhrmann uses a variety of techniques to destabilize audience expectations and then inscribe familiar scenes with unexpected meanings. He places the action of the film in a world where Shakespeare is as much a relic as the monolithic ruin that dominates the film's imagery. Shakespeare survives mainly as a figure of the past through the language of signs and advertisements. This is a post-catastrophic, post-apocalyptic world in which nature is contained and mediated, fabricated from images and genres to which it constantly alludes, a world in which the deaths of Romeo and Juliet remain an isolated event with no indication that their sacrifice will have any positive effect on the world. The opening of the film presents a pattern of Luhrmann constructing images by taking the elements of the original and then recontextualizing them through borrowing from other genres. Luhrmann's allusive technique tends to subvert rather than reinforce the meanings displayed on the screen, and it often blurs the line between media representation of events and the events themselves by drawing on the conventions of television and print reporting. The ending of the film, less often discussed in terms of how it differs from previous versions, provides a good example of how Luhrmann radically reshapes events and draws on a variety of film conventions to create a very different story. His film is not just a change from Zeffirelli's youth affirming green world in terms of visual content and style. What Luhrmann does is appropriate a very different set of motivations and sensibilities to propel his characters through the events of Shakespeare's play.

"Both Your Houses"

Several articles discuss the locations in Luhrmann's film as representative of real places and real ethnic divisions. Early reviews in particular argued that Luhrmann was describing a Miami/Cuban or Los Angeles/Mexican environment, or some other border place dominated by divisions between Latino and Anglo cultures.[4] Alfredo Michel Modenessi, on the other hand, writing as an insider, interestingly explores Luhrmann's use of actual locations in Mexico City, affirming, however, that "we are probably not meant to identify this place as anything other than a shimmering no-place" (70). More recently, Philippa Sheppard argues that "Luhrmann's selection of Latin American culture as the dominant one in his film ... is crucial to the ways in which Luhrmann explores urban postmodern multiculturalism" (242).

To get a better sense of how a Shakespeare adaptation might explore or exploit Latin culture, we need only to consider two examples. In *West Side Story* (1961), Arthur Laurents, Leonard Bernstein, and Stephen Sondheim adapt Shakespeare's division of families to reflect issues of immigration and assimilation. The Sharks are recent Puerto Rican immigrants, and the Jets are first-generation Americans, the children of Polish and Italian immigrants. Comments about being "American" in this film are deliberately tinged with immigrant irony that clearly has no precedent in Shakespeare's citizens of Verona. In addition, a song like "America," with its contrasting choruses on the attractions and difficulties of being in America ("Ev'ry thing free in America / For a small fee in America"), illustrates and emphasizes the misgivings of the Latinos in the film.[5] James Gavin Bedford's adaptation of Shakespeare's *Richard III* provides a second example. In *The Street King* (2002), Richard becomes "King Rikki" (an alternate title for the film), and Bedford turns the conflicts of that play into turf wars between Latino gangs, the blue *Norteños*, located north of Bakersfield and the red *La Eme* in southern California. The film opens with a spray paint rendition of the Folio Shakespeare portrait being painted over to include a red bandana, sunglasses (shades), a gold crucifix earring, and a goatee, changing the Elizabethan playwright into a contemporary, hip *vato*. On either side, the words *plata* (silver, money) and *plomo* (lead, bullets) appear, alluding to Columbian drug lord Pablo Escobar.[6] Clearly, however, this kind of exploration is very much not the kind of thing Luhrmann is doing. Even if we concede that Luhrmann's "depiction of Verona Beach and its inhabitants' attitudes to Latinity bears striking parallels with Shakespeare's Verona and Elizabethan assumptions about Spain and Italy" (Sheppard 243), it is still difficult to show that Luhrmann's film deliberately explores ethnicity beyond what is necessary to demonstrate a fundamental difference between the two families.

The three major film versions of *Romeo and Juliet* prior to Luhrmann's have in common an attempt to capture the original time and place of the events. Reportedly, producer Irving Thalberg, who cast his thirty-five year old wife, Norma Shearer, as Juliet, wanted to film in Italy but settled for sending "distinguished British designer Oliver Messel with a camera crew to Verona" (Flamini 245). Although Cukor's "Hollywood set was designed in detail from carefully selected photographs of Italian renaissance architecture" (Davies 154), designer Cedric Gibbons had the final say, and the sets "are on a characteristic M-G-M scale, detailed and colossal architectural behemoths that tend to dwarf the actors" (Flamini 247). H. R. Coursen cites a study guide prepared for the film's release which states that Gibbons "designed fifty-four models, actual reproductions of historical Veronese buildings ... so that there might be a faithful atmosphere of the fifteenth century capital of Northern Italy" (44).

Filming his *Giuliete e Romeo* in Italy, Castellani seems obsessed, according to Anthony Davies, with "insistently filling the frame with authentic architectural and artistic detail" (156). Roger Manvell writes that Castellani's film was "a splendidly colourful reincarnation of fifteenth-century Italy in Technicolor, the period to which the play was moved forward so that the more splendid resources of art could be drawn upon for costumes, settings and locations" (97),[7] and Patricia Tatspaugh comments that Castellani even "interpolated sequences to portray Renaissance Verona, its rigid class system, Roman Catholicism and feuding families" (138).[8] The film is notable both for its realistic settings and for its use of period art as a pattern for many of its visual effects. Although the architecture tends to enclose and isolate its characters, its details spring out as one notices a dress from Botticelli, a fresco from Fra Angelico, or the door from San Zeno Maggiore.

In a somewhat different way, Zeffirelli also emphasizes the Italian origins of the Romeo and Juliet story, but his Verona consistently contrasts open and natural places, such as Juliet's garden, with the spaces of the city itself. According to Ace Pilkington, "For Zeffirelli, the Italian towns which became his Verona (Tuscania, Pienza, and Gubbio) are part of the plot, an 'additional character' indeed, with the beauty of Renaissance Italy but also a sinister energy which drives the tragedy inexorably on." In fact, he adds, "The town seems to crowd and compress the characters so that the individual violence and riots look like attempts to escape from a maze" (172). Viewed alongside Castellani's dark and claustrophobic vision, however, Zeffirelli's version seems light, open, and spacious, as a comparison of similar scenes would demonstrate. While Cukor's lovers touch hands, and Castellani's do not touch at all, Zeffirelli's Romeo sees his Juliet in a low-cut gown sitting on the edge of a long and spacious balcony that wraps part way around the building. Framed in the greenery of the Capulet garden, the lovers discover each other, and then Romeo impulsively climbs a tree, and suddenly he is on the balcony with her. All three films draw from similar sources, and for each the aim is to create some sense of Italy and the Renaissance world, however differently they might use that world. Luhrmann's version contains a very different set of references suited to a very different purpose.

Meditation on the Ruins

Luhrmann's film presents a world that is a "Never-never land" (Rothwell 241), "a no-place that stands for anyplace" (Arroyo 8), a "meta city" (Jess-Cooke, *Shakespeare* 66), that "reduces its Mexican landscape to a trope for the postmodern city" (Modenessi 70). For Jose Arroyo, it is "a 'constructed' world, one that is different enough from a 'real' one to allow for different ways of knowing, but with enough similarities to permit understanding," a kind of "parallel universe" that is "like ours but different," a creative technique that he traces to comics books, science fiction, and fantasy novels (121). It is also a place where nothing seems experienced in and of itself, where things are instead filtered through media. In fact, as Peter Donaldson writes, "the film works ... consistently to weaken the sense of place, because every place is equally a construction of a pervasive media culture" ("'All Which it Inherit'" 198). Worthen explains this phenomena as an example of the film's "alertness to the process of surrogation, its simultaneous invocation and displacement of the 'original,'" and he argues that "[t]he film marks its fidelity to Shakespeare's *Romeo and Juliet* at the precise moment that it marks it distance from it, when it cites the text (e.g. 'long sword') as text — a text that is instantly replaced by performance; refigured as both a cultural commodity and as an item in commodity culture" ("Drama" 1104). This interest in invoking and displacing extends to the entire list of components in the film, including Shakespeare himself, the original play, previous film versions of the play, other films and film genres that Luhrmann uses to develop his alternative view of the Romeo and Juliet story, the very media which permeates nearly every piece of our experiencing the film, and even Mexico City itself.[9] Samuel Crowl notes that in this film, "'This place we see' does at least partially, emerge from a place we know: other films" (127). It is, in short, as virtually every writer on the film has noted either in praise or exasperation, very much a postmodern film.[10]

    In many cases identities and significances are constructed, or reconstructed, as we watch. One notable example is the construction of gender that occurs through paralleling Gloria Capulet and Mercutio as they prepare for the party. We see the process begin with Lady Capulet, who is dressing and being dressed even as she tells Juliet about young Paris, preparing her daughter for her own role as a young woman in Verona. Gloria Capulet's comically exaggerated movements, her southern accent, and the allusions perhaps to the corset fastening scene in *Gone with the Wind* (1939), all emphasize the artificial, and to finish it off she appears as Cleopatra, perhaps an allusion to Elizabeth Taylor's starring role in the eponymous film (1963). Shortly after this scene, Mercutio appears outrageously dressed, somewhat like Lady Capulet in wig and sequined dress. Commenting on the results, Donaldson contends that the "thin line between femininity as masquerade and as reality is underscored by the way in which this sequence exactly repeats Lady Capulet's earlier descent of the same staircase" ("'In Fair Verona'" 71).

    At another level, other elements of the film define a specific set of connections and suggest a kind of symbolic geography, with the Christ statue and the image of the Virgin Mary defining fundamental oppositions. These two images mediate between the warring families. The Christ statue appears as a kind of divide between the towers marked Montague and Capulet, and the image of the Madonna marks the church into which both Capulet and Montague can retreat. Romeo meets Friar Laurence there, marries Juliet there, and it is there that Juliet is laid to rest. The Montague world is connected with images of Christ and the crucifixion. The Montagues themselves exist for the most part in public space — on the beach, wearing open shirts, riding in an open convertible. The Capulet world is connected with images of the Blessed Virgin Mary. Juliet's room is a virtual shrine to Mary. Their spaces are interior and closed. The Capulet party and Juliet's room are expected images, but other reinforcements of this motif include Capulet's office, then the elevator, steam room, and den in which Capulet and Paris meet to discuss Juliet. At the Capulet mansion, Juliet and Romeo must meet in other enclosures: the elevator and in the pool, where the security system simply adds another layer of enclosures as the lovers appear on the multiple small screens. Although others have noted that water images are often associated with Romeo, the water images occur most often at the Capulet mansion or in direct connection with Juliet. Romeo, in Juliet's home, immerses his face in water, then, a few minutes later, he stares through water when he first sees Juliet. He falls into the pool with her twice after the party and then again when he leaves her room after they consummate their marriage.

Catherine Martin, Luhrmann's set director and now wife, comments that since they "clash" the language of Shakespeare "with a modern context, the language is clarified because it is articulated in familiar images" (qtd. in Luhrmann). Consider briefly the often discussed opening of the film. The fundamental elements of the action are, of course, there: the prologue followed by the quarrel that spills out into the city and draws in both elders and citizens and stops only when the Prince intervenes. Writing about Luhrmann's version, Philippa Hawker says, "This scene is filled with glancing references to and overt borrowings from the cinema of violence: the Western, the gangster movie, the kung-fu pic, the urban drama, the action comedy" (7). More importantly, Sergio Leone and John Woo, the influences most often noted for this scene, practice very stylized approaches to violence, and it is that mediated kind of violence that is most significant for what Luhrmann attempts here.[11] In the fight at the gas station, for example, Tybalt's stylized actions invoke a number of sources, including the "slow-motion shots of the leaping Tybalt firing two guns at once," which Loehlin says is "a parody of, or homage to, the Hong Kong director, John Woo" (126),[12] but, drawing from another spectrum, his movements sometimes suggest a toreador placing *banderillas*, or a dancer, sometimes ballet, sometimes flamenco, an allusion perhaps to Luhrmann's own first film, *Strictly Ballroom* (1992). Certainly the sequence of Tybalt genuflecting, crossing himself, and kissing the pistol — an extraordinary pause in the rapid action of the fight — constitutes another example of the very stylized and ritualized action of this opening that often becomes comic exactly because of these elements. The point is simply that, as Martin claims, the film does reconstruct the opening fight through this extensive vocabulary of performance sources, but these elements do not amount to an innocent rendering from one medium to another.

One indication of the effect of this change is that, on another level, simultaneously undercutting and emphasizing all of this bravado and danger, everything we see in this opening is also both introduced by a variety of new formats and then rapidly transformed into still more of them. Courtney Lehmann comments that "[t]he prevailing feel of this bizarre opening sequence is pure pastiche: evening-soap fiction meets evening-magazine 'real life,' but the lines separating titillation from truth, melodrama from docudrama, are fuzzy at best" (134). In its shift from reportage to action to television live action to newspaper print and magazines, the opening also oddly recalls the opening of Cukor's 1936 version, which introduces the characters by family, as Luhrmann does, then shows what appears to be a tapestry, which dissolves into a drawing, and then suddenly becomes a stage tableaux as the central figure begins to say the lines of the Prologue, after which the scene seems to change back into a drawing, then cuts to an overhead painting of the city of Verona, then to the middle of the city where it places the viewer in the town square as the Capulets, then the Montagues, enter in formal procession. Cukor seems to be trying to impress his audience with the authenticity of his film, but in Luhrmann's version, as Anthony Guneratne points out, "a certain ironic self-awareness (not unlike Shakespeare's) allows the film a certain distance from, even ambivalence toward, the genres it cites insistently: reality TV, the teen pic, MTV, the Bollywood extravaganza, and, of course, the previous film adaptations of Robbins and Wise" (240).[13] Maurice Hindle calls attention to yet another effect of this opening when he says it becomes possible to generalize "that communications through screen and image in modern culture are so pervasive that there is little difference between our experience of reality and its media representations" (178). When Romeo meets Benvolio, a few lines later (about four minutes later in the film), the events of the fight are already on the television news and on the headlines of *The Verona Beach Herald*.

Dominating this constructed world is the image of the ruin, the Sycamore Grove Theater, the embodiment of that post-apocalyptic dystopian

vision. Judith Buchanan sees the image of the ruined Sycamore Grove Theatre as part of the "elegiac symbolism" that Luhrmann used to comment on
the death of "public performative arenas — both theatres and cinemas ... left
to crumble in spaces no longer fashionable, memorials to their own outmod-
ishness" (236). Perhaps more than that, the ruin also recalls similar elements
in other post-apocalyptic films. It is somewhat like the image of the broken
Statue of Liberty at the end of *Planet of the Apes* (1968), the ruins of Washington, D.C., in *Logan's Run* (1976), the remnants of civilization in the *Mad
Max* series (*Mad Max* 1979, *The Road Warrior* 1981, *Mad Max Beyond Thunderdome* 1985), and the recurring images of the destructive wars between
humans and machines in the *Terminator* series (*The Terminator* 1984, *Terminator 2: Judgment Day* 1991, *Terminator 3: Rise of the Machines* 2003), or
the monolithic structures in films such as *Metropolis* (1927) or *Blade Runner*
(1982). The theater is a signifier of a world that is presented as missing. This
sense of a missing world extends both to the ruins of Shakespearean architecture and to the ruins of Shakespeare's language. The ruined arch appears
three times, displacing more conventional locations for the actions that
Luhrmann moves to this site. Benvolio mentions "the grove of sycamore /
That westward rooteth from this city side" (1.1.119–120), and most often film
versions portray the location as a wooded, isolated place, but Luhrmann's
film tends to exclude or marginalize nature rather than incorporate it as a
refuge. The beach and Mantua, for example, are both barren and bleak. The
natural havens that exist in other filmed versions of the play are absent from
this one. The ruin appears a second time a few scenes later (1.4) when Romeo,
Mercutio, Benvolio and others are on their way to the party, a scene that
other versions place in a street. The final appearance occurs at the point
where Tybalt kills Mercutio (3.1), a scene that other versions clearly place in
the square, which is to say, in the central part of the city. Luhrmann instead
places these events at the most marginal edge of the city, a place where the
mere shell of a building is allowed to stand undisturbed as a monument to
what is missing.

By moving all of these scenes to the ruined theater, Luhrmann is able
to link them together and emphasize the theatricality of each scene. In the
first, Romeo sits writing framed by the arch of the ruin as the sun rises
behind him. Buchanan notes that these first "shots of the ruined theatre are
given more potential symbolic weight than any single image that has preceded them by virtue of the fact that for once the camera is allowed a moment
of pause" (232). This image of the poet Romeo perhaps intentionally suggests images of writer/singer Kurt Cobain and of DiCaprio's previous image
as a writer in *The Basketball Diaries* (1995). Michael Anderegg points out
that "his image is constructed in a theatrical, self-conscious fashion: ciga-

rette in hand, hair tousled, sport coat over his 'Hawaiian' shirt, jotting his Petrarchan conceits in a small notebook" (*Cinematic* 75). In the second appearance of the ruin, it is night and the Montague boys are costumed and dancing on the stage as they prepare to go to the party. In a sense, it is the staging area where Mercutio delivers his "Queen Mab" speech while the fireworks from the Capulet celebration fill the background. It is here that Romeo takes the drugs which distort his vision until he sees Juliet at the party. For the last scene, Luhrmann stages the fight between Mercutio, Tybalt, and Romeo that ends in Mercutio's death. According to Buchanan, "The symbolism of the ruined theatre becomes most delineated ... in its final appearance"; it is here, she says, that Mercutio "self-consciously performs his own death," and he "is left, dramatically framed by the desultory theatre arch until, with deliberate stylization, the lights are brought down on them both" (234). In a sense, the introduction of Romeo at this site and the introduction of Mercutio in the same place prepare the way for the most dramatic scene, the turning point in the story, the death of Mercutio. Interestingly, Tybalt's death does not occur here in the same location as Mercutio's death, though it does in the other film versions.

Part of what is missing, however, is Shakespeare himself. In *Shakespeare Remains*, Lehmann uses auteur theory to examine Shakespeare, because "the concept of auteur renders visible what *remains* after all is said and undone, by drawing attention to how the plays themselves — and recent film adaptations of them — generate intriguing traces that testify to an authorial presence despite historical conditions of erasure" (19).[14] Her point is perhaps paralleled by Donaldson's claim that "[t]he setting of the film evokes Los Angeles, but it is generalized and de-localized, and, one might say placed under erasure by being unabashedly named 'Verona'" ("'All Which it Inherit'" 198). In a very real sense, Shakespeare is history in this film. Luhrmann presents a world in which Shakespeare appears as a figure of the past, absent, under erasure. Lines and images that we might ordinarily connect to him seem free to detach themselves from their original context and become reconnected to the decayed, the fallen, and the trivialized products of consumerism. It can be argued that most Shakespeare adaptations maintain the illusion that the characters are enacting the play script as though it were a kind of archetypal pattern of action. This seems especially true in cases where the play has been recontextualized in a time that is remote from Shakespeare's own and the characters seem to be driven by impulses from a very different narrative world. Only a few adaptations consciously present a post–Shakespearean world, one that openly acknowledges Shakespeare as an historical figure rather than an archetypal guiding spirit. Two versions of *Lear*—Godard's *King Lear* (1987) and Kristian Levring's *The King Is Alive*

(2000)—present characters who actually reconstruct Shakespeare's play. In *10 Things I Hate About You,* Shakespeare is taught in the classroom, and in *Tromeo and Juliet* (1996) the character Cappy, that film's version of Old Capulet, dies when Tromeo beats him to death with a copy of the *Yale Shakespeare Complete Works.*

At the same time, Luhrmann's film incorporates Shakespeare in a way that is very nearly the opposite of *Shakespeare in Love* (1996), the other immensely popular variation of the Romeo and Juliet story that dominated Shakespeare on film at the turn of the century. *Shakespeare in Love,* according to Michael Anderegg, works "to collapse past and present, to deny that there is such a thing as 'pastness' altogether. 'History,' from this point of view is always 'now'" ("James Dean" 69). This film transports our own contemporary language, images, and attitudes into a humorous explanation of how *Romeo and Juliet* was written. The anachronistic language and images of this film prompted the winking eye of the knowing film viewer, and was the basis of a considerable amount of the enjoyment. Luhrmann's film, by contrast, drags the remnants of Shakespeare's world into this very constructed world in which the reenactment of the Romeo and Juliet roles and language often seems out of sync with the visual and aural elements of a world that is a parallel to our world.

In this film, Shakespeare's language becomes the source of advertising copy. On the DVD commentary, Catherine Martin explains that Tania Burkett, listed as both "Graphics Designer" and "Title Designer" in the credits, had worked in advertising and "put her hand to all the Shakespearean advertising in the movie, and some of it is absolutely wonderful" (qtd. in Luhrmann). However clever some of the ads are, they are also indicators of this post–Shakespearean world. Lehmann believes that the ads "refigure the high-cultural status of Shakespearean verse as an homage to postmodern consumer culture" (141), and Hodgdon adds that the film "knowingly flaunts how that culture consumes 'Shakespeare'" (89). Shakespeare the author is dead and survives as advertising copy and a brand name. Worthen also calls attention to what he calls "gags," such as "the Post Haste mailing company that Friar Laurence used to contact Romeo in Mantua," adding that "the visual texture of the film is replete with allusions that extend beyond the lines of Shakespeare's play to the texture of Shakespeare the author and cultural icon" ("Drama" 1103).

Another area of changed meanings involves what might be called the "Pierre Menard" effect, in which the significance of some of the characters, places, and events are changed simply because time has passed since Shakespeare wrote the play, so that things that might on the surface seem very similar in function are really very different because of their new circumstances. Pierre Menard, in the famous story by Jorge Luis Borges, rewrites Cervantes's *Don Quixote* in the early twentieth century, but even as he reproduces the exact words Cervantes wrote, they convey something very different in their new historical context. The film is filled with examples of this phenomenon, such as the connotations of taking drugs, but this change in significance is especially apparent in some of the characters. Escalus, Prince of Verona, seems to retain something like his name, but as Captain Prince he cruises the city in a helicopter; the associations for the Alchemist in Shakespeare's time are very different from the disheveled drug dealer (listed in the script as "Pharmacist") who runs "The Globe" pool hall; finally both Tybalt and Juliet, because of their presentations as Latins, take on significations beyond those of the originals. Discussing Tybalt, Arroyo claims that the character's "pride, temper and the importance he attaches to family honour are far more understandable to present-day viewers as Hispanic stereotypes than as the values of a Renaissance nobleman. Likewise, Juliet's refusal of her father becomes more transgressive when read through her ethnicity" (123).

Shootout at the Sanctuary

The ending of Luhrmann's film, Shakespeare's last act, makes radical changes from previous film versions of the play. For the most part, these changes reflect the world Luhrmann has established throughout the film by unmooring expected meanings and recontextualizing them as post-apocalyptic through film, gesture, and media. It is a world in which the efficacy of suffering does not apply, a world without redemption, a world in which the dominant image of the ruin stands for other kinds of absence. Burt comments on some of the changes when he observes that "Luhrmann's film recodes the play in terms of a doomed youth culture and offers a sociological reading of contemporary (gang) youth: Romeo and Juliet are not innocent flower children destroyed by a stale, older, violent generation; they no longer have any distance from violent, drugged-out gang thuggery but participate in it fully (both wield guns, for example)" (*Unspeakable* 229). In fact, Luhrmann draws on three types of film influences to construct his ending. First, he criminalizes Romeo and Juliet in a way that seems to draw on the film tradition of lovers on the run, a group that includes Fritz Lang's *You Only Live Once* (1937), Nicholas Ray's *They Live by Night* (1949), and Joseph H. Lewis's *Gun Crazy* (1949), along with the several descendents of these films, such as Arthur Penn's *Bonnie and Clyde* (1967), and Robert Altman's *Thieves Like Us* (1974). Luhrmann's film, more than other film versions, heightens various elements to dramatize that sense of transgressive youth.

Following Burt's suggestion, we might consider the following reading of the action from that point of view. The fanciful and apparently innocent "Queen Mab" speech cleverly becomes a description of the drug that Mercutio gives to Romeo, who meets Juliet while he is coming off a high. Mercutio is stabbed to death in a gang fight that echoes the opening conflagration, and he dies dramatically on a stage as a tropical storm darkens the sky. Romeo drives into the darkness, finds Tybalt and shoots him dead, then drives off after Tybalt's body splashes backward into the water at the foot of the Christ statue that dominates the city and, in the opening scenes, divides the Montague from the Capulet towers. Juliet holds a pistol to her head, forcing Friar Laurence to find a way to keep her from marrying Paris, and then, reinforcing the drug motif, she takes drugs to feign suicide. Romeo sneaks back into the city to buy a lethal and illegal drug from a dealer, while police helicopters aim search lights into the dark streets, and heavily armed and armored police marksmen open fire on Romeo. He escapes them only by taking a hostage on the church steps. Inside, he takes the poison, and Juliet fulfills her earlier threat by shooting herself. By contrast, in Castellani's film, the only one that suggests the fugitive theme, Romeo creates a distraction with his horse so that he can sneak past the guards to the walled city. Zeffirelli's version abbreviates the ending so that Romeo arrives at the door of the tomb and enters it unchallenged.

A second line of influence, described by Richard Benjamin, is the "youth apocalypse film" that evolved during the 1990s, a time when "an ill defined sense of purposelessness and anxiety fueled teen anomie" (35). These films "share violent and extremely dark orientations"; and among these he includes both "hand-held-camera, direct-cinema style" films such as *Menace II Society* (1993), *American History X*, and *Kids*," and "the fragmented, hyperkinetic, music-video expressionism of *Basketball Diaries*, *William Shakespeare's Romeo and Juliet*, and *Doom Generation*" (35), as well as *Natural Born Killers* (1994), *Fight Club* (1999), and *Requiem for a Dream* (2000). The third type of film that influences the ending of *Romeo + Juliet* developed in the 1980s and 1990s as a general vogue of futuristic, often violent, post-apocalyptic films, beginning perhaps with George Miller's *Road Warrior* series and John Carpenter's *Escape from New York* (1981) and continuing through such films as *Brazil* (1985), *The Running Man* (1987), *Total Recall* (1990), *Waterworld* (1995), *Strange Days* (1995), and *12 Monkeys* (1995). It is these contexts into which we might place Luhrmann's film.

Luhrmann changes the ending of *Romeo and Juliet* in ways that alter Shakespeare's play to reflect the concerns and images of these three types of films. Specifically, he borrows from the "shoot out at the sanctuary" pattern found in a number of films, but particularly featured in two films that most critics agree have influenced Luhrmann's work — Nicholas Ray's *Rebel Without a Cause* (1955) and John Woo's *The Killer* (1989). In both of these films, the final scenes take place when the main characters must take refuge in a place of sanctuary. To retreat to the sanctuary is, of course, to seek protection, but it is also a way of defining the opposition. In the original play, and in the film versions by both Cukor and Castellani, Romeo's fight is with Paris, so that the battle is between the secret husband and the presumptive husband, person to person, and based on confusion. In Luhrmann's version, the conflict is moved to a very different scale. Eliminating Paris in the final section of the film and presenting Romeo as a fugitive criminal suggests that larger things are at stake. Lurhmann's Romeo is pitted against Captain Prince and the law enforcement system, and this opposition has very little directly to do with the love story. Romeo is not so much fighting against fortune as against the official law enforcement structure of his society, which musters an amazing amount of fire power to subdue him. Like many of the young protagonists in the lovers on the run films, he is sympathetic and, in a sense, innocent. Especially in his last desperate act, returning to die with Juliet, he is presented as blameless, at least in part because Luhrmann eliminates the fight with Paris, although the film conventions invoked in this section all point to the fact that there is no way Romeo is getting out of there alive.

In *Rebel Without a Cause*, the location is the Griffith Observatory, in which John "Plato" Crawford (Sal Mineo) takes refuge after he has fired at both the gang members who pursue him and at the police. In *The Killer*, it is an actual church where Inspector Li Ying (Danny Lee), Jeffrey (Chow Yun Fat), and the blind girl Jenny (Sally Yeh) take refuge from pursuing gangsters. In both cases, the characters must shoot their way into the refuge, and the walls of the building provide protection and define the divisions between the opposing forces. In the case of *Rebel Without a Cause*, Plato's isolation is modified by the presence of Jim Stark (James Dean) and Judy (Natalie Wood), the young couple that he thinks of as surrogate parents, even though they are his age. In this fifties parable, Jim tries to fill the parental role that Plato lacks and that Jim's own father cannot seem to provide. In *The Killers*, the odd relationship between the Inspector and Jeffrey — in the midst of the fight they nickname each other Dumbo and Mickey Mouse — as well as the visual image of the church filled with candles, may have influenced Luhrmann as he developed the images in the church and the earlier relationship between Romeo and Mercutio. The defining element in these scenes is the isolation of the protagonists in a confined space while they are surrounded by an opposition that threatens at various levels, including, of course, the gunplay that is important to this scene in all three films. In both *Rebel Without a Cause* and *The Killers*, important characters die, and the standoff precipitates a real change in the remaining members of society. That kind of change does not seem to occur in Luhrmann's film.

Ironically perhaps, the efforts of Romeo and Juliet to find privacy in the middle of a crowd has been an especially important issue in this film. Cukor, in his film, isolates the lovers at the party scene by simply pulling them out to a balcony away from the other dancers. Castellani attempts the same thing by having them exchange their first conversation wearing masks. Zeffirelli's Romeo speaks his first lines to Juliet while she is watching the other dancers and then pulls her behind a pillar to kiss her. In Luhrmann's version, the lovers retreat to an elevator and speak their lines as the camera whirls around them, and they are moving from floor to floor. The garden scene abandons Zeffirelli's overgrown foliage, and instead presents a smaller walled-in area, with security lights, where guards watch the activity through closed-system monitors. Again, the lovers must work to wrest privacy out of a public place. Their most relaxed time together is, perhaps, the brief night they spend together before Romeo must go to Mantua, but even there Luhrmann alludes to the sense of enclosure by having the sheets billow up over the lovers, making them seem like children at play and shutting them off from the room around them, until, of course, the Nurse and Lady Capulet intrude, and Romeo must sneak out the window. The scene in the church when Romeo escapes the police and shoots his way in to see Juliet must, therefore, remind an audience of that desperate attempt to find the private in the middle of a public scene.

Because of this isolation and because Luhrmann draws on the "shootout at the sanctuary" motif, this Romeo and Juliet seem unusually alone when they die. Friar Laurence, for example, who hurries nervously out of the tomb in Zeffirelli's version, is kept away from the site in Luhrmann's film, and we see him only in four brief scenes as he wakes with a premonition that his plan has gone wrong and tries to find out at the Post Haste delivery company office whether his message to Romeo was delivered. The shots in Luhrmann's film primarily juxtapose Romeo and Captain Prince, at least until the moment when Romeo is safely inside the church with Juliet. It is important to notice that this is the church in which Romeo and Juliet were married and their reunion in this space seems to suggest an extension of that ceremony. Their deaths become, however, very much a private matter to the extent that there is no resulting resolution on the larger scale of the injured society. If their deaths might be looked at as sacrificial in some versions, the same cannot be said about the events in Luhrmann's film. Donaldson declares that the "hundreds of neon crosses, with their techno-baroque religiosity, convey the triumph of the spectacle over the lovers. The final moments are unbearably bleak" ("'All Which it Inherit'" 200).

Romeo (Leonardo DiCaprio) clutches a hostage in Baz Luhrmann's version of the "shootout at the sanctuary" in his *William Shakespeare's Romeo + Juliet* (1996).

The organization of images at their death, however, seems significant and may provide more evidence for how we are to read this ending. When Juliet fires the bullet into her head, the camera pulls back, and in an overhead crane shot, the dead lovers seem momentarily like figures in a painting, surrounded by jewels, reminiscent of the work of Gustav Klimt. The hundreds of candle flames that surround them seem to morph into the bubbles of their underwater kiss, resolving the fire and water dichotomy that pervades the film's imagery. The memory montage here recalls the events of their brief time together, but it also fits with the several foreshadowing scenes earlier. It is, again, as if the reality of their lives exists only in those moments. At this point, according to Hodgdon, "the candle-flames dissolve into bubbles to freeze frame the lovers' underwater kiss," and "a long fade to white, accompanied by the *liebestod*'s final strains, dissolves in turn to the 'social real'—a white-sheeted body on a hospital trolley" (97). This emphasis on the "social real" is unrelieved by the final scenes. All three of the previous film versions, to varying degrees, include the reconciliation described in the play when each father, Montague and Capulet, promises to build a gold statue of the other's child, so that when the Prince says "all are punished," the implication might be that there has been a communal suffering followed by repentance. Luhrmann's version, as Anderegg explains, "sacrifices Shakespeare's finely held balance between the personal tragedy of the lovers and the larger social implications of the feud" (*Cinematic* 63). In addition, when the deaths of Romeo and Juliet shift from their moment of apotheosis to the grainy image on the television reportage, the shift in perspective suggests that their lives have become just another story on the news. The difference between the image of them inside the church, lying very nearly enshrined, contrasts markedly with the reality of their being loaded into the ambulance. Their achievement, however, ends with their lives, since it seems to have no repercussions in the world outside. Captain Prince reiterates "All are punished," and the more balanced line, "Some shall be pardoned, and some punished" (5.3.307), is uttered by the newscaster before the screen turns to visible noise.

Other readings of the ending of the film emphasize other elements, and Crowl nicely summarizes some of these, commenting on the "lively critical debate about how ironically (or pessimistically) we are meant to read the media's enclosure of Shakespeare's tale" (134). Examining the film from the point of view of the post-apocalyptic, however, it seems that Luhrmann has placed the action in a largely unrealistic framework, anticipating what he later does with the Bollywood inspired *Moulin Rouge!* (2001), the last film in his Red Curtain Trilogy, a grouping intended to underscore the heightened and theatrical nature of these films. Within that framework, Luhrmann's choices do not really emphasize the conflict between generations that animated Zeffirelli's version. Then again, as Anderegg points out, "To understand the play as primarily concerned with the 'generation gap' and with teen suicide is to misrepresent its essence" (*Cinematic* 80). In his ending to this film, Luhrmann continues to destabilize audience expectations and to insert post-apocalyptic images, reconstructing both action and motivation by drawing on these film subgenres. Romeo and Juliet in Luhrmann's film reflect the "purposelessness and anxiety" that Benjamin ascribes to teen apocalypse films, and they live in the world of the stylized, even glamorous, violence found in post-apocalyptic science fiction films of the closing decades of the last century. Their criminalization and their sense of alienation guarantee that the only triumph available to these lovers will be a personal and private one.

This same romanticized division between public failure and private victory occurs in many of the lovers on the run films, which often become examples of how "violent delights have violent ends" (2.6.9). In *You Only Live Once*, Eddie Taylor (Henry Fonda) carries the dying Jo Graham (Sylvia Sidney) toward safety when he is shot to death by lawmen. When Bowie (Farley Granger), in *They Live by Night*, is shot down, Keechie (Cathy

O'Donnell), who is pregnant with his child, finds a letter in which he declares his love for her. *Gun Crazy*'s Bart Tare (John Dall) shoots Annie Laurie Starr (Peggy Cummings), and then falls next to her when he is shot to death. Finally, in *Bonnie and Clyde*, perhaps the most eroticized of these films, Bonnie (Faye Dunaway) and Clyde (Warren Beatty) exchange a brief loving glance just before their bodies are riddled by bullets in a parody of sexual embrace. Although the device of having Juliet awake soon enough to see Romeo die but too late to save either herself or him is, most likely, borrowed from eighteenth century theater actor and impresario David Garrick, Luhrmann's *Romeo + Juliet* draws on the conventions and imagery of these crime films which create sympathy for lovers who clearly have no place in the world in which they find themselves, either alive or dead. As in other tales of last survivors, their final accomplishment is simply to assert their existence, which they do by ending it.

Notes

1. All textual references are based on both the Arden Shakespeare *Romeo and Juliet* and *William Shakespeare's Romeo & Juliet: The Contemporary Film, the Classic Play*, a volume marketed as a tie-in with the film.

2. Jack J. Jorgens discusses the film as a "'youth move' of the 1960s which glorifies the young and caricatures the old, a Renaissance *Graduate*" (86).

3. James N. Loehlin claims, for example, that in some scenes Luhrmann matches the Zeffirelli version "almost shot for shot" (127).

4. Richard Alleva, for example, says "the action is in Florida," as do Desson Howe, Stanley Kauffmann, Rita Kempley, Janet Maslin, and Donald Lyons, who comments that it is "the Miami Beach of Brian De Palma's *Scarface*," while Lynda Boose and Richard Burt say that Verona Beach is "a Cuban-American community" (18); some writers, such as Gary Crowdus, claim it is part Miami and part Mexico City; Brian D. Johnson and Alex Ross each see allusions to Miami and Los Angeles, with Richard Gyde calling it "a downtown L. A.–style cityscape," and Courtney Lehmann suggesting it is at least partly "LA's Venice Beach" (134); Jim Welsh writes that it as "a Hispanic ghetto called Verona Beach," while David Ansen and Yahlin Chang say it is "a teaming, violent, multicultural Latin metropolis" (73) and Anthony Lane calls it "a Lurid Latino dump patrolled by a pair of rival gangs" (66). W. B. Worthen summarizes some of these claims, explaining that "Luhrmann's Verona registers a range of locations" (*Shakespeare* 135–136). Alfredo Michel Modenessi writes that "Verona Beach is built upon signs easily recognizable as originating on *either* side of the U.S.–Mexico border, but *most* of them are rooted in the Mexican landscape and religious iconography" (69), and Barbara Hodgdon says "it takes place, not in a Euorcentric culture, but in a multicultural borderland — a mythic geographical space open to variant readings (Miami, California, Mexico)" (95).

5. Stephen Sondheim's lyrics are available at *The Official West Side Story Site*, among other places. See Alberto Sandoval Sanchez's article "*West Side Story*: A Puerto Rican Reading of 'America'" for a discussion of specific Latino issues in that film.

6. Carolyn Jess-Cooke's discussion of the film in "Screening the McShakespeare" is helpful and explains the *plata o plomo* allusion in more detail (167–168).

7. According to Manvell, "locations included the Ca d'Oro in Venice (for the balcony and ballroom scenes), the Plazza del Duomo in Sienna (for the Romeo-Tybald duel,

with an artificial fountain set in the middle), the walls of twelfth-century Montagnana (for the opening scene with Friar Laurence, who is discovered gathering herbs), the San Zeno Maggiore, with its bronze door and huge interior (for certain of the later scenes)" (100). In addition, "the paintings of Uccello, Piero, Botticelli and many other painters were drawn on for costumes and properties," for which he gives several examples (100).

8. Tatspaugh writes, "Guards at the gate to Verona welcome farmers who carry their produce to a market held in the piazza dominated by the cathedral; the Capulets and Montagues pursue each other through narrow streets lined with mellow stone buildings; Capulet's mansion, with its large courtyard and grand rooms, his comfortable study, his numerous servants, and his elaborate feast, testify to his wealth and status; monks announce Friar Laurence's visitors and sing a steady round of devotional services in their Romanesque chapel" (138–139).

9. Worthen, in *Shakespeare and the Force of Modern Performance*, mentions that "the film seems to cite Mexico and displace it, a gesture typified by the digitalized image of Christ that replaces the Monument to Independence on Paseo de la Reforma" (140).

10. Modenessi provides a useful summary of this view: "Practically no review I have read, nor any colleague with whom I have discussed the film, has failed to label Luhrmann's version of *Romeo and Juliet* 'postmodern.' Every readily recognizable feature of this now comfortably numb category may be invoked with examining the movie: furious juxtaposition; re- and de-contextualization; rejection of representation; seemingly random self- and cross-reference and allusion; media- and genre-jumbling; undermining plot and character (and of their conventions in general: conflict, motivation); and, of course, the quintessential denial of totalizing and totalizing meaning" (64).

11. In the case of Tybalt, as James N. Loehlin explains, "close-up slow-motion and freeze-frame shots of Tybalt lighting a cheroot, then crushing out the match with the silver heel of his cowboy boot, quote shots of Clint Eastwood in *A Fistful of Dollars* and Charles Bronson in *Once Upon a Time in the West*" (126). Our first view of Max in the western film influenced *Mad Max* (1979) follows that same slow revelation of feature by feature before the whole man is present on screen.

12. The leaping two-handed shot occurs in several John Woo films, notably in *The Killer* (1989), and it also appears in *Face/Off* (1997), a film he made for American audiences the year after *Romeo + Juliet.*

13. Guneratne goes on to point out, "The montage (concluding with a sequence of flash-forward vignettes) that follows the narration parodies the credit sequences of docudramas, each character's name being associated with his or her dramatic function" (241).

14. Commenting on a somewhat different set of circumstances, Richard Burt asserts, "As the distinction between the Shakespeare canon and the Shakespeare apocrypha dissolves before us, it may soon be time to speak of the Shakespeare apocalypse" (227).

Works Cited

Alleva, Richard. "The Bard in America: 'Looking for Richard' & 'Romeo.'" *Commonweal* 6 Dec. 1996: 18–19.

Anderegg, Michael. *Cinematic Shakespeare.* Lanham, MD: Rowman & Littlefield, 2004.

_____. "James Dean meets the pirate's daughter: passion and parody in *William Shakespeare's Romeo + Juliet* and *Shakespeare in Love.*" *Shakespeare the Movie II.* Ed. Richard Burt and Lynda E. Boose. London and New York: Routledge, 2003. 37–55.

Ansen, David, and Yahlin Chang. "It's the '90s, So the Bard is Back." *Newsweek* 4 Nov. 1996: 73+.

Arroyo, Jose. "Kiss kiss bang bang." *Film/Literature/Heritage.* Ed. Ginette Vincendeau. London: British Film Institute, 2001. 120–125.

Benjamin, Richard. "The Sense of an Ending: Youth Apocalypse Films." *Journal of Film and Video* 56.4 (2004): 34–49.

Boose, Lynda E., and Richard Burt, eds. *Shakespeare the Movie: Popularizing the Plays on Film, TV, and Video.* London and New York: Routledge, 1997.

Buchanan, Judith. *Shakespeare on Film.* Harlow, England: Pearson Longman, 2005.

Burt, Richard. "*Shakespeare in Love* and the End of the Shakespearean: Academic and Mass Culture Constructions of Literary Authorship." *Shakespeare, Film, Fin de Siècle.* Ed. Mark Thornton Burnett and Ramona Wray. New York: St. Martin's Press, 2000. 203–231.

_____. *Unspeakable ShaXXXpeares: Queer Theory and American Kiddie Culture.* New York: St. Martin's Press, 1998.

Coursen, H. R. *Shakespeare in Production: Whose History?* Athens: Ohio University Press, 1996.

Crowdus, Gary. "Words, Words, Words." *Cineaste* 23.4 (1998): 13–19.

Crowl, Samuel. *Shakespeare at the Cineplex: The Kenneth Branagh Era.* Athens: Ohio University Press, 2003.

Davies, Anthony. "The Film Versions of *Romeo and Juliet.*" *Shakespeare Survey* 49 (1996): 153–162.

Donaldson, Peter. "'All Which It Inherit': Shakespeare, Globes and Global Media." *Shakespeare Survey* 52 (1999): 183–200.

_____. "'In Fair Verona': Media, Spectacle, and Performance in *William Shakespeare's Romeo + Juliet.*" *Shakespeare After Mass Media.* Ed. Richard Burt. New York: Palgrave, 2002. 59–82.

Flamini, Roland. *Thalberg: The Last Tycoon and the World of M-G-M.* New York: Crown Publishers, 1994.

Guneratne, Anthony R. *Shakespeare, Film Studies, and the Visual Cultures of Modernity.* New York: Palgrave, 2008.

Gyde, Richard. "Baz Luhrmann's *William Shakespeare's Romeo and Juliet*—A Review." *Shakespeare on Line.* July 1997. 9 July 2007 <http:www.shakespeare–online.com/essays.RJG.html>.

Hawker, Philippa. "DiCaprio, DiCaprio, Wherefore Art Thou, DiCaprio." *Meanjin* 1997: 6–25.

Hindle, Maurice. *Studying Shakespeare on Film.* New York: Palgrave, 2007.

Hodgdon, Barbara. "*William Shakespeare's Romeo + Juliet*: Everything's Nice in America." *Shakespeare Survey* 52 (1999): 88–98.

Howe, Desson. "This 'Romeo' Is Bleeding." *Washington Post* 1 Nov. 1996. 6 June 2008 <www.washingtonpost.com>.

Jess-Cooke, Carolyn. "Screening the McShakespeare in Post-Millennial Shakespeare Cinema." *Screening Shakespeare in The Twenty-First Century.* Ed. Mark Thornton Burnett and Ramona Wray. Edinburgh: Edinburgh University Press, 2006. 163–184.

_____. *Shakespeare on Film: Such Things As Dreams Are Made Of.* London and New York: Wallflower, 2007.

Johnson, Brian D. "Souping Up the Bard." *Maclean's* 11 Nov. 1996: 74–75.

Jorgens, Jack J. *Shakespeare on Film.* Lantham, MD: University Press of America, 1991.

Kauffmann, Stanley. "Blanking Verse." *New Republic* 2 Dec. 1996: 40–41.

Kempley, Rita. "Romeo and Juliet Do the New World." *The Washington Post* 1 Nov. 1996. 6 June 2008 <www.washingtonpost.com>.

Lane, Anthony. "Tights! Camera! Action! *The New Yorker* 25 Nov. 1996: 65–77.

Lehmann, Courtney. *Shakespeare Remains: Theater to Film, Early Modern to Postmodern.* Ithaca: Cornell University Press, 2002.

Levy, Emanuel. *George Cukor, Master of Elegance: Hollywood's Legendary Director and His Stars.* New York: William Morrow, 1994.

Loehlin, James N. "'These Violent Delights Have Violent Ends': Baz Luhrmann's Millenial Shakespeare." *Shakespeare, Film, Fin de Siècle.* Eds. Mark Thornton Burnett and Ramona Wray. London: MacMillan, 2000. 121–136.

Luhrmann, Baz, dir. *William Shakespeare's Romeo + Juliet.* 1996. DVD. Twentieth Century Fox, 2002.

Lyons, Donald. "Lights, Camera, Shakespeare." *Commentary* Feb. 1997: 57–60.

Manvell, Roger. *Shakespeare and the Film.* New York and Washington: Praeger, 1971.

Maslin, Janet. "Soft! What Light? It's Flash, Romeo." *The New York Times* 1 Nov. 1996. 7 June 2008 <http://movies.nytimes.com/movie/review>.

Modenessi, Alfredo Michel. "(Un)Doing the Book 'without Verona walls': A View from the Receiving End of Baz Luhrmann's *William Shakespeare's Romeo + Juliet.*" *Spectacular Shakespeare: Critical Theory and Popular Cinema.* Ed. Courtney Lehmann and Lisa S. Starks. Madison, NJ: Fairleigh Dickinson University Press, 2002. 62–85.

Pilkington, Ace G. "Zeffirelli's Shakespeare." *Shakespeare and the Moving Image: The Plays on Film and Television.* Ed. Anthony Davies and Stanley Wells. Cambridge: Cambridge University Press, 1994. 163–79.

Ross, Alex. "Leonardo and Juliet." *Slate* 6 Nov. 1996. 6 June 2008 <http://www.slate.com/id/3195>.

Rothwell, Kenneth S. *A History of Shakespeare on Screen.* Cambridge: Cambridge University Press, 1999.

Sanchez, Alberto Sandoval. "West Side Story: A Puerto Rican Reading of 'America.'" *Latin Looks: Images of Latinas and Latinos in the U. S. Media.* Ed. Clara E. Rodriguez. Boulder, CO: Westview Press, 1997. 164–179.

Shakespeare, William. *Romeo and Juliet* (The Arden Shakespeare). Ed. Brian Gibbons London and New York: Methuen, 1980.

Sheppard, Philippa. "Latino Elements in Baz Luhrmann's *Romeo + Juliet.*" *Latin American Shakespeares.* Ed. Bernice W. Kliman and Rick J. Santos. Madison, NJ: Fairleigh Dickinson University Press, 2005. 242–262.

Sondheim, Stephen. "America." *The Official West Side Story Site.* 2001. 15 Sept. 2008 <http://westsidestory.com/site/level12/lyrics/america/html>.

Tatspaugh, Patricia. "The tragedies of love on film." *The Cambridge Companion to Shakespeare on Film.* Ed. Russell Jackson. Cambridge: Cambridge University Press, 2000. 135–159.

Welsh, Jim. "Postmodern Shakespeare: Strictly *Romeo.*" *Literature/Film Quarterly* 25 (1997): 152–153.

William Shakespeare's Romeo & Juliet: The Contemporary Film, The Classic Play. Screenplay by Craig Pearce and Baz Luhrmann. Play by William Shakespeare. New York: Bantam Doubleday, 1996.

Worthen, W. B. "Drama, Performativity, and Performance." *PMLA* 113 (1998): 1093–1107.

_____. *Shakespeare and the Force of Modern Performance.* Cambridge: Cambridge University Press, 2003.

5

Celluloid Revelations: Millennial Culture and Dialogic "Pastiche" in Michael Almereyda's *Hamlet* (2000)

Melissa Croteau

Hello, hello, hello, hello,
With the lights out, it's less dangerous,
Here we are now, entertain us.
   — Kurt Cobain with Nirvana, "Smells Like Teen Spirit" (1991)

GenX existed the moment it announced itself, in its own voice, to itself.... A generation saw itself in the mirror for the first time and realized that its own reflection was unique. What characterized its uniqueness ... is this very quality of self–reflexiveness.... "Look at me looking at me!"
   — Douglas Rushkoff, *The GenX Reader* (10)

The reviews of independent filmmaker Michael Almereyda's *Hamlet* (2000) were extremely divergent, some savagely panning it and others dubbing it a masterpiece. The opinions seemed to depend a great deal on the position each critic took toward what we call postmodernism. One thing most critics agreed upon, however, is that the sad, "modern moping malcontent," Peruvian wool cap-wearing, "GenX slacker" persona of Ethan Hawke's Hamlet is a major drawback in the film (cf. Rosenthal 34; Hoberman; Howell; LaSalle). What these critics seem to have missed is that the generation formerly known as X is, in fact, the first generation to be brought up entirely in the postmodern era of mass media-saturated consumer capitalism. We are the first "postmodern generation," if you will. Director Michael Almereyda, being born in 1960, is an early "GenX-er" (generally defined as those born between 1961 and 1981), and his *Hamlet* film reveals that he has learned all the lessons our culture has taught him. Douglas Rushkoff elaborates on GenX culture:

> Faced with a culture and media in which personalities, images, and ideologies were formulated solely to sell products, politicians, and lifestyles, kids growing up in the 1970s learned to appreciate this landscape of iconography as a post-modern playground.... GenX is the nightmare of a postindustrial, postmodern age. We are a marketing experiment gone out of control. Like any youngsters, we learned the language we were taught when we were kids ... the language of advertising.... [W]e celebrate the recycled imagery of our media and take pride in our keen appreciation of the folds within the creases of our wrinkled popular culture.... [GenX has] an ability to derive meaning from the random juxtaposition of TV commercials, candy wrappers, childhood memories, and breakfast treats. [GenX has] a willingness to deconstruct and delight in the Toys "R" Us wasteland of cultural junk while warding off the meaningless distractions of two-party politics, falling interest rates, and phantom career opportunities [Rushkoff 4–6].

The above quotation precisely describes Almereyda's approach to his film *Hamlet* as well as his and Hawke's interpretation of the character of Hamlet. It is a definitively postmodern film and this Hamlet is a postmodern man, as expressed in the relentless self–reflexivity and *mise-en-abîme* in the film, the self–conscious and expressive cinematography, and the *mise-en-scène* of cold, reflective glass and polished metal skyscrapers, communicating the obsession with surfaces, images, and commodities. Almereyda notes that "nearly every scene in the script features a photograph, a TV monitor, an electronic recording device of some kind" because "[t]he film admits that images currently keep pace with words, or outstrip them, creating a kind of overwhelming alternate reality" (x). The director exploits his GenX inculcation and mines his own experience to create a *Hamlet* which generates meaning through juxtaposition of myriad cultural images; and for a postmodern twist of genius, Almereyda makes Hamlet an experimental videographer who splices together an alternate reality of his own. In a sense, Almereyda mechanically reproduces himself as Hamlet in this film, and why not? The likes of Sir Laurence Olivier and Kenneth Branagh chose to direct themselves playing the great Dane in their film adaptations of the play. Appropriately, Almereyda chose to give Hawke a *toy*, the defunct Fisher-Price PXL-2000 Pixelvision camera, to record his personal development of the character of Hamlet and his experience in making the film (Chang). This "toy," then, became an instrument of "postmodern play"; Hawke records himself rehearsing various Hamlet speeches while he is technically not "performing" for the super 16mm camera with which Almereyda shot the actual film. These are often private moments illustrating Hawke's struggles with the character as much as Hamlet's struggles with his existential and familial quandaries (cf. Hawke in Almereyda xv). However, when Almereyda puts these rough, pixilated black-and-white images into the film *Hamlet*, these images read as Hamlet's video diary, not Hawke's; although Hawke, not Almereyda, is the auteur governing the pixel text. There is a collision between Hawke's "real" world on Pixelvision, which appears to the audience as a digital video text within a cinematic text, and Hamlet's world in the film. We see in this orchestration of images a fascinating *mise-en-abîme*, "a play of signifiers within a text, of sub–texts mirroring each other" (Hayward 231): the audience watches Hamlet watch himself in his "video-diary," which is actually Ethan Hawke's video-diary, all of which is contained in the 16mm frame of Almereyda's film *Hamlet*. Clearly, as has been noted by several scholars, this is a film that deals graphically with what Fredric Jameson calls the "fragmentation" and Lacanian "schizophrenia" of the postmodern subject (Jameson, *Postmodernism* 14, 26). However, unlike Fredric Jameson, Jean Baudrillard, and Theodor Adorno, who make apocalyptic prophecies about the vitiated and meretricious mass-mediatizeded consumer society and its perplexing pastiche, depthless surfaces, "packed emptiness," and lack of historical consciousness, I embrace the views of Mikhail Bakhtin regarding the fecundity of intertextuality, particularly as laid out by prominent film scholar Robert Stam.

Bakhtin, of course, is not the only eminent scholar to celebrate the proliferation of "voices" or texts in literature and culture, but his views are the most extensively developed. Although he never wrote about film, his theories of *dialogism, heteroglossia,* and *polyphony* can be applied to it with quite rewarding results. A brief look at the way I will be using these terms will be useful. Bakhtin's term *heteroglossia* refers to the "conflict between 'centripetal' and 'centrifugal,' 'official' and 'unofficial' discourses within the same national language. [It] is also present, however, at the (q.v.) microlinguistic scale; every utterance contains within it the trace of other utterances, both in the past and in the future" (Morris 248–49). In applying this term to our world, and the film's world, of globalization and multinational corporate culture, I will be expanding the meaning of *heteroglossia* to include the interaction and conflict between all *texts*, regardless of national affiliation or system of signification (e.g., spoken, written, video, film). *Dialogism* is the "basic trope" and foundation of all Bakhtin's work:

> Dialogism is the characteristic epistemological mode of a world dominated by heteroglossia. Everything means, is understood, as a part of a greater whole — there is a constant interaction between meanings, all of which have the potential of conditioning others. Which will affect the other, how it will do so and in

what degree is what is actually settled at the moment of utterance [Holquist 426; Morris 247].

Polyphony is often confused with the term *heteroglossia,* but Bakhtin uses the former term mainly to describe Dostoevsky's "multi–voiced" novels, "whereby author's and heroes' discourses interact on equal terms" (Morris 249). For our purposes, therefore, *polyphony* refers to the plurality of distinct "voices" within any text that dialogue with each other, generating intertextual meanings. Describing the importance of polyphony and heteroglossia in film studies, Stam writes that both terms

> point not to mere heterogeneity as such but rather to the dialogical angle at which voices are juxtaposed and counterposed so as to generate something beyond themselves.... The notion of polyphony, with its overtones of harmonious simultaneity, must be completed by the notion of heteroglossia, with its undertones of social conflict rooted not in random individual dissonances but in the deep structural cleavages of social life [Stam, *Subversive* 229, 232].

Almereyda's *Hamlet* is set in a hard, grey world of concrete, metal, and glass. This *mise-en-scène* makes evident the "deep structural cleavages" of our postmodern, hyper–real urbanity. Cinematographer John de Borman captures the juxtaposition and the irony of human insignificance in a "cave" of man-made skyscrapers by taking very low-angle shots of the characters as they walk down the streets of New York City. These dramatic shots seem to embody Albert Einstein's declaration, "It has become appallingly obvious that our technology has far surpassed our humanity." The cityscape dwarfs the human in an overwhelming capitalist carnival of neon signage, ubiquitous advertisements, ever-rolling stock tickers, and frenzied media gathering and dissemination. Jameson calls this type of environment "postmodern hyperspace" and argues that it has "finally succeeded in transcending the capacities of the individual human body to locate itself, to organize its immediate surroundings perceptually, and cognitively to map its position in a mappable external world" (*Post.* 44).[1] This kind of disorientation in the treacherous, unstable postmodern wilderness is an apt metaphor for the mental state of Shakespeare's character Hamlet. Hawke's Hamlet may be a "slacker dude" or a "perpetual graduate student," but this seems a typically defensive response to the confusion and alienation of his familial and political situation as presented in the play. The now renowned instability of this particular play with its three texts (Q1, Q2, and F) is apposite to the characteristic fragmentation, recycling, and replication we now associate with postmodernism. In these observations, I am not interested in chasing the chimera of "fidelity to the play text"; I am, however, drawing parallels between the themes and tropes of the play and film.

Famed experimental stage director Charles Marowitz writes, "When you have a large, multinational corporation such as the Shakespeare Industry, it goes without saying that it attracts people of easy virtue" (1). Although several critics ascribed such "bardolatrous harlotry" to Michael Almereyda and Ethan Hawke, this film is more than just another clever adaptation of the overdone classic; it is an innovative look at the relevance of *Hamlet* to a disillusioned generation in our millennial era. It may not be "Shakespeare's Hamlet," much to the chagrin of many newspaper film reviewers, but early modern scholars are well aware that the story of Hamlet certainly never "belonged" to Shakespeare. He was simply offering yet another telling of the ancient tale of the Danish prince, and the Renaissance audience would have known this. George Bernard Shaw once said that Shakespeare could tell a wonderful story "provided someone else had told it to him first" (*Biography*, qtd. by Stanley Wells). This is meant to be humorous, but it is true. The extant versions of "Shakespeare's" *Hamlet* leave us with many unanswered questions about authority and authenticity.

Almereyda himself does not claim that his film has an authentic relationship to Shakespeare's text; he explains that he had "no wish to illustrate the text, but to focus it, building a visual structure to accommodate Shakespeare's imagery and ideas" (x). Although he paradoxically entitles his published shooting script *William Shakespeare's* Hamlet: *A screenplay adaptation by Michael Almereyda*, he has a particular agenda in this film, and he is not afraid to state it outright. In Almereyda's screenplay, he clarifies the message behind his striking *mise-en-scène*:

> From what I can tell, global corporate power is as smoothly treacherous and absolute as anything going in a well-oiled feudal kingdom, and the notion of an omnipresent Denmark Corp. provided an easy vehicle for Claudius's smiling villainy. But this was a key for opening a wider door. It's more meaningful to explore how Shakespeare's massive interlocking themes — innocence and corruption, identity and fate, love and death, the division between thought and action — might be heightened, even clarified, when colliding with the spectacle of contemporary media-saturated technology [x].

This sort of dialogical "collision" of texts communicates multiple and often contradictory meanings and messages. The heteroglossia of Almereyda's *Hamlet* presents us with a film that is far greater than the sum of its parts. To accomplish this postmodern aesthetic, Almereyda uses four closely inter-related concepts: "simulation, which is either parody or pastiche; prefabrication; intertextuality and bricolage" (Hayward 277). These concepts all have to do with the self–conscious interweaving of a dialogic textual collage for the purpose of signification. In fact, director Almereyda, has no qualms about telling his audience that in his film, "[e]ntire scenes were dropped,

Shakespeare's text was ... trimmed and torn, and the result is, inevitably, an *attempt* at *Hamlet*— not so much a sketch but a collage, a patchwork of intuitions, images and ideas" (Almereyda, *Hamlet* xii). In true GenX form, Almereyda unapologetically announces his commitment to creating meaning through montage (in its most basic definition)[2], not to reverently reproducing the sacrosanct text of *Hamlet*.

There are a great many vivid and ingenious examples of postmodern aesthetics in *Hamlet* (2000). However, for my purposes here, I will focus on one particularly infamous scene and its prolific "matrix of communicative utterances" (Stam, *Film* 201–02). Almereyda's depiction of Hamlet's "To be, or not to be" soliloquy has generated much comment, some adulatory and some derogatory or disdainful. The soliloquy itself is split into three distinct scenes, which include a dizzying and provocative array of images, sound, and speech. The audacious fragmentation of this most famous of soliloquies communicates what Jameson calls the "schizophrenic experience": "an experience of isolated, disconnected, discontinuous material signifiers that fail to link up into a coherent sequence" ("Postmodernism" 195). In this case, however, the lack of coherence generates polyphony and heteroglossia that cause this speech to explode with meaning and possibilities.

The first in the sequence of "To be..." scenes appears directly after Polonius tells Ophelia to stay away from Hamlet (Almereyda 36–37). There is no analogue in the play to the scene Almereyda interpolates here. It opens in Hamlet's cluttered bedroom with a medium shot of the television and VCR pulling in to a close-up on the screen featuring the Buddhist monk Thich Nhat Hanh. He is explaining in a tranquil voice, "We have the word 'to be,' but what I propose is the word 'to inter–be.' Because it's not possible to be alone, to be by yourself. You need other people in order to be" (Almereyda 37). Almereyda is editorializing on the famous speech, playing with the audience and humorously alluding to their knowledge of the coming soliloquy. He cuts to a shot of Hamlet crossing the room holding his clam-shell monitor as Hanh is heard in voice-over continuing his lesson: "Not only do you need mother, father, but also uncle, brother, sister, society. But you also need sunshine, river, air, trees, birds, elephants and so on" (37). After another brief close-up of the television close-up of Hanh, Almereyda cuts to a medium shot of Hamlet sitting on his bed, staring intently into the clam-shell monitor. We then see a point-of-view shot of a pixel image of Ophelia in bed, trying to shield her face from the camera with a book. Finally, she lifts the book and looks directly into the camera with a long, somber stare. We hear Hanh finishing his speech as Ophelia occupies the screen within the screen: "So it is impossible to be alone. You have to inter–be with everyone and everything else. And therefore 'to be' means 'to inter–be'"

(37). When the words have finished, we see the Pixelvision pull in to an extreme close-up on Ophelia's face, followed by a reaction shot of Hamlet's face. The grammar of these shots connects these two characters, creating a strange sort of "inter–being" in which Hamlet communes with the absent presence of Ophelia's black-and-white pixel image. Interestingly, Hanh's final words tell us how to "read" Hamlet's soliloquy in a similar way to Olivier's voice-over announcement at the start of his 1948 *Hamlet* film: "This is the tragedy of a man who could not make up his mind." Almereyda's interpolated words, like Olivier's, seem to be directed at the audience, not at any of the characters in the film. Hawke's Hamlet is never shown looking at Hanh on the television screen, only the camera's gaze is watching, and from the shots of Hamlet enthralled in images of Ophelia, it would seem that he is not paying any attention to the guru's message. Hanh's wisdom is for the audience, and it is unclear how we are to apply this information to Hamlet's upcoming contemplation on life and death. Hanh's idealistic ontological philosophy, although earnestly presented, can be read as an ironic joke in this world of fleeting mass-mediatized images; but it also can be read as a comment on Hamlet's solipsism or his refusal to acknowledge his interrelatedness to others. This Hamlet constructs his relationships with others, along with his memories of them, on his video screen, where he is shown editing pixel images of his father and mother, Ophelia, and himself throughout the film. He negotiates his relationships through media, claiming the identity of the alienated postmodern, GenX subject. Perhaps the words of this Buddhist monk deconstruct the myths surrounding this notion of the postmodern subject.

Mark Thornton Burnett argues that the Thich Nhat Hanh interpolation does *not* anticipate Hamlet's soliloquy but instead serves "to underscore Hamlet's distance from any sense of communal interaction" ("Contemporary" 279). While the scene certainly depicts Hamlet's sense of isolation, it also reveals his specific desire and obsessive longing for Ophelia. In her ground-breaking essay "Visual Pleasure and Narrative Cinema," feminist film scholar Laura Mulvey incisively discusses two types of pleasure offered by the cinematic gaze that reinforce patriarchal concepts of subjectivity: scopophilia and identification. In this scene, Hamlet directs what Mulvey terms an "active/male" gaze at the "passive/female" Ophelia on the small monitor, where she is rendered powerless and eroticized not only in that he is staring at the filmic image of her that he has captured, but also because she is shown at a vulnerable, sexually suggestive moment, in bed, trying to block the camera's eye with her book (Mulvey 750). Indeed, this scene portrays Hamlet's "scop–Ophelia," his love of looking at this particular woman. Hamlet's double objectification of Ophelia, both as filmmaker and subsequent spectator and owner of the footage, casts some doubt regarding the nature of his relationship with her, or at least the quality of his feelings toward her. Does he love Ophelia, as he later so vehemently claims over her grave, or does he love his objectified image of her, the perfect woman he has created through his lens and in the editing process? Is this Hamlet, like Pygmalion, narcissistically constructing his beloved out of the media he is striving to master, to sculpt it into the ideal shape of his desire? (Ovid 232–34) As for Ophelia's desires, we see in this Pixelvision footage that she tried but could not escape Hamlet's invasive camera and thereby has unwillingly become "the woman as icon, displayed for the gaze and enjoyment of men, the active controllers of the look" (Mulvey 753). Interestingly, this scene reifies the patriarchal specular economy of film as it has been laid out by Mulvey, and I do not believe Almereyda is presenting Hamlet's look uncritically. Hamlet's scopophilia here reveals that he is complicit in the oppressive media mechanisms that he attempts to undermine. Although Hamlet endeavors to present a new, less totalizing perspective in his postmodern films (or film fragments), he is unable to break free from the "voyeuristic active/passive" apparatus that the Denmark Corporation uses to exploit its consumers. However, whereas Hamlet seems unaware of the power structures implicit in his gaze at Ophelia, in this sequence, Almereyda is acknowledging Hamlet's, and therefore his own, inevitable collusion with the ideological underpinnings of conventional narrative film. This metafilmic self-critique and revelation of complicity is consistent with Almereyda's postmodern project.

In this scene, Hamlet's fixed gaze on Ophelia's face in the clamshell monitor is both a tacit acknowledgment of his desire to "inter-be," at least on his terms, and a sad testament to the impossibility of this connection. Despite the fact that Hamlet himself does not speak a word, this key moment in the film divulges a great deal about his character, adding to his complexity. Mark Thornton Burnett asserts that this "inter-be" episode robs Hamlet of "the exclusive ownership of Shakespeare's most celebrated intellectual deliberation: the famous speech, in this multinational universe, has been both ethnically pluralized and philosophically transformed by the new media establishment" ("Contemporary" 279). I believe this is an oversimplification of the intricate dialogism of the scene. Is Hanh's doctrine being *sold* to Hamlet by "the new media establishment"? It must be noted that the footage of Hanh appears on the television in Hamlet's bedroom; it is chosen by him rather than hurled at him from outside sources (e.g., the big screen and stock tickers in Times Square, neon signs, advertisements). Although even this distinction could be questioned, Hamlet does have the power to turn Hanh off if he wishes. While the allusive representation of this Vietnamese monk does pluralize "Hamlet's" soliloquy, it is not necessarily an example of nefarious colonization (or globalization).[3]

This film constantly draws attention to the pluralism of its subject and of its own construction (particularly in the bricolage film-within-a-film, *The Mousetrap*). In the *Hamlet* screenplay, Almereyda claims that this film was influenced most by two "foreign" adaptations of *Hamlet*, Akira Kurosawa's *The Bad Sleep Well* (Japan, 1960) and Aki Kaurismäki's *Hamlet Goes Business* (Finland, 1987), and by the work of Swedish stage and film director Ingmar Bergman (133). Almereyda's emphasis on the ethnic and philosophical plurality of his own "sources" casts the integration of Hanh's Vietnamese, Zen Buddhist voice in a positive rather than oppressive light. However, the Hanh clip featured in *Hamlet* also can be read as an advertisement for the video from which it is excerpted, *Peace Is Every Step*, a product that sells for about thirty-five dollars, substantially more than Almereyda's *Hamlet* costs on DVD. Is this a case of product placement, a genuine statement of enlightened philosophy, or something else altogether? Once again, Almereyda leaves his text open. Hanh's speech represents one more provocative voice in the proliferation of texts and textual influences in this film. His doctrine of "inter-being" inspires the audience to reflect upon the famed soliloquy in communal rather than existential terms. Ironically, the Hanh piece was not only Hamlet's apparent viewing choice in this particular scene; it was Ethan Hawke who discovered the Buddhist monk's video and, thinking it would be a good choice for inclusion in the film, passed it along to Almereyda. The director thought Hanh's concept of "inter-being felt like a perfect ramp up to Hamlet's most famous soliloquy" (Almereyda ix). Almereyda seems to have nonchalantly "tossed it [the footage] into the mix," yet he insists that this clip is "[t]he one pre-recorded voice, I'd like to think, that Shakespeare wouldn't consider an intrusion" (ix). Almereyda believes that Hanh and his Zen philosophy are able to enter into a meaningful dialogue with the multifarious voices circulating in this film text, and, in my opinion, this is precisely what the interpolation achieves. Moreover, Almereyda states that his *Hamlet* film is not trying to "illustrate [Shakespeare's] text"; rather, it is "a collage, a patchwork of intuitions, images and ideas" (x). The words and images of Thich Nhat Hanh are a stimulating intertextual addition to this extraordinary *Hamlet* "collage."

The second piece of the "To be or not to be" soliloquy can be found following the scene in which a distraught Hamlet shows up at Ophelia's East Village flat (a depiction of Ophelia's report in 2.1) and gives her his "Doubt not the stars are fire" poem. Almereyda cuts from Ophelia's apartment to a shot of Hamlet from behind, sitting at his desk in his room. We are looking over his shoulder at the television, which is wired to the small clam-shell monitor in the lower right corner of our frame. We can see that Hamlet, with his right hand, is controlling the identical images on the television and small monitor, as Almereyda's camera slowly zooms in closer to the screens, intensifying our focus on them. Both screens show an extreme Pixelvision close-up of Hamlet's face gazing blankly into the camera. In this unsteady shot, apparently Hamlet's of himself, there is always a part of his physiognomy cut off by the frame; he is never "all there." He is holding a gun in his right hand and neurotically raises it to his temple, puts it in his mouth and back to the temple, places it under his chin, then finally rests the gun against his temple again. At this point Hamlet speaks those ubiquitous lines, "To be, or not to be"; it is graphically clear that he is contemplating suicide. However, these images seem more like a performance of a suicide game than a genuine attempt to exterminate himself. This is made clear when the pixilated Hamlet finishes his line, pauses briefly, and begins to grin as he shifts his eyes to face the camera directly. Until this split second, Hamlet's eyes have been glancing to the right, away from the camera's gaze. Pausing at this point, Hamlet the director rewinds the recording so that we see and hear it in reverse, then plays the clip with the line again, rewinds once more, and compulsively plays it a third time, "To be, or not to be," before the picture fades out (Almereyda 41). In this dramatic thirty-five-second scene, another interpolation to the play text, we watch Hamlet watching what seems to be his rehearsal of the "big speech." Is this Hamlet graphically struggling with himself and his mortality *aided* by media devices that help him reflect repeatedly on the ideas which plague him? Or is this Hamlet just obsessed with creating the perfect image, the perfect performance? Does he possess "that within which passes show"? This adaptation evokes these questions, which are meant to be contemplated but not definitively answered. Almereyda makes this clear in his preface to the screenplay, declaring that *Hamlet*, "Shakespeare's most inexhaustible play — an echo chamber, a bottomless well, a hall of mirrors, an untamable beast — keeps throwing back infinite answers" (xii). It was Almereyda's goal not to limit the text but to open it up to further voices and discourses.

In the very short scene I have just described, for instance, Almereyda alludes explicitly to Mel Gibson's performance as Martin Riggs in Richard Donner's popular action film *Lethal Weapon* (1987). This is a rich and complex reference. We are drawn to make connections between the Riggs character in *Lethal Weapon*, Gibson's performance as *Hamlet* in Franco Zeffirelli's 1990 film, Hawke's portrayal of Hamlet, and Almereyda's direction in this film. Zeffirelli is one of the great auteurs of Shakespearean film, and Almereyda obliquely gives him a nod here. Zeffirelli's *Hamlet*, like Almereyda's, is marked and even sometimes defined by the actor portraying

Hamlet. Harry Keyishian writes that "Zeffirelli's *Hamlet* is, among other things, a Mel Gibson movie, with discernable connections to his earlier films," and notes that "[t]he director has said that he cast Gibson in the role after seeing his character contemplate suicide in the first *Lethal Weapon* film" (74). The character of Martin Riggs contemplates suicide early in *Lethal Weapon* because his wife recently has died in an auto accident and he sees no reason to continue his lonely life. He speaks none of Shakespeare's words, but when the agitated Riggs puts a gun to his temple, then puts it in his mouth, tears streaking down his cheeks, it is clear this film is referencing Hamlet's grief and desire to "end / The heart-ache and the thousand natural shocks / That flesh is heir to" (3.1.60–62). During this intense scene, Riggs is sitting across from cartoons playing on his television; these images of popular culture trivialize Riggs' torment in the same way that the "signs" of consumer culture in Almereyda's film belittle Hamlet and his suffering. As in the play *Hamlet*, the repeated question asked by the characters in *Lethal Weapon* is whether or not Riggs is insane. Almereyda's parody of the "suicidal" action film scene is hardly an "empty signifier." His reworking of the Gibson scene is another act of copying in the swirl of popular culture imagery, but it also alludes to the endless recycling and simulation (what Jameson calls "cannibalization" [*Post.* 18]) that goes on in the world of film and culture: *Lethal Weapon* is the first of four *Lethal Weapon* movies; *Hamlet* has been adapted to film "at least forty-three times" (Almereyda viii); ten years before he played Hamlet, Mel Gibson made a name for himself as the avenging action hero in the three dystopic, post–apocalyptic *Mad Max* films (1979, 1982, 1985); and Ethan Hawke brings with him to the part of Hamlet all his previous performances as an over–educated, under-employed, and alienated GenX artist-philosopher (cf. *Reality Bites* [1994], *Before Sunrise* [1995], *Great Expectations* [1998]). Thus, the seemingly straightforward heteroglossia in this scene can send us off in myriad directions, each adding to the significance and meanings of this scene and the film text as a whole.

The third and final representation of Hamlet's "To be, or not to be" soliloquy has garnered much attention from journalists and scholars. Some critics vilified the scene, claiming that it is irreverent or overly contrived or just too obvious; others found it brilliant, innovative, and brimming with intertextual gems. I am of the latter school of thought. This now infamous scene was shot entirely in a Blockbuster Video store. Unlike the previously offered derivations and fragments of the soliloquy, this scene is placed in the traditional sequence of the play (i.e., in 3.1 [cf. Q2 and F], after Polonius's conversation with Claudius and Gertrude) and gives us the whole speech. This is neither a commentary on nor a rehearsal of the legendary contemplation on human mortality; this is finally the thing itself with its promised end. The juxtaposition of language and *mise-en-scène* is striking. The beauty and the rhythm of Shakespeare's words share the screen with cylinders of Pringles chips, numerous identical Blockbuster Video boxes, and a multiplicity of mundane "Action" signs marking the aisle in which Hamlet is strolling while he asks himself why he and all the other creatures "crawling between earth and heaven" do not their own "quietus make" to escape this abominable and crushing world (Shakespeare 3.1.127–28; 3.1.74). These are lofty ruminations to be uttered in such a vulgar, synthetic environment. The scene begins with a medium shot of Hamlet from behind. As he speaks the first line, he slowly pivots to face the camera. This immediately cuts to a medium tracking shot of the prince that follows his back down the "Action" aisle while he is decrying the "slings and arrows of outrageous fortune" (3.1.57). We hear a shotgun blast in the background at the end of this line as Hamlet goes on to speak of "tak[ing] arms against a sea of troubles" (3.1.58). This ironic sound effect draws the viewer's attention to its source: the three video screens looming side-by-side above Hamlet's head (see below). The televisions are set into the top of the wall facing the "Action" aisle, and they are all showing the same scene from the film *The Crow: City of Angels* (1996), giving us a horizontal line of three identical frames within the film frame. The parallel video monitors are an Andy Warhol–esque collage of replicated images in the age of mechanical reproduction, once again reminding the audience that late capitalism operates by feeding consumers

Hamlet's (Ethan Hawke) existential contemplation at Blockbuster Video in Michael Almereyda's *Hamlet* (2000) (Photofest).

endlessly repeating images. Almereyda is also playing with the idea of *mise-en-abîme* here by portraying a flat, linear line of repetition (like a factory assembly line), rather than the depth of infinite regress that generally characterizes the *mise-en-abîme* aesthetic. However, in that *The Crow: City of Angels* footage is a sub–text that mirrors the larger text in which it is embedded, the frames within the frame create the effect of a *mise-en-abîme* because of their reflexivity and their potential for intertextual commentary on (or deconstruction of) *Hamlet* as well as the three *Crow* films (Hayward 231). It is significant that the screens flickering above Hamlet's head in Blockbuster Video are portraying *prefabricated* film images that function in the parodic mode as opposed to the pixilated images that Hamlet is controlling. Almereyda's choice to interpolate clips of director Tim Pope's 1996 film opens up a fascinating deluge of intertextual dialogue.

Like several other films referenced in *Hamlet*, *The Crow* (1994) spawned more films: *The Crow: City of Angels*, *The Crow: Salvation* (2000), and *The Crow: Wicked Prayer* (2005). *The Crow* films are themselves adaptations of the "gothic" comic book series and comic strip of the same name by James O'Barr. These four *Crow* films represent four different cinematic visions of the same source, just as *Hamlet* is one in a line of over forty different cinematic interpretations of the classic play. Almereyda is making a characteristically postmodern (and GenX) gesture here by embedding a pop culture text adapted from a subcultural text (comics) inside the very centerpiece (the "To be" soliloquy) of a rendition of a play that has come to epitomize high culture in the last century. Jameson asserts that one fundamental feature of postmodernism is the "effacement" and "erosion of the older distinctions between high culture and so-called mass or popular culture" (Jameson, *Post.* 2; Jameson, "Post." 186). In this scene, these distinctions have completely disintegrated. Aspects of *The Crow: City of Angels* are woven into Almereyda's *Hamlet* both obviously and obliquely; while Shakespeare's work, particularly *Hamlet*, is frequently alluded to and even quoted in *The Crow: City of Angels*. There is a reciprocal textual exchange between *The Crow* films and Shakespeare's language: these texts bleed into each other in varying degrees, illuminating each other in significant ways. The most recognizable and consistent features of *The Crow* films are their revenge tragedy plots and dark, post–apocalyptic urban *mise-en-scènes*. It is not difficult to identify the connections between the *Hamlet* plot and the *Crow* narratives: a young man loses a loved one and returns to his home to hunt down and execute the killers. The major differences lie in the *The Crow's* "comic book" plotline in which the protagonist and his beloved are murdered, and then the tragic hero is resurrected in his old body by a nebulous avian spiritual power in order to wreak vengeance on his enemies. What is most interesting in Almereyda's choice to quote and emulate the second *Crow* film is that it is the only one of the three about a father and son being murdered together, rather than a man and his female beloved. Like *Hamlet*, this is a story about father-son relationships, a grief-stricken young man, murder, revenge, and corrupt power in a vicious world. It also includes a "gothic romance," a powerful love thwarted by circumstance. *The Crow* comics and films were designed to appeal to the "goth" subculture, which grew out of the countercultural punk movement of the 1970s. Self-proclaimed "goths" tend to wear all black clothing, often made of leather or fishnet, and black make-up over an artificially whitened face. They customarily put on a melancholy persona and are obsessed with death and cemeteries. In light of this albeit superficial description, it is not difficult to imagine why Hamlet has been declared "the first fully developed goth" by many members of this subculture, including Peter Murphy, former front man for the classic goth band Bauhaus (Wolff 34).[4] As a group, goths have appropriated Hamlet as their role-model. The goths repudiate the world of corporate consumerism by focusing on the great equalizer: death. They have paid close attention to the gravedigger scene in *Hamlet* and claim to be demystifying death by "swallowing" images of death (metaphorical necrophagia), as Hamlet stares into the empty sockets of Yorick's skull (Wolff 49).

Burnett asserts that Almereyda's quotation of *The Crow: City of Angels* serves simply to focus attention on "Hamlet's intellectual impasse": his unique inability "to master 'consummation' or 'resolution,'" unlike the ghostly rock musician who revenges himself on urban hoodlums in Tim Pope's conflagration-obsessed [film]" ("To Hear" 57). (Actually, the undead protagonist, aptly name Ashe, is not a glorified rock musician, but a humble motorcycle mechanic.) Surely, a juxtaposition is set up between the explosively avenging father on the Blockbuster screens and Hamlet the sauntering philosopher kvetching about his abulia and inaction. However, the heteroglossia these quotations generate goes far beyond this obvious dichotomy. In fact, there are significant allusions to *The Crow: City of Angels* outside of the "To be, or not to be" scene, including the Halloween setting combined with Day of the Dead imagery, the use of a hyper-urban *mise-en-scène* containing a profusion of reflective surfaces (functioning as metaphors for the unconscious), overt biblical and theological references, and the use of illuminated signage to communicate states of mind.

Returning to the scene of the soliloquy, we find our Hamlet still strolling down the "Action" aisle, musing about self–inflicted death while the three screens above his head show Ashe the undead avenger annihilating his foes. As Hamlet begins the equivocating second sentence of his soliloquy, "To die, to sleep —/ No more —" (3.1.59–60), we see Ashe in triplicate setting fire to a highly flammable drug warehouse, burning his enemy alive, and exiting the exploding structure unharmed. Although this is not one of Hamlet's soliloquies in which he bemoans his inability to act on his "bloody thoughts" (i.e., those in 2.2 and 4.4 [Q2 only]), the images of Ashe's blazing revenge flashing above him seem to communicate that it is Hamlet's "coward conscience" that restrains him from both escapist suicide *and* violent retribution. As Hamlet continues his soliloquy, the camera cuts to a frontal medium close-up of Hawke, and we can now see a television screen in the background above the cashier exhibiting a much later scene in *The Crow: City of Angels* in which Ashe shoots punk trendsetter Iggy Pop's wicked character, Curve, off of his motorcycle with a large rifle. (This is the same scene we heard in the background a few moments ago when Hamlet was lamenting the "slings and arrows of outrageous fortune"). We see Curve blasted backward, flying through the air. Almereyda's camera then cuts to a close-up of the three television screens we just saw above the "Action" aisle. The shot slowly zooms in on the screens until only the center screen is fully within our frame, the other two are bisected by the frame of the 16mm film camera. The orchestration of this shot self–reflexively reminds us that we are watching frames within a frame. As the camera focuses on the screens, the unseen Hamlet goes on, "To die, to sleep, / To sleep perchance to dream" (3.1.63–64), and we see the video picture of what we have heard twice before in this scene: Ashe shooting the rifle directly at the camera (aimed at Curve), Curve's motorcycle exploding, and Curve hurtling backward again. The rapid repetition of this revenge-killing scene in various fragments and fragmented forms (i.e., through sound only, then on a single screen far in the background, and finally on the three screens in a zoom-in close-up) express Hamlet's fractured, disoriented, and obsessive psychological state. Almereyda's next cut disorients the audience, for we believe that the close-up on the three screens is a point-of-view shot and that Hamlet is watching the screens as he speaks of death. However, the film cuts to a medium close-up of Hamlet as he declares "Ay, there's the rub" (3.1.64), and we discover that, having veered right down another aisle while off-screen, he now has hit a wall of comedy videos, causing him to turn back toward the "Action" aisle. As in the earlier "To be" scene with Hanh, the camera's gaze does not present Hamlet's point of view (cf. Mulvey 756–57). *The Crow* scene may be modeling Hamlet's subconscious, or his "dreams," but that revelation is meant solely for the audience, not for Hamlet. As Hamlet continues his soliloquy, he turns left, pauses briefly, and walks up the "Action" aisle once again. This time, the camera frames him in a medium close-up tracking shot, and when he pauses for a moment, we see him in a tableau, surrounded by innumerable identical Blockbuster Video boxes, spaced precisely the same length apart as if in a grid. They are visual evidence of the loss of individuality and identity in the age of mechanical reproduction. But they also evoke the question, if all movies are the same, or if photography and cinematic production are simply about mindless copying, then what are we watching on the screen before us and in the screens within that screen? Yes, this film is one in a long line of *Hamlet* "reproductions," but this *Hamlet* is vastly different from Branagh's (1996), and Branagh's is nothing like Zeffirelli's (1990), despite the fact that these *Hamlet* films were made within ten years of each other. Perhaps these repetitive adaptations of *Hamlet* are not "empty signifiers," but rather signify the infinite possibilities and fecundity of Shakespeare's text.

As Hamlet goes on to list the terrible experiences that should move one to end his "weary life," the three screens above Hamlet display a high-angle long shot of Curve floating in a disgustingly brown, polluted river that ironically runs through the "City of Angels." The dying Curve is facing upward, arms outstretched as if he were on a cross, and he is surrounded by bright marigolds, which are being scattered down on him by an old woman standing above who repeats, "Flores para los muertos" ("Flowers for the dead"). It is the Day of the Dead. This shot of Curve eerily mirrors the pre–Raphaelite painting of *Ophelia* by Sir John Everett Millais (1852), although it exchanges Millais' romanticized context of lush flora with the *mise-en-scène* of a debased, putrefying dystopia, a post–apocalyptic metropolis. The screens above Hamlet have now become a premonition of what is to come in Hamlet's own story and perhaps what is to come for the urban civilization of conspicuous consumption.

Further irony ensues when Hamlet speaks the last few lines of his soliloquy in the "Action" aisle:

> Thus conscience does make cowards of us all,
> And thus the native hue of resolution
> Is sicklied o'er with the pale cast of thought.
> And enterprises of great pitch and moment
> With this regard their currents turn awry
> And lose the name of action [Almereyda 52; Shakespeare 3.1.82–87].

When Hamlet reaches the penultimate line, he stops at the end of the aisle and turns his head "awry" to look back through the multiplicity of "Action" signs to the three video screens once more. The Curve shooting scene has now jumped back to the moment just after Curve's body has slammed into the ground following the rifle shot. Almereyda cuts from a close-up of Hamlet's profile to a tight close-up on the center video screen (although the edges of the other two screens still peek in on either side). We hear Hamlet speak his closing line as Ashe emerges unharmed through the flames of the motor-

Ashe (Vincent Perez) the avenger wearing his priestly leather coat in Tim Pope's *The Crow: City of Angels* (1996) (Photofest).

cycle explosion, wearing a long black leather coat that looks like a priest's robe and making a gesture that closely resembles the sign of the cross. The word "action" concludes the scene in the Blockbuster "Action" section while the screen within our screen is displaying a violent avenger appearing as a pseudo-sacred figure. Are we to think that the undead father Ashe is also urging Hamlet to take action? If so, the action indicated is not narcissistic self–destruction but self–sacrificial retribution.

In Michael Almereyda's eccentric and infamous rendering of the "To be, or not to be" soliloquy, we see the compelling use of all four major concepts of the cinematic postmodern aesthetic: simulation, prefabrication, intertextuality, and bricolage (Hayward 277). Fredric Jameson describes postmodernism as being bereft of "parody's ulterior motive, without satirical impulse, without laughter, without that still latent feeling that there exists something normal compared to which what is being imitated is rather comic" ("Post." 188–89). He insists that what we encounter in postmodern culture is not parody but "pastiche," which he defines as "blank parody, parody that has lost its sense of humor" ("Post." 189). Whether you call aesthetic mimicry and quotation "pastiche" or "parody," I would suggest that it is *never* barren of meaning. This kind of heteroglossia and synergy is always greater than the sum of its parts, generating fresh meanings out of new relationships or juxtapositions. Angela McRobbie points out that Jameson fails to recognize "that those elements contained within his diagnosis of postmodernism — including pastiche, the ransacking and recycling of culture, the direct invocation to other texts and other images — can create vibrant critique rather than an inward-looking, second-hand aesthetic" (176). This is clearly evident in Michael Almereyda's *Hamlet*. McRobbie goes on to explain that a great proportion of Gen X-ers find postmodernism appealing because

> they themselves are experiencing the enforced fragmentation of impermanent work, and low career opportunities. Far from being overwhelmed by media saturation, there is evidence to suggest that [they] are putting it to work for them. This alone should prompt the respect and the attention of an older generation who seem at present too eager to embrace a sense of political hopelessness [178; written in 1989].

Perhaps our mass mediatized, hyper–consumer capitalist world is not stripping us of the ability to communicate and is not devoid of depth; perhaps it does not signal the end of meaning or "the beginning of the new nihilism" (McRobbie 178). Even Burnett, who dwells a great deal on Jameson's and Baudrillard's negative postmodern ideologies, contends that "[t]his version of *Hamlet*, ... while successfully echoing millennial concerns, also finds concomitantly animating logic in the communicative virtues of a postmodern aesthetic" ("To Hear" 49). While "playing" with his Pixelvision camera,

Hawke's GenX prince reconstructs his memories in black-and-white pixel images, and with his digital editing equipment, he crafts an "abstract and brief chronicle" of his family out of found footage, resulting in his *Mouse-trap* film. Hamlet is acutely aware of the power of technology and media images, and he is adept at manipulating them for his own purposes, even as he recognizes the corruption and coercion represented by Claudius and the Denmark Corporation's dominance in the global multimedia market.

In this way, Almereyda bears an uncanny resemblance to his protagonist. In his published screenplay, Almereyda expresses his frustration at being criticized for the "product placement" in this film and confesses that he "paid for the privilege of parading certain logos and insignia's across the screen" (xi). The filmmaker goes on to elucidate his "intended point":

> "Denmark is a prison," Hamlet declares early on, and if you consider this in terms of contemporary consumer culture, the bars of the cage are defined by advertising, by all the hectic distractions, brand names, announcements, and ads that crowd our waking hours. And when, in this *independent* film, the ghost of Hamlet's father vanishes into a Pepsi machine, or Hamlet finds himself questioning the nature of existence in the "Action" aisles of a Blockbuster video store, or Shakespeare's lines are overwhelmed by the roar of a plane passing overhead — it's meant as something more than casual irony. It's another way to touch the core of Hamlet's anguish, *to recognize the frailty of spiritual values in a material world*, and to get a whiff of something rotten in Denmark on the threshold of our self–congratulatory new century [xi, my emphasis].

Almereyda self–consciously refers to his film as "independent," implying that his film controls and manipulates the icons and imagery of mass media rather than the other way around. The context and intertextuality of this "independent film" produce dialogic irony, not "blank parody." Like his alter ego, Hamlet the GenX filmmaker, Almereyda the GenX filmmaker utilizes postmodern aesthetic concepts and film techniques to entertain his audience *and* to present it with a reflection of our world that "must give us pause" (3.1.67; Almereyda 50). With *Hamlet*, Almereyda proves that a film which so brazenly proclaims "Look at me looking at me!" can reach beyond superficial narcissism to inspire genuine ontological contemplation. It is this quality that makes the film, in Almereyda's words, a "distinctly American, millennial *Hamlet*" (Almereyda 133).

Notes

1. It should be made clear that Jameson is not necessarily claiming that there is, or ever was, such a thing as a "mappable external world," nor does he state that the ability to "locate" oneself within such a world is a positive accomplishment. Henri Lefebvre writes about the spatial/architectural illusion of stability, unity, and homogeneity (i.e., a map-

pable external world) (292–351). He asserts that the "legitimating ideology" of "contradictory space" manipulates inhabitants by presenting, "incoherence under the banner of coherence, a cohesion grounded in scission and disjointedness, fluctuation and the ephemeral masquerading as stability, conflictual relationships embedded within an appearance of logic and operating effectively in combination" (308–09). Therefore, unlike Jameson, Lefebvre overtly contends that the notion of a "mappable world" was always already a reductive façade masking fragmentation.

2. Film's infinite potential for generating meaning through the counterposing of images was noted on the most fundamental and profound level by renowned early twentieth century Russian filmmaker Sergei Eisenstein, who asserted that it is imperative that the makers and audiences of film possess "an understanding of montage as not merely a means of producing effects, but above all as a means of *speaking*, a means of *communicating* ideas, of communicating them by way of special film language, by way of a special form of film *speech*.... The very production of simple meanings rises as a process of juxtaposition" (245–46). Like Bakhtin, Eisenstein takes verbal language as his model in his writings on signification and communication: the film "speaks" through montage. It is important to note that Eisenstein uses the term *montage* here specifically to refer to the practice of film editing, hence to the juxtaposition of images over a span of time. Each image must be read in dialogue with the images that have come before it. In noting the vernacular use of *montage*, which includes the concept of diverse juxtaposed images through various methods, including superimposition, it is not a stretch to apply Eisenstein's notion of montage to postmodern *mise-en-abîme* as well as editing practices in film and video.

3. It is of course significant that the monk is Vietnamese. The history of the relationship between the United States and Vietnam is fraught with debates concerning "American colonialism," and the many guises that assumed, during the Vietnam War. In fact, interviews with American Vietnam War veterans appear elsewhere on the video excerpted in this *Hamlet* scene, entitled *Peace is Every Step* (1998). Furthermore, Hanh's usurpation and transformation of the "To be, or not to be" soliloquy also could be making a statement about the potential colonization of iconic texts such as this one. The Merchant-Ivory film *Shakespeare Wallah* (1965) also takes up this issue in an intriguing manner, focusing on the fate of Shakespeare's plays in post–colonial India.

4. One could pursue the irony and intertextuality further here in regard to the renowned *Bauhaus* school of architecture, design, and applied arts, which was established in Germany in 1919. The leaders of the Bauhaus school and their protégés had a broad influence on architecture and design, particularly after the school's dissolution by the Nazis in 1933. The Bauhaus architects propagated the Modernist philosophy of Functionalism, also called the International Style, which resulted in much of the formulaic, postmodern urban architecture extant in American and European cities today. One of the chief principles of so-called Functionalism was to erase individuality by constructing a homogeneous built environment (cf. Lefebvre above). Architectural structures were to adapt to the new, modern technological culture; in other words, form follows function. For a detailed account of the Bauhaus and its impact on architecture, see *The New Architecture and the Bauhaus* (1965) by Walter Gropius, director and founding architect of the school. For an account of Functionalism and its place in the history of twentieth century architecture, see Alan Colquhoun's *Modern Architecture* (2002) in the Oxford History of Art series.

Works Cited

Almereyda, Michael. *William Shakespeare's* Hamlet *adapted by Michael Almereyda.* London: Faber & Faber, 2000.

Biography—William Shakespeare: Life of Drama. Dir. Bill Harris. Host Peter Harris. Videocassette. A&E Home Video, 1996.

Burnett, Mark Thornton. "Contemporary Film Versions of the Tragedies." *A Companion to Shakespeare's Works: Vol. 1, The Tragedies.* Ed. Richard Dutton and Jean E. Howard. London: Blackwell, 2003. 262–83.

_____. "'To Hear and See the Matter': Communicating Technology in Michael Almereyda's *Hamlet* (2000)." *Cinema Journal* 42.3 (2003): 48–69.

Chang, Chris. "The Pleasures and Terrors of Michael Almereyda." *Film Comment* May/June 2000: 56+. *ProQuest.* San Diego State University, Love Library. 26 Feb. 2004 <www.proquest.umi.com>.

The Crow: City of Angels. Dir. Tim Pope. Perf. Vincent Perez, Mia Kirshner, and Iggy Pop. 1996. DVD. Miramax/Dimension, 2003.

Eisenstein, Sergei. *Film Form: Essays in Film Theory.* Ed. and trans. Jay Leyda. San Diego: Harcourt Brace & Co., 1949.

Hamlet. Dir. Franco Zefferelli. Perf. Mel Gibson, Glenn Close, Alan Bates, and Helena Bonham Carter. 1990. DVD. Warner, 2004.

Hamlet. Dir. Kenneth Branagh. Perf. Kenneth Branagh, Kate Winslet, Derek Jacobi, and Julie Christie. 1996. Videocassette. Castle Rock, 2000.

Hamlet. Dir. Laurence Olivier. Perf. Laurence Olivier, Jean Simmons, Basil Sydney, and Eileen Hurlie. 1948. Videocassette. Hallmark, 1995.

Hamlet. Dir. Michael Almereyda. Perf. Ethan Hawke, Julia Stiles, Kyle MacLachlan, Diane Venora, and Bill Murray. 2000. DVD. Miramax, 2003.

Hayward, Susan. *Cinema Studies: The Key Concepts.* 2nd ed. London: Routledge, 2000.

Hoberman, J. "Vanity Fare: *Hamlet.*" *The Village Voice* 16 May 2000: 135. *ProQuest.* San Diego State University, Love Library. 17 Nov. 2003 <www.proquest.umi.com>.

Holquist, Michael, ed. *The Dialogic Imagination: Four Essays by M.M. Bakhtin.* By Mikhail Bakhtin. Trans. Caryl Emerson and Michael Holquist. Austin: University of Texas Press, 1981.

Howell, Peter. "Hip Hamlet Smells Like Teen Spirit." *Toronto Star* 26 May 2000, Ontario ed.: F03. *ProQuest.* San Diego State University, Love Library. 17 Nov. 2003 <www.proquest.umi.com>.

Jameson, Fredric. "Postmodernism and Consumer Society." *Movies and Mass Culture.* Ed. John Belton. New Brunswick: Rutgers University Press, 1996. 185–202.

_____. *Postmodernisn, or, The Cultural Logic of Late Capitalism.* Durham: Duke University Press, 1991.

Keyishian, Harry. "Shakespeare and Movie Genre: The Case of *Hamlet.*" *The Cambridge Companion to Shakespeare on Film.* Ed. Russell Jackson. Cambridge: Cambridge University Press, 2000. 72–81.

LaSalle, Mick. "'Hamlet'—21st Century Guy: Fresh look at classic too staid to succeed." *San Francisco Chronicle* 19 May 2000: C1. *ProQuest.* San Diego State University, Love Library. 17 Nov. 2003 <www.proquest.umi.com>.

Marowitz, Charles. *Recycling Shakespeare.* London: Macmillan, 1991.

McRobbie, Angela. "Postmodernism and Popular Culture." *Postmodernism: ICA Documents.* Ed. Lisa Appignanesi. London: Free Association Books, 1989. 165–79.

Morris, Pam, ed. *The Bakhtin Reader: Selected Writings of Bakhtin, Medvedev and Voloshinov.* London: Arnold, 1994.

Mulvey, Laura. "Visual Pleasure and Narrative Cinema." *Film Theory and Criticism: Introductory Readings, Fourth Edition.* Ed. Gerald Mast, Marshall Cohen, and Leo Braudy. New York: Oxford University Press, 1992. 746–57.

Ovid. *Metamorphoses.* Trans. A. D. Melville. Oxford: Oxford University Press, 1986.

Peace Is Every Step, Meditation in Action: The Life and Work of Thich Nhat Hanh. Perf. Thich Nhat Hanh. Narr. Ben Kingsley. Videotape. Mystic Fire, 1998.

Philpot, Robert. "Ethan Hawke as Hamlet was Not Meant To Be — Movie Review: 'Hamlet.'" *The Patriot Ledger* 20 May 2000: 42. *ProQuest.* San Diego State University, Love Library. 17 Nov. 2003 <www.proquest.umi.com>.

Rosenthal, Daniel. *Shakespeare on Screen.* London: Hamlyn, 2000.

Rushkoff, Douglas. *The GenX Reader.* New York: Ballantine Books, 1994.

Shakespeare, William. *The Riverside Shakespeare.* Ed. G. Blakemore Evans. Boston: Houghton Mifflin, 1974.

Stam, Robert. *Film Theory: An Introduction.* Malden, MA: Blackwell Publishers, 2000.

_____. *Subversive Pleasures: Bakhtin, Cultural Criticism, and Film.* Baltimore: Johns Hopkins University Press, 1989.

Wolff, Justin. "Leave Me Alone: San Diego's Goths." *San Diego Weekly Reader* 8 Feb. 2001: 28–49.

6

The Revenger's Tragedy in 2002: Alex Cox's Punk Apocalypse

GRETCHEN E. MINTON

The past two decades have seen a proliferation of film adaptations of Shakespeare's plays. From smash hits such as Baz Luhrmann's *William Shakespeare's Romeo + Juliet* to the series of Kenneth Branagh's films to Michael Almereyda's *Hamlet*, there has been ample material for viewing and for study.[1] However, just as Shakespeare has overshadowed many of his contemporaries who were equally popular in his day, so other Renaissance dramatists have suffered from a lack of attention in popular filmmaking. The list of film versions of Shakespeare's contemporaries is quite short and, aside from BBC and student productions, is limited only to a handful of experimental ventures, such as Derek Jarman's overtly political version of Christopher Marlowe's *Edward II* (1991).[2]

Making a film by a non–Shakespearean dramatist is a risky business because of the lack of name recognition, coupled with the standard difficulties of language and accessibility, as well as a perceived historical remoteness. Ben Jonson declared that Shakespeare was "not for an age, but for all time," but was Jonson himself? Yet, given the surprisingly effective ways that Shakespeare has been adapted to our screen, there is every reason to believe that film versions of certain Renaissance dramas also could work particularly well. Perhaps Julie Taymor's success in making a film out of the bloody and until recently unpopular *Titus Andronicus* owes much to the film culture that enabled Quentin Tarantino's success (exemplified by the academy award for *Pulp Fiction* in 1994). No Renaissance drama seems as well-suited to this type of commentary on violence as *The Revenger's Tragedy*, now widely accepted to be Thomas Middleton's play, written around 1607.[3] This drama is wickedly funny, revelling in its own parody of the genre of revenge tragedy that had become popular with Thomas Kyd's *The Spanish Tragedy* and *Titus Andronicus* in the late 1580s and early 1590s. The main character of *The Revenger's Tragedy*, Vindice, named for revenge itself, is a hero who becomes so obsessed with the business of his revenge that he completely loses perspective on what he is doing. He devises ever more creative ways to kill his enemies — the Duke and his family — until he loses his own sense of morality, which makes him not entirely different from those he seeks to destroy. Vindice is as melancholy as Hamlet, but much less ponderous, and the violence in the play is so over-the-top as to be funny rather than horrific (an attribute it potentially shares with *Titus*). The apocalyptic symbolism employed by Middleton (exemplified by such signs as thunder and comets) also capitalizes on the sensationalism of the book of Revelation in ways that seem familiar to contemporary audiences.

The filmmaker who saw the potential of *The Revenger's Tragedy* was Alex Cox, whose scintillating version of the play was released in the UK in 2002. This *Revengers Tragedy* was directed by Cox and adapted for the screen by Frank Cottrell Boyce; it stars an impressive cast, including Derek Jacobi as the Duke, Christopher Eccleston as Vindice, Eddie Izzard as Lussurioso, Carla Henry as Castiza, and Andrew Schofield as Carlo (called Hippolyto in the original play).[4] The film also features a soundtrack by Chumbawamba and has a Chinese proverb as its motto: "Let the man who seeks revenge remember to dig two graves." This *Revengers Tragedy* fascinates on several levels, not the least of which is the risk of putting not Shakespeare's but instead one of his contemporary's plays on the screen. Although it certainly was no box office hit, Middleton's play does lend itself extremely well to the kind of postmodern punk that is also present in Shakespeare movies such as Luhrmann's *William Shakespeare's Romeo + Juliet* and to the postmodern self-reflexivity that characterizes Almereyda's *Hamlet*. Furthermore, Cox manages to create a film version of Middleton's play that is reminiscent of *A Clockwork Orange* (Stanley Kubrick, 1971) and *Blade Runner* (Ridley Scott, 1982). while also alluding to political preoccupations of our time, such as the veneration of Lady Diana, sports fans inciting riots, terrorism, and nuclear explosions. By interweaving and juxtaposing the seventeenth and twenty-first centuries through language, music, and strikingly disjunctive visual devices, Cox's film embraces the full range of Middleton's macabre humor and scathing political commentary. Because Middleton's play is rife with allusions to the apocalypse, it is interesting to see this pervasive aspect of early modern theater transferred to a new age that is itself obsessed by notions of Armageddon. Indeed, this film trades upon the apocalyptic discourses surrounding Shakespearean film that are discussed in this collection. In this chapter, I will be talking more specifically about where Cox's film fits with respect to other Shakespearean and non–Shakespearean films, showing how it employs postmodern techniques that trace the intersections between the camera, God, and the apocalypse.[5]

The Post-Apocalyptic Setting

Cox's *Revengers Tragedy* opens with a satellite view of the earth revealing a ravaged globe missing land masses such as France, Spain, and southern England. The premise of the film is that a comet destroyed these lands in 2001 (an appropriately millennial date) and now it is the year 2011, ten years after this apocalyptic event.[6] The Duke and his demented family, ostentatiously decorated with tattoos, piercings, make-up, and punk clothing, reign supreme in a post-apocalyptic Liverpool (now the seat of power since London has been destroyed).[7] The theme of surveillance is established by the satellite, which carries the brand name "Duke Satellites" and an accompanying logo — a D enclosed in a circle (we later see this symbol on money as well, which emphasizes the total control of this Duke). The camera focuses on Liverpool as Vindici[8] returns from his self-imposed exile aboard a bus that crashes because all of the other inhabitants, including the driver, have been killed by some unnamed force. Like a displaced hero from a spaghetti western (one of Cox's favorite genres), Vindici stumbles off the bus as cell phones ring in the dead passengers' hands and flies buzz around the corpses. Walking down the street while shaving his head, Vindici is assaulted by a gang of punks who demand "are you a cockney?" He nonchalantly beats several of them up and scatters the rest; then an eerie giant screen on an abandoned building flashes advertisements and a voice announces, "Welcome stranger!" and encourages him to "stop off for a drink, or a dance, at Duke's" while visiting Liverpool. Vindici's next stop is the crypt that houses the shrine of his dead love Gloriana; here he talks to her skull, to which her long red hair is still attached. Remembering "the form that living shone so bright," he utters words from *The Revenger's Tragedy* itself: "Thou sallow remnant of my poisoned love…" (1.1.14).[9] Vindici then has a flashback (again spaghetti-western style) to his wedding day, when he danced happily with his beautiful bride, both dressed in white, until the reception turned into a nightmare as most of the guests as well as the bride were poisoned by the caterers — "Duke and Sons." The victims cough blood all over their white wedding outfits and champagne glasses crash to the floor. Returning to thoughts of the present, Vindici becomes a ventriloquist, speaking for the skull as well as himself and shouting "Revenge! Revenge! Revenge!"

This opening sequence shows how Cox's post-apocalyptic setting creates a sense of postmodern dislocation. Vindici, as a displaced hero in a corrupt world, becomes emblematic of the film's emphasis on disjunctions in time, place, and language. Part of the point of the play, as with most early modern tragedies, is that "time is out of joint" (*Hamlet*, 1.5.188) — thus the characters inhabit a world that is inherently flawed, and the ruling class is reflective of an entirely corrupt society. Cox emphasizes these temporal disjunctions with frequent use of anachronisms that draw parallels between the twenty-first and seventeenth centuries. We have become accustomed to seeing modern-dress Shakespeare productions, as well as cars and guns incorporated in the midst of what purports to be drama from several centuries ago. However, this anachronistic technique has interested Cox for a long time. His 1987 film *Walker*, which is about a violent invasion of Nicaragua in 1855 by an American, includes "a variety of twentieth-century anachronisms (tape recorders, copies of *Newsweek*, personal computers and helicopters) as a reminder to viewers of America's continued interference with the Central American country" (Davies, *Alex Cox* 100). Reflecting upon this film later, Cox lamented that he passed up the effectiveness of more such anachronisms; he explains, "In the very opening scene, when Walker tries to take over Mexico and fails, it should have ended with a Mexican bus driving through. Also, when Vanderbilt meets Walker in the desert, he should have been talking on a cellular phone! It was a directorial error on my part not to have had the anachronisms in from the start" (Davies, *Alex Cox* 100).

In the opening scene of *Revengers Tragedy*, Cox is already taking advantage of those missed opportunities, showing us a bus and cell phones in this Jacobean play. Various modes of transportation and communication continue to be employed throughout the film, portraying a world in which all real connections are lost, broken apart by the reign of the evil Duke. This world's sorrow is that there is a radical sense of dislocation and disconnectedness in the midst of a world obsessed with communication. Vindici arrives on a bus that originated from nowhere, and his fellow passengers who lie dead cannot answer the phone calls of their loved ones. Later in the play a "nobleman" kills the Duke's bastard, Spurio, while holding a cell phone to his ear with one hand and shooting his gun with the other.

Setting the film in a post-apocalyptic Liverpool that is subject to gang violence as well as the licentious whims of its rulers underlines the corruption of this society. Cox apparently liked the idea of filming in his home town because of the city's "epic" qualities, for, as production designer Cecilia Montiel points out, "Liverpool has everything the project needs, ... [c]atacombs, long-forgotten, half-flooded tunnels, palaces, red-stone cathedrals of impossible dimensions, bunkers, gigantic warehouses, rusting cranes, abandoned docks.... In all, a concentration of symbols of might, ingenuity and ruthlessness that fits perfectly with the play's characters" ("*Revengers Tragedy*

Prod. Info.—Creating the Look"). This setting illustrates just how broken down society has become, but it also displays a complex landscape that is itself out of joint because it includes modern architecture as well as remnants of a much older society, creating an architectural palimpsest that echoes the film's layered effect.[10]

The film's language is also strikingly disjunctive; Boyce uses a substantial portion of Middleton's text while also frequently interjecting modern words, phrases, and expletives into the dialogue. The effect is at once jarring and appropriate; we are encouraged to embrace the chaotic connections between the two centuries while also becoming uncomfortable about how little has changed. Middleton's language, in part because of its irregularities and occasional sing-song quality, actually translates better to a contemporary setting than much of Shakespeare. Rather than struggling with densely packed speech with complex metaphors, we are given a sort of jingle, inspired by Middleton's more frequent use of rhymes, contractions, and end-stopped lines. This is more in keeping with our sound-byte culture, adapted as we are to commercials and brief news updates. Nonetheless, Cox and Boyce allow us to be jarred by the early modern speech in the mouths of these punks. A close-up of the hilariously demented Supervacuo (the Duke's second, and indeed vacuous, stepson), with his blonde spiked hair and pierced face, creates just the right kind of surprise when he says, "Drop one, and there lies t'other" (5.1.192), as he relishes the sound of the odd contraction on his pierced tongue and smiles at the audience.[11] Like the awkwardly archaic speech of *A Clockwork Orange* (e.g., "How art thou, thou globby bottle of cheap stinking chip oil?"), these aliens of society speak a tongue that is and is not ours. Vindici's ventriloquist act with Gloriana's skull also underlines the linguistic disjunction — the words that he speaks are his as well as hers, just as the film speaks in words that are Middleton's as well as ours.

The disjunctions in time, place, and language in *Revengers Tragedy* ally it not just with recent Shakespearean films, but also with other futuristic dystopian films such as Ridley Scott's *Blade Runner* or George Miller's *Mad Max* trilogy (1979–85), which also take place in lawless desiccated worlds and feature deeply flawed heroes on a path of violence and destruction. The assumption of all these films that set themselves at (or after) the apocalypse is that society is permeated by violence. The obsession with violence and the bloodlust of the characters in *Revengers Tragedy* are also reminiscent of *A Clockwork Orange*.[12] Although he does not break into choruses of "Singin' in the Rain" as the protagonist of *A Clockwork Orange* does while brutally raping a woman, Vindici does have a little tune that he hums as he brushes the poison onto the skull's teeth, singing "up and down, up and down, till they're clean and sparkly." This ditty shows Vindici's own lust for violence, and its eerie playfulness is all the more unsettling because of its deadly message. Later we hear Vindici humming the same tune as he brushes his own teeth, completely enamored with his creativity in the business of revenge (and foreshadowing his ultimate self-destruction).

Playing songs as the background to extreme acts of violence has become a postmodern cliché of sorts as happy tunes accompany and thus amplify horrific events. Another such famous moment in recent movie history is the scene in Quentin Tarantino's *Reservoir Dogs* (1992) in which Michael Madsen dances around and sings "Stuck in the Middle with You" while he's cutting a policeman's ear off. The final scene of *Revengers Tragedy*, in which all of the brothers kill each other in quick succession, also lends itself quite nicely to a Quentin Tarantino sense of domino-effect murders (as in *Reservoir Dogs*). All of these movies portray a desensitized society that creates cold-blooded killers. In his previous films, Cox focused on the connection between such violence and consumer culture; thus, *Repo Man* (1984) shows the protagonist as a product of his job stocking shelves that all bear generic labels. This technique returns briefly in *Revengers Tragedy* when Vindici shows his poison — a plain white bottle with the white generic label that reads, simply, "poison." The enjoyment that Vindici and his siblings experience from watching the Duke's lips eaten away with generic poison is indicative of the lawless violent society created by the film's post-apocalyptic setting.

Social Commentary: The Media

The emphasis on violence in *Revengers Tragedy* makes it very much in the same vein as its near contemporary *Titus*, with its insistent focus on modern violence, filtered through the eyes of young Lucius as if it were a video game. However, Cox's dark commentary on our society focuses on the ubiquitous presence and invasion of the camera — something that it shares most in common with Almereyda's *Hamlet* (in which Hamlet's self-reflexivity is expressed through the lens of an inward- as well as an outward-aimed video camera). The attention to *looking* in these films connects to the providential nature of apocalyptic — the eye of the media replaces the eye of God, suggesting that all events are being watched and controlled by a higher theological power. Again, like *Blade Runner* (in which the omniscient Tyrell Corporation controls Los Angeles through a giant eye that sees and knows all), Cox's film emphasizes the dark underbelly of technological "development" that leaves humanity itself in a perilous position in the future.

The most striking impact of the media in *Revengers Tragedy* relates to the rape of Lord Antonio's wife. In the film she is given the name Imogen and is played by Sophie Dahl, a British model and actress; she is young and beautiful in contrast to a much older and somewhat lecherous-looking Antonio (played by Anthony Booth). He is in the news constantly, with her, which is what causes Junior (the Duke's youngest son) to lust after her and to commit the rape; early in the play we see him looking at TV coverage of her following Antonio out of a limousine, then lasciviously licking the TV screen. The central news event at the beginning of the movie is a sporting contest between "The Duke's boy" and "Antonio's lad." Being prepared for something truly athletic, we are instead treated to large muscular men playing foosball in the middle of a stadium (set at Liverpool's Aintree racecourse). The televised broadcast is cheered and gambled on by people throughout the city with no less enthusiasm than they would have for a genuine soccer match. Antonio's cheering becomes ugly, and he does not even notice the disappearance of his wife from the scene. Directly after the rape, she stumbles into an alleyway screaming for help and is rescued by Vindici's sister, Castiza, who is a much more frequent presence in this film than she is in Middleton's play (this modern Castiza actually plots the murders with her brothers and takes a very active role in the preservation of her virginity from the advances of Lussurioso; she also participates in a knife-throwing show for a living and is perfectly capable of using these knives to defend herself as well).

When Imogen appears at Junior's trial, she looks like popular representations of the Virgin Mary, her face and blonde hair shining, with a modest blue scarf covering her head. She is the archetypical female victim, sitting in the courtroom in beautiful innocence. Meanwhile, Antonio's political fortunes are rising (people stand outside the courthouse chanting his name). After her death, Antonio is immediately seen giving the media an official account of what happened; an "eye" icon appears in the bottom corner of the screen — this symbol for Antonio's media network gradually replaces the ubiquitous presence of the Duke's symbol of the D within a circle. The entire event seems staged; when Antonio looks at Imogen's dead body as reporters stand by and cameras flash, he appears to "discover" the prayer book in her hands and then spontaneously reads the Latin epigram written there, which he tearfully translates, "Better to die virtuous than to live dishonored." Antonio is clearly playing with the public's sympathies in order to incite a riot, using Imogen's death to his own political advantage. The people rage through the streets in anger; at one point, they even surround the royal brothers' car and vandalize it in retaliation for the mysterious death of the adored Imogen. In a bar, we see two commoners talking about Antonio's speech, and one says that the bullet entered through the back of Imogen's head, so clearly it was not a suicide.[13] At the suggestion that Antonio engineered the suicide, the other man becomes very angry and a fight develops. Of course it is particularly silly to see this violent outbreak originating from the point of a foosball match. Cox is commenting on the role of the media and sports in inciting violent riots, such as the 1989 soccer stampede in Sheffield that killed 94 fans and injured 170 others. Here we see how quickly and seamlessly cheering for a sporting event has turned into a politically-charged bloodbath.

After Imogen's death, the parallels between her and Lady Diana become patently obvious. The media coverage does not stop, the people are all in public mourning, images of her are everywhere, and teary-eyed school children arrive by bus every day to place teddy bears honoring Imogen on a public set of stairs. Even at the end of the movie when Antonio rises triumphant, the crowd stands outside his window holding up giant signs with his dead wife's picture on them. Like Diana, Imogen is completely deified by the media that was in some sense responsible for her demise. Cox's portrayal of the media in the film is a scathing satire that casts nearly everyone in the play, including Antonio, in a negative light. The macabre humor of this veneration reaches its absurd culmination when one group of schoolchildren goes to pay the usual homage to the departed Imogen, only to end up screaming hysterically as they find the dead Duke's decaying head among the teddy bears. Alex Cox, like Vindici, has a wicked sense of humor.

The sense that surveillance cameras and spies watch all is underlined by the constant media coverage of everything that happens in Liverpool. As the spectators walk into the trial, they pass a newsstand where a tabloid headline announces, "Junior up before Senior." The tabloids also explode with the gossip about the illicit affair between the Duchess and Spurio (including an incriminating and graphic picture), and Lussurioso angrily shows the front page to his family at breakfast the morning the news breaks. Near the end of the film, the tabloids change from news about the royal family to news about the approaching comet (a headline that is more understandably alarming when we remember that apparently such a comet was horribly destructive a decade earlier).[14] Thus the apocalyptic resonance of this film intersects with its critique of the media's omniscient eye, raising important questions about current political and ethical issues.

Political Context

In every interview Cox gave about his inspiration to do a film of *The Revenger's Tragedy*, he explained his first discovery of the play:

> It was 1976 ... and I was sitting in the college library, intending to revise for my law exams. Unfortunately I was a very poor student and couldn't concentrate on

the law books in front of me. There were all these other books on shelves all around me — big, leather-bound olde bookes from the previous century. So I dragged down this two or three volume collection called *The Works of Cyril Tourneur* ... and started browsing through it. And in among the poems and rather undistinguished plays was this one called *Revengers Tragedy* ["*Revengers Tragedy* Prod. Info.—Comedy"].

The image of Cox as a disgruntled law student is, of course, apt, because it echoes so clearly (and self-consciously?) Vindice's self portrait when he appears "like himself" to Lussurioso later in the play. Cox's dissatisfaction with studying law and with the political establishment of the 1970s becomes part of a political framework within which he appropriates Middleton.

Cox's first encounter with the play seemed to him particularly reflective of the 1970s milieu; he explains, "In 1976 the punk movement was beginning, in part as a gesture of frustration and opposition to all the royalist obeisance and blather about the Royal Jubilee. In the cinema we had *Night of the Living Dead* and *Bring Me the Head of Alfredo Garcia*— the same insanity, the same societal death-cult as *Revengers Tragedy*. 1607 or 1976, there was no difference" ("*Revengers Tragedy* Prod. Info.—Comedy"). Despite this universalizing statement that we may be apt to dismiss, it is important to see that Cox did believe that the play could cross over the centuries and speak to our own times. But what effect does delaying the dream to produce a movie of this play for nearly thirty years have on Cox's vision? The punk feel of the movie seems to at least one reviewer to smack of Cox's original view: "The result has a slightly dated feel: its rebellious mood might have been perfect for Queen Elizabeth's Silver Jubilee in 1977, but looks less representative of Blairite, Golden Jubilee Britain, perhaps partly due to Cox's long absence from the country" (Johnston).[15] Yet this is an incomplete assessment of the film. Cox's political views about the Iraq war and American foreign policy are very much part of the film's makeup — there can be no doubt that this is a post–9/11 movie and an indictment of Blair's Britain.[16]

For Cox, Shakespeare was a reactionary playwright upholding the Tudor agenda, whereas Middleton belonged to a generation of political radicals who did not shrink from the idea of regicide. Therefore, Cox's film is self-consciously different because it is *not* Shakespeare. In this respect, Derek Jarman is the obvious precursor, with his satirical films *Jubilee* (1977), *The Last of England* (1988), and also with *Edward II* (1991).[17] The last of these is particularly relevant to Cox's project; by mixing the strikingly postmodern with the Elizabethan and throwing out the supposed sacredness of Marlowe's language, Jarman created a film that violently addressed the politics of homosexuality in the 1980s and early '90s. Jarman chose *Edward II* because the play itself seemed subversive to him —"Marlowe outs the past — why don't we out the present?" (Jarman dedication). Similarly, Cox is famous for working against the Hollywood grain and producing anarchic films. Therefore, to Cox, Shakespeare is to be avoided because he is the consummate establishment playwright (which, to a certain extent, he is; Hollywood is not any more likely to embrace Middleton than it is to embrace Cox).[18]

Cox's *Revengers Tragedy* ends quite literally with a bang, and accompanying political suggestions. Vindici and his family, including his blind mother, Gratiana, are eating lunch with Antonio. As Vindici departs, saying that he will not remain in Liverpool any longer, Antonio attempts to pay him off for helping to avenge the deaths of both wives (a significant addition to the play that casts Antonio in a more negative light). Vindici refuses the money, and as he walks away Antonio says he is puzzled about "how the old Duke came murdered" (5.3.111). Vindici confesses and provides proof of his single guilt by saying that his penknife could be found in the Duke's body. One of Antonio's men holds up the "evidence" of this knife in a plastic bag, thus confirming that Vindice killed the Duke.[19] However, the Duke in question here is Lussurioso, not the "old Duke." Therefore, the movie fails to make the necessary connection between what Antonio asked and what ensues, while also leaving questions about whether Antonio knows that Vindice killed the original Duke. Following this confusing exchange, Vindici pulls a gun and the entire family surrounds Antonio and walks him down a long staircase as Vindici and Carlo split Vindici's final soliloquy, ending with the lines, "We're well, our mother turned, our sister true; / We die after a nest of dukes" (5.3.145–6). At the bottom of the staircase, they are met by dozens of people who are aiming guns at them, from policemen with riot gear, to common citizens, to the long-wigged judge with an oxygen tube in his nose who presided over Junior's trial. When Vindici attempts to shoot Antonio, it turns out to be a fake gun with a "bang" banner — theatrical antics have at last gotten the better of the revenger. Carlo exclaims "shit!" and then Vindici says, as he does in the play, "adieu" and is answered by his family with their own "adieu" (which does not occur in the play). As we hear the endless rounds of gunfire (presumably wiping out Antonio and his men as well as Vindici and family), the camera lifts to focus on a picture of Queen Elizabeth II at the top of the stairs.

The painting of the queen dissolves into the film's final image: an atomic bomb exploding while we hear again the words that Vindici had ventriloquised to the skull at the beginning: "Revenge! Revenge! Revenge!" Originally, Alex Cox had planned to show footage of the twin towers collapsing on 9/11, but he was prevented from doing so by the film's backers.[20] This image would have been much more powerfully specific than the atomic bomb explosion reminiscent of *Dr. Strangelove* (Stanley Kubrick, 1964). Tying the word "revenge" to the terrorist attack on the World Trade Center is a very daring move and also one that could easily be construed as anti–American (undoubtedly what the backers of the film feared, especially because this is in keeping with Cox's long-standing criticism of the United States). Thus, Cox manages in his final flair to take aim at both American and British powers at a time — 2002 — when Britain was the United States's most vocal supporter.

Cox allies his politics with those of Middleton, explaining why he prefers this playwright: "Shakespeare ... is the greatest playwright in the English language, but his politics are fairly square. The greatest crime in a Shakespeare play is to murder the king. For Middleton it's like, 'Kill the king? Why not?' It's inspirational — nobody is above being brought down. It's a revolutionary message" (qtd. in Davies, DVD cover). It is, of course, rather odd to take this message from Middleton of all playwrights. The ending of *The Revenger's Tragedy*, like that of *Women Beware Women*, ties things in a neat bow that Shakespeare would have avoided at all costs. Vindice must die because his job is done, and because he has lost sight of morality and even *brags* about his murders. Middleton does in fact have a tendency toward moralization: it is morally defensible to kill the Duke of *The Revenger's Tragedy* because he is evil, but even so, Vindice is caught up in the bloodlust and inevitably must die for his crimes too. By making Antonio as power-hungry and opportunistic as the rest, Cox erases Middleton's political message and replaces it with a much more subversive one. The disruptive force in Middleton's play must be controlled and contained at the end by the "silver age" promised by Antonio's rule, but in Cox's film there is no comfort of a better day to come — we are already past the apocalypse. Vindice does not die alone with his brother as in Middleton's play, but instead takes everyone down with him. Like Jarman, Cox is willing to alter the text so that his own anarchic chaos can shine through the drama.

Metatheatricality and Apocalypse

Because *The Revenger's Tragedy* was probably written around 1607, it is no surprise that it contained quite a bit of apocalyptic imagery. The apocalypse had been a popular topic since the Reformation, but under the reign of James it gained a new currency. The King himself was interested in the book of Revelation and wrote his own commentary on it. Obviously, others held the same interest; Shakespeare's dramas with the most allusions to the apocalypse come from this period — most notably *King Lear* and *Antony and Cleopatra*. In *The Revenger's Tragedy*, Vindice casts himself as a sort of horseman of the apocalypse, helping heaven expedite the vengeance that he thinks is strangely slow in coming. Vindice angrily asks, after he discovers that his mother is willing to become a bawd to his sister,

> Why does not heaven turn black, or with a frown
> Undo the world? Why does not earth start up,
> And strike the sins that tread upon't? [2.1.254–6]

With these words, Vindice calls for apocalyptic vengeance in a world gone mad with sin — not just in the Duke's family, but in his own. Therefore, Vindice takes complete control of every situation, orchestrating the murder of the Duke, the downfall of the royal family, and the reformation of his own mother. By the end of the play, even the heavens seem to obey him. Referring to Lussurioso, Vindice says,

> O thou almighty Patience! 'Tis my wonder
> That such a fellow, impudent and wicked,
> Should not be cloven as he stood,
> Or with a secret wind burst open!
> Is there no thunder left, or is't kept up
> In stock for heavier vengeance? [*Thunder is heard*] There it goes!
> [4.2.199–204]

The thunder comes on cue, making the nature of the apocalypse self-consciously theatrical. Just as in *The Spanish Tragedy*, in which Revenge watches from above, vengeance here seems tied directly to a theatrical device — Vindice is not so much a person as he is the personification of Revenge.

There is indeed a providence shaping the ends of the characters in *The Revenger's Tragedy*; Vindice's acceptance of the situation at the end makes it clear that he is ready to bow to his fate in this regard. Speaking to Lussurioso about the sins that take place at night, Vindice asks, "Who can perceive this, save that eternal eye / That sees through flesh and all?" (1.3.65–6). This line serves as a sort of motto for Cox's film, for here the eternal eye is a very powerful force — the insignia for the media, the source of surveillance, and the force watching over the entire city. The emphasis on this omniscient eye provides a thematic link between the role of god (or lack thereof) in apocalyptic vengeance, metatheatricality, and postmodern self-awareness. The sign of this eye is frequently shown in the film with a pyramid — a uniquely American symbol (featured on the one dollar bill) representing the "providential" mission of the U.S.

The comet that appears toward the end of the play also adds a sense of impending doom for the royal family. Lussurioso is very angry that such a comet could persist during his rise to power, for it does seem to portend a higher law that will not allow him to reign for long. Though the comet is a stage prop, Middleton seems to stop just short of claiming Vindice and the drama itself as the absolute controllers of the situation. Though Kyd projects his own power as author onto the character of Revenge, Middleton's own portrait of revenge must itself be destroyed. Despite the potential for special effects in contemporary films, Cox does not attempt to make the comet that ominously appears in acts 4 and 5 realistic. Instead, it is as artificial as the Duke's punk Machiavellian sons. Thus, the film is entirely appropriate to the play in which Vindice calls for a justice that is provided by the theater itself. Cox intensifies this feeling by playing up Middleton's own use of asides — the kind of direct address to the camera that works so well in movies such as Richard Loncraine's *Richard III* (1995), in which Ian McKellan looks knowingly at the camera, winks, and invites the audience to limp down the hallway with him. Similarly villainous, Derek Jacobi's Duke plays the piano and talks directly to the camera about his decision to release Lussurioso from prison; later he confesses knowingly to the camera, "Age hot is like a monster to be seen; / My hairs are white, and yet my sins are green" (2.3.132–3). As Vindici says the above lines that call for thunder while he talks to Lussurioso in a Liverpool bar, the thunder comes on cue, and Vindici looks at the camera and winks. After the murder of Lussurioso and the others, Vindici gives the camera a "thumbs-up" and says gleefully, "most fitting revels!" In this film, the all-seeing eye is not that of Providence, but that of the camera itself.

Reviewer Maximilian Le Cain says that "[i]t is as if Cox allows fate to hand over control of events to Vindici for the specific purpose of destroying the Duke, only to cruelly wrest it from him when this is accomplished — all part of a nihilistic, cosmological joke with the last laugh on Vindici, who has been laughing throughout." However, such a statement is much more appropriate to Middleton's *Revenger's Tragedy* than to Cox's: it is Vindici's disembodied voice gleefully shouting "Revenge!" during the explosion. There are no cosmological jokes here, only cinematographic ones.

Middleton wrote *The Revenger's Tragedy* a few years after a new century had begun, but it was not the dawn of a glorious new age; the reign of James was characterized by financial troubles, rising religious tensions, and a perceived corruption in the court. It is no wonder that *The Revenger's Tragedy* seems at once so funny and so bitter in its satire on the corruption of power. Cox revived this play not just at the early stages of a new century, but also of a new millennium. Once critical of Thatcher's England, Cox shows a similar disaffection with the Blair UK and the ominous presence of the U.S. over all. In this light, to say that *The Revenger's Tragedy* translates well across the centuries is actually an understatement.

To show a world on the verge of apocalypse is, as it always was, a way of commenting on the corruption of contemporary society. Films such as the *Mad Max* trilogy, *Blade Runner*, and *Revengers Tragedy* show the remnants of a post-apocalyptic world. The disaster has already happened, and the survivors are left to scrape out a meagre existence on what remains of the earth. For so many years leading up to the year 2000, however, books, films, and popular thought focused on the disaster to come. Having passed the official millennium, we are, like the characters of Cox's *Revengers Tragedy*, living in a post-apocalyptic world. Yet doomsday prophecies do not stop, and some version of a comet invariably threatens overhead. This film speaks to our own sense of being "stuck in the middle" — between apocalyptic events that are alarming precisely because they are insistently deferred (or, like Y2K, disturbingly anti-climactic). By underlining the theatrical nature of the apocalypse while also showing the very real physical horror the violence of our society creates, Cox's film stages a provocative revival of *The Revenger's Tragedy*.

Notes

1. See, for instance, *Shakespeare After Mass Media*, ed. Richard Burt (New York: Palgrave, 2002); *Shakespeare and the Moving Image: The Plays on Film and Television*, ed. Anthony Davies and Stanley Wells (Cambridge: Cambridge University Press, 1994); *Shakespeare, Film, Fin de Siècle*, ed. Mark Thornton Burnett and Ramona Wray (London: Macmillan, 2000); *Shakespeare the Movie: Popularizing the Plays on Film, TV, and Video* (London and New York: Routledge, 1997).

2. For a bibliography of film versions of plays by Shakespeare's contemporaries, see Philippa Sheppard, "A Renaissance Filmography," *Approaches to Teaching English Renaissance Drama*, ed. Karen Bamford and Alexander Leggatt (New York: MLA, 2002), 13–19.

3. Some copies of the title page are dated 1607, and others 1608. The title page also says that the play was performed by the King's Men (presumably at the Globe). For Middleton's authorship, see MacDonald P. Jackson, *The Revenger's Tragedy Attributed to Thomas Middleton* (Toronto: Associated University Presses, 1987) and David J. Lake, *The Canon of Thomas Middleton's Plays: Internal Evidence for the Major Problems of Authorship* (London and Cambridge, 1975).

4. Cox made a point of following the 1607–8 quarto in not putting an apostrophe in the title ("*Revenger's Tragedy* Prod. Info.— Apocalyptic"). Therefore, when I am referring to Cox's film I use no apostrophe, though when I refer to Middleton's play, following modern editors and commentators I am including the customary apostrophe. Cox's choice to call Hippolyto Carlo is based on a single instance in the play, where the character is called Carlo by his mother: "What news from court, son Carlo?" (1.1.108).

5. Throughout this paper, I am using the term "apocalypse" in the popular sense of the word (events related to the end of the world), rather than the more literal notion of an unveiling.

6. Art director Sandoval explains, "We envisaged southern England and part of mainland Europe half-vaporised by a massive comet; a cloud of debris hanging over the remains.... In the Elizabethan play they are afraid of comets as portents; in our film they are just afraid of them. We imagined a world shocked and frozen in time — a glorious dissection of humankind's grandeur and folly" ("*Revengers Tragedy* Prod. Info.— Creating the Look").

7. In a nod to the play's formerly assumed author, Cyril Tourneur, the screenplay gives the Duke and his family the last name Tourner.

8. Although the character is called "Vindice" in most versions of the play, he is called "Vindici" in the film and thus I will use this spelling when referring to the character in Cox's film.

9. The play reads "picture," not "remnant."

10. Patrick Cook further suggests that another important effect of the Liverpool setting is the distinctiveness of its dialect: the native accents, such as those of Vindici and his family, contrast with the more "Shakespearean-sounding" Duke, who seems to be a ruler from the outside (86).

11. This is actually Ambitioso's line in the play.

12. In another nod to *A Clockwork Orange*, when Vindici murders the Duke he gives him a pill which prohibits him from blinking so that he can watch the horrible vision of his Duchess fornicating with his bastard son (reminiscent of the torture device in Kubrick's film that forces Alex to keep his eyes open).

13. As Cook (86) points out, this is clearly a parody of the conspiracy theories surrounding the assassination of John F. Kennedy.

14. "Both in the film and in the play, such heavenly violence is caused by a comet hurtling towards the earth. Cottrell Boyce's decision to set his screenplay in the aftermath of destruction caused by a comet makes sense of, and makes more credible, the fear of comets towards the end of the play" (Spiller 13).

15. Cox has spent most of his time over the past two decades in Mexico.

16. The *Revengers Tragedy* website has included from its beginning a running tally of the cost of the war in Iraq (see <www.alexcox.com/rt>).

17. See Johnston.

18. However, Cox's embracing of Middleton includes its own kind of historical misunderstanding—he repeatedly refers to Middleton as a Jacobean playwright and to Shakespeare as an Elizabethan playwright. Furthermore, as Jarman showed with his film of *The Tempest*, Shakespeare can also be appropriated for an anarchic message. See also Cox, "Stage Fright."

19. An earlier scene showed these men performing an autopsy on Lussurioso and locating Vindice's penknife.

20. See Davies, DVD cover.

Works Cited

A Clockwork Orange. Dir. Stanley Kubrick. Warner Brothers, 1971.

Cook, Patrick. "Adapting *The Revengers Tragedy*." *Literature/Film Quarterly* 35.2 (2007): 85–91.

Cox, Alex. "Stage Fright." *The Guardian* 9 Aug. 2002.

Davies, Steven Paul. *Alex Cox: Film Anarchist*. London: Batsford, 2000.

_____. *Revengers Tragedy* DVD cover. Tartan DVD, 2003.

Jarman, Derek. *Queer Edward II*. London: British Film Institute, 1991.

Johnston, Sheila. Rev. of *Revengers Tragedy*. *ScreenDaily.com* 6 August 2002. 1 April 2008 <www.screendaily.com>.

Le Cain, Maximilian. Rev. of *Revengers Tragedy*. *Senses of Cinema* Jan.-Feb. 2003. 1 April 2008 <www.sensesofcinema.com/contents/03/24/revengers.html>.

Middleton, Thomas. *The Revenger's Tragedy*. *English Renaissance Drama*. Ed. David Bevington, et al. New York: W.W. Norton, 2002. 1303–67.

Revengers Tragedy. Dir. Alex Cox. Screenplay by Frank Cottrell Boyce. 2002. DVD. Fantoma, 2004.

"*Revenger's Tragedy* Production Information for the Pathé Film Distribution — Apocalyptic Apostrophe." *Revengers Tragedy*. 2002. 1 April 2008 <www.alexcox.com/rt/prodinfo.html>.

"*Revengers Tragedy* Production Information for the Pathé Film Distribution — Comedy and the Dance of Death." *Revengers Tragedy.* 2002. 1 April 2008 <www.alexcox. com/rt/prodinfo.html>.

"*Revengers Tragedy* Production Information for the Pathé Film Distribution — Creating the Look: Design." *Revengers Tragedy.* 2002. 1 April 2008 <www.alexcox.com/rt/ prodinfo.html>.

Spiller, Ben. "'Today, Vindici Returns': Alex Cox's *Revengers Tragedy.*" *Early Modern Literary Studies* 8.3 (2003): 1–14.

7

The Plague in Filmed Versions of *Romeo and Juliet* and *Twelfth Night*

CARL JAMES GRINDLEY

> What an vnmatchable torment were it for a man to be bard vp euery night in a vast silent Charnell-house? hung (to make it more hideous) with lamps dimly & slowly burning, in hollow and glimmering corners: where all the pauement should in stead of greene rushes, be strewed with blasted Rosemary: withered Hyacinthes, fatall Cipresse and Ewe, thickly mingled with heapes of dead mens bones: the bare ribbes of a father that begat him, lying there: here the Chaplesse hollow scull of a mother that bore him: round about him a thousand Coarses, some standing bolt vpright in their knotted winding sheets: others halfe mouldred in rotted coffins, that should suddenly yawne wide open, filling his nosthrils with noysome stench, and his eyes with the sight of nothing but crawling wormes.
> — Thomas Dekker, *The Wonderful Yeare*, 1603

The world Shakespeare inhabited had been battling the plague since the disease first made its way from Asia to British soil in the mid-fourteenth century (Bean 423). This catastrophe swept "through the city again and again, spreading panic, wiping out whole families, decimating neighborhoods" (Greenblatt, *Will* 163). In 1563, for example, a highly contagious illness struck London in a manner unseen since the collapse of feudal England and managed to wipe out a staggering number of people per week until an unusually cold period of weather stopped the disease in its tracks (Creighton 304–306). Similar outbreaks of equally virulent infectious diseases occurred throughout the 1580s and early 1590s. Some of these so-called plague years were accompanied by the closing of public playhouses or were shadowed by potential rebellion or at least the threat of social unrest. Even relatively minor

148

outbreaks of disease were significant, and these outbreaks occurred almost with clockwork precision during the summer months of 1581, 1582, 1587, 1591, 1592, 1597, 1599, 1602 and 1605 (M.F. Hollingsworth and T.H. Hollingsworth 133). Indeed, the 1592–1593 outbreak was so severe that Elizabeth "abandon[ed] London" for a tour of rural England (Cox 1). That was not the first time that Elizabeth's center failed to hold; during the 1563 epidemic, for example, she had fled to Windsor Castle and ordered that anyone attempting to visit her would be immediately hanged on a brand new set of gallows that had been constructed for that very purpose.

As Robin B. Barnes notes,

> Even in times of relative peace, most of Europe did not escape cycles of severe dearth, typically seen as God's punishment upon a sinful world. The pale horse, finally, was disease and death. Diseases both old and new helped to produce an atmosphere in which disaster was always either threatening or at hand; the resulting individual and social anxiety commonly took on apocalyptic dimensions [264].

Shakespeare grew up in this milieu and was only three months old when the 1563 plague finally managed to make its way to Stratford in 1564, carrying off one out of every seven people. It has even been suggested that Shakespeare's would-have-been elder sister died of the disease some months before he was born. But for a writer whose background and culture was accompanied and informed by the plague in so many very real and tactile ways, his plays are seen as being only periodically concerned with the actual disease. Nothing could be further from the truth, and indeed, the plague's subtle presence in many of his works helps to foster a sort of nebulous apocalypticism.

By a "nebulous apocalypticism" I do not mean that Shakespeare was merely expressing a general despair over a decaying civilization, but also that he was engaged in a uniquely secular attempt at the "disclosure of divine purpose to history, to which common usage has added the dimension of immediate crisis" (Reeves 40). According to Lorenzo DiTommaso, apocalypses are texts of "crisis and consolation focusing on history and politics" (251), and Shakespeare's imagery conforms to this general pattern. In Shakespeare, the apocalyptic is usually preceded or presented concurrently with some form of optimistic but ultimately failed revelation, a horrid pre-millennial angst with no real blissful payoff. This is not to say that Shakespeare is prophetic in the sense that some of his near contemporaries would have recognized — popular writers of the Protestant Reform such as Robert Crowley and John Bale provided the true texts of the genre, taking their cues from writers of the proto–Reformation, including poets such as William Langland. Not only did Shakespeare's religious sentiments lean towards Catholicism, but he studiously avoided writing anything with more than a whiff of traditional Eschatology, and he obviously preferred to present his societal critiques from a distance — the vast majority of his plays, for example, are set in the past, either historical or mythical. Nevertheless, I think that many of Shakespeare's plays shared a number of traits with the kind of texts penned by late Medieval apocalyptic writers of the Reformist tradition: "very realistic and, in certain ways, very reactionary in their treatment of the present time. Whatever new-found optimism they may have held for the future, pessimism regarding the present was widespread ... [an] odd combination of grim pessimism and tenacious optimism, reactionary indignation and unflagging hope for large-scale renewal" (Kerby-Fulton 5).

Certainly, the Pale Horse of plague stalks the stage in a number of his plays (*Lear* 2.4, for example, contains a grotesque likening of Goneril to a pus-filled bubo; similarly, the plague gains a few passing references in *Timon of Athens* and *The Tempest* among others), but for the most part, Shakespeare refrains from giving the disease a starring role in any of his works. Instead, the plague forms a lexical residue — synonyms for it are used to construct all-purpose insults, oaths, exclamations and so on. This sort of linguistic behavior can be tracked quite easily with a standard concordance, the use of which reveals that Shakespeare's usual approach to the "pestilence" (14 uses), the "plague" and its variants (104 uses), the "pox" (24 uses), or the "contagion" (7 uses) was to apply it as a general-purpose curse — something he did across his entire oeuvre. These curses occur with some predictability but rarely form clusters with other plague terms. That is, someone might desire a pox on another character, but seldom do they want a pox, a pestilence, three plagues and a sickness to visit a single household.

In at least two instances, however, the plague does take a much more important role, although it still is not entirely in the spotlight. In *Romeo and Juliet* and *Twelfth Night,* the disease resides in a pivotal space, informing not only plotlines but also character arcs and settings. These two plays represent opposite ends of the same spectrum — one end providing the obvious dramatic convenience of Friar John's delay, the other embodying a more sophisticated understanding of the plague's overall influence on the social fabric of a community, in this case, Illyria's.

Of the two situations, the one represented by the text of *Romeo and Juliet* is the simplest to outline. A good portion of the tragedy hinges on a delay caused by an outbreak of the plague. Friar Laurence's letter to Romeo explaining Juliet's apparent death is held up by the plague:

> FRIAR LAURENCE. This same should be the voice of Friar John.
>   Welcome from Mantua! What says Romeo?
>   Or if his mind be writ, give me his letter.

FRIAR JOHN. Going to find a barefoot brother out —
　　One of our order — to associate me,
　　Here in this city visiting the sick,
　　And finding him, the searchers of the town,
　　Suspecting that we both were in a house
　　Where the infectious pestilence did reign,
　　Sealed up the doors, and would not let us forth,
　　So that my speed to Mantua there was stayed.
FRIAR LAURENCE. Who bare my letter then to Romeo?
FRIAR JOHN. I could not send it — here it is again —
　　Nor get a messenger to bring it thee,
　　So fearful were they of infection [5.2.2–16].

Out of all of the potential causes of Romeo's and Juliet's deaths, the plague is the most direct. Without the ongoing feud, obviously there would not have been much of an impediment to the young couple's romance. Without Tybalt's death, Romeo would not have been exiled. Without the Friar's continuous meddling, Romeo would not have been turned into a poor man's Petrarch, nor would there have been a secret marriage, and so on. But it is the plague that puts in motion the play's final descent into tragedy.

Scholarly opinion ranges considerably on Shakespeare's overall wisdom in hinging so much of his play on such a creatively feeble gambit. Back in 1928, Walpole claimed that the plague in *Romeo and Juliet* was "a purely 'external' event, not elsewhere used or even mentioned in the play" (213), calling its use as a dramatic convenience "certainly a flaw" (213). Wentersdorf, some sixty years later, instead calls Friar John's sealing up "a commonplace" (437). Indeed, judging from Shakespeare's contemporaries, sealing people up in their homes was exceedingly common. The only real dramatic issue with John's confinement is the relatively trivial anachronistic jolt that it provides: after all, the distant and historical Romeo and Juliet lived and died long before the plague arrived in Europe, but the device was not Shakespeare's innovation, and besides, Shakespeare routinely fills even his history plays with anachronisms, so it hardly matters.

The plague also appears in *Romeo and Juliet* in a more surreptitious role. At first glance, it is easy enough to blame poor parenting for both keeping Juliet unmarried beyond an appropriate age and for inciting in her a certain level of unacceptable disobedience, but on a closer reading (following Q2), it seems possible that the plague is also to blame for these issues:

CAPULET. But saying o'er what I have said before.
　　My child is yet a stranger in the world;
　　She hath not seen the change of fourteen years,
　　Let two more summers wither in their pride
　　Ere we may think her ripe to be a bride.

> PARIS. Younger than she are happy mothers made.
> CAPULET. And too soon marred are those so early made.
>   The earth hath swallow'd all my hopes but she,
>   She is the hopeful lady of my earth:
>   But woo her, gentle Paris, get her heart;
>   My will to her consent is but a part,
>   And, she agreed, within her scope of choice
>   Lies my consent and fair according voice [1.2.7–17].

In the Q2 reading, "The earth," Capulet explains to Paris, "swallowed" all of his children except for Juliet, who — due to Juliet's mother's extremely young age — presumably would have been his eldest child, although there is nothing in the play that indicates that Juliet's mother is his first wife. Interestingly, although Shakespeare inherited Friar John's delay from Arthur Brooke, he did not acquire Juliet's dead siblings from him. Brooke describes Capulet's selection of Paris and Juliet's position in the family quite simply:

> And Capulet, the maiden's sire, within a day or twain,
> Conferreth with his friends for marriage of his daughter,
> And many gentlemen there were with busy care that sought her;
> Both for the maiden was well shapéd, young, and fair,
> As also well brought up, and wise; her father's only heir [1877–1881].

Likewise, Capulet's characterization in Brooke does not bear much resemblance to Shakespeare's overly indulgent Capulet. Shakespeare has manipulated the drama so that the premature deaths of his other children created an unreasonable permissiveness in Capulet's parenting. Not only does he claim to Paris that he will offer Juliet absolute choice in love and marriage, but his wife attempts to persuade Juliet rather than simply inform her of what must occur. I believe that both Q2's reading and the Folio's reading are authorial and that Shakespeare deliberately backtracked from his initial depiction of Juliet's afflicted family.

In *Romeo and Juliet,* the plague serves several important functions. By having Juliet's only-child status being caused by some sort of series of unexplained deaths, Shakespeare is able not only to better justify Brooke's plague delay of Friar John, but he is also able to explain Juliet's permissive upbringing. In a way, Juliet — and a similar case could be made for Romeo — has been commoditized by the plague. Without it lurking in the background, she would have just been another disobedient child in a presumably large family.

From the perspective of what I have called a "nebulous apocalypticism," the plague in *Romeo and Juliet* helps to form the play's pre-millennial backdrop. Other aspects of this backdrop include such obvious features as the violence and chaos of Verona, the breakdown of traditional family structures, the abuses of friars, and the inability of the Prince to provide sound governance, but also include more subtle features such as Shakespeare's nearly continuous use of astrological imagery — usually read in the context of the protagonists' idolatrous relationship, but also important as a warning against prophecy as the stars reveal themselves to be both harbingers of doom and untrustworthy emblems of prosperity. At the same time Shakespeare crafts this disturbing milieu for his characters to occupy, he also presents a vision of a golden age, a world where warring families are reconciled, where a Prince exercises a just and considered rule, where civic peace rules, and where the old structures are brushed aside and love rules the day. Like the traditional texts of Reformist Apocalpyticism — the *Piers Plowman C-text* immediately comes to mind — *Romeo and Juliet* ends in a flourish of disgraced hope. The original prophecy is ruled out — the families' war has grown more costly, the unaffiliated inhabitants of Verona are close to rebellion, the Prince is exposed as being utterly impotent, and the lovers are dead — but the play's concluding lines hint that the future will indeed be brighter.

The plague's appearance in *Twelfth Night* is slightly more difficult to analyze. In this case, it is helpful to consult a concordance. As usual, Shakespeare's lexical practice is to form anomalous clusters of terms that point to a play's grander thematic interests. In *Twelfth Night*, disease exists as a *dark other*, a force that either directly runs through the play's action or informs its dramatic origins.

A basic analysis of Shakespeare's language in *Twelfth Night* reveals that "plague" occurs four times, "pestilence" once and "contagion" once. The play contains one use of "corpse," five uses of "sick," four uses of "ill," eight uses of "death," six variants of "die" and four in-context uses of "grave" (as opposed to one use of "grave" as an adjective). This sort of pattern of usage is easily one of the more unusual features of the play. The obvious conclusion is that this is a rather large number of unpleasant lexical items for what should be a happy little play: until it is remembered that *Twelfth Night* is actually a play characterized by and frequently criticized for a lack of emotional and societal balance. The characters of *Twelfth Night* inhabit a world where there is a shortage of genuine or well-developed feelings, a world that becomes increasingly confusing as its sometimes nasty and threatening action progresses. Even Olivia's first recognition of love is couched in contradictory imagery:

> OLIVIA. "What is your parentage?"
> "Above my fortunes, yet my state is well:
> I am a gentleman." I'll be sworn thou art.
> Thy tongue, thy face, thy limbs, actions and spirit,
> Do give thee five-fold blazon. Not too fast. Soft, soft —

> Unless the master were the man. How now?
> Even so quickly may one catch the plague?
> Methinks I feel this youth's perfections
> With an invisible and subtle stealth
> To creep in at mine eyes. Well, let it be [1.5.259–268].

Here, Olivia likens love to a dangerous and contagious illness. Ordinarily, a reasonable impulse would be simply to acknowledge Shakespeare's obvious debts to standard Petrarchan conceits. Yet, through Olivia and the other characters, Shakespeare out–Petrarchs Petrarch, and it should be noted that only a few lines earlier, Olivia had used sickness not as a metaphor for love, but as an excuse to avoid it. This is not the last time that love will be seen in such an odd way:

> FESTE. Come away, come away death,
>   And in sad cypress let me be laid.
> Fie away, fie away breath,
>   I am slain by a fair cruel maid.
> My shroud of white, stuck all with yew,
>   O prepare it.
> My part of death no one so true
>   Did share it.
> Not a flower, not a flower sweet
>   On my black coffin let there be strewn.
> Not a friend, not a friend greet
>   My poor corpse, where my bones shall be thrown.
> A thousand thousand sighs to save,
>   Lay me O where
> Sad true lover never find my grave,
>   To weep there [2.4.50–65].

Unlike Olivia's measured poetry, Feste's song owes little to Petrarch save some of the imagery. It is a strange song in a strange play, but then again, *Twelfth Night's* most notable plot device (the cross-dressing) is only necessary because Viola fears rape. In addition, the wooing of Olivia would have been much different had her father and brother not died under unusual circumstances less than a year apart. Death and comedy usually do not go hand in hand. In very few of Shakespeare's other major comedies is there such a surplus of dead characters. As Viola recognizes, Illyria is far removed from harmless. Indeed, she obviously fears strongly for her life. To her, even Sir Andrew Aguecheek, fop and a half that he is, is a plausibly dangerous foe.

    Illyria — like the Verona of *Romeo and Juliet*—seems to bear more than a passing resemblance to Petrarch's descriptions of Florence when that city was besieged by disease. In one section of his plague narrative, Petrarch describes how people would hold up flowers to their noses to ward off the

Black Death; of course it did not work, but in *Twelfth Night*, the Duke seems to mirror Petrarch's observations by retiring to his flowered gardens:

> DUKE ORSINO. Why, so I do, the noblest that I have.
>   O, when mine eyes did see Olivia first
>   Methought she purged the air of pestilence;
>   That instant was I turned into a hart,
>   And my desires, like fell and cruel hounds,
>   E'er since pursue me [1.1.17–22].

What better setting for a Petrarchan lover than the world of Petrarch, a world of the plague where loved ones die with astonishing regularity and gamesmanship takes precedence over rational thought. *Twelfth Night*, like *Romeo and Juliet*, seems to present a collision between the sonnets of Petrarch and the dissipated world of Boccaccio's *Decameron*, where moderates and wastrels, rich and poor alike attempt to will the world of death out of existence:

> Among whom there were those who thought that to live temperately and avoid all excess would count for much as a preservative against seizures of this kind. Wherefore they banded together, and, dissociating themselves from all others, formed communities in houses where there were no sick, and lived a separate and secluded life, which they regulated with the utmost care, avoiding every kind of luxury, but eating and drinking very moderately of the most delicate viands and the finest wines, holding converse with none but one another, lest tidings of sickness or death should reach them, and diverting their minds with music and such other delights as they could devise. Others, the bias of whose minds was in the opposite direction, maintained, that to drink freely, frequent places of public resort, and take their pleasure with song and revel, sparing to satisfy no appetite, and to laugh and mock at no event, was the sovereign remedy for so great an evil: and that which they affirmed they also put in practice, so far as they were able, resorting day and night, now to this tavern, now to that, drinking with an entire disregard of rule or measure, and by preference making the houses of others, as it were, their inns [Boccaccio 21–22].

Indeed, once this background reading is established, much of *Twelfth Night's* action is explained. Olivia's odd behavior in locking herself away is rational: she is behaving no differently than did Queen Elizabeth when her kingdom was under threat. Likewise, the bizarre drunkeness of Toby Belch, Andrew Aguecheek and Feste the Jester suddenly makes sense. These characters remain intoxicated throughout most of the action in much the same way that Boccaccio observed during the plague of 1348. Even *Twelfth Night's* temporal setting makes sense — the two references to summer are purposeful. The plague was always much worse during the hot months.

The plague is not the only pre-millennial feature of *Twelfth Night's* background structure. Like *Romeo and Juliet*, the play also creates a world inherently hostile to strangers and dangerous to women, showcases a breakdown in family structures and civic responsibilities, and, through Feste's portrayal of the priest Sir Thopas, the play also provides a traditional criticism of clerical excesses and a brief foray into eschatology. *Twelfth Night* also makes a series of failed predictions: Malvolio's hope that class structures will vanish, Viola's hope that inequalities between the sexes may be simply transgressed, the Duke's that he will actually realize a distinctly Petrarchan love and so on. The play ends on a distinctly reactionary note, with Viola's marriage to the Duke and Olivia's odd surrender to a man she does not know. Far from an idealized future, the play closes with Malvolio's ominous promise of future revenge.

Although it is initially troubling to recognize the centrality of the plague to *Romeo and Juliet*, once the observation is made, the play's debt to apocalypticism becomes an interesting feature of the work's dramatic structure. Likewise, once it is suspected, it is easy enough to confirm disease's place in the background of *Twelfth Night* and then recognize an apocalyptic framework similar to that seen in *Romeo and Juliet*. At least in these two plays, the plague is not merely a feature of setting, but instead is an essential and informing aspect of mood, theme and structure. In both *Twelfth Night* and *Romeo and Juliet*, Shakespeare appears to invoke apocalypticism as a stable framework on which to fashion his works. At the time that Shakespeare wrote these plays, these structures would have carried cultural resonance for his audience, but over time, the hallmarks of apocalypticism have become less obvious or less important, and are now ignored by many of his readers. It is, therefore, particularly interesting to consider whether any contemporary filmmakers — the most publicly-motivated of Shakespeare's readers — have either accidentally or intentionally recognized or preserved any of these apocalyptic features in their works. In particular, how has cinema treated both the obvious plague references in *Romeo and Juliet* and the subtle ones in *Twelfth Night*? Perhaps more importantly, when the matter of analogue, adaptation and translation are concerned, what happens to Shakespeare's apocalypticism?

In the last few decades, *Romeo and Juliet* and *Twelfth Night* have been adapted for the screen a number of times, making it easier to come up with a general impression of Shakespeare's contemporary readers by considering a few scenes in detail. First, Juliet's dead siblings and Friar John's delay in Franco Zeffirelli's *Romeo and Juliet* (1968) and Baz Luhrmann's *William Shakespeare's Romeo + Juliet* (1996) will be balanced against the general depiction of the plague in John Madden's *Shakespeare in Love* (1998). Then, I will discuss Olivia's dead family and the dissipated court of Duke Orsino in Trevor Nunn's traditional vision of *Twelfth Night* (1996) and Andy Fickman's witty analogue, *She's the Man* (2006).

Zeffirelli's approach to *Romeo and Juliet* focuses on the two lovers, and the Italian director is happy to edit Shakespeare in order to bring the teenagers into sharper relief. For example, although he pares 1.2 down, discarding the entire device of the illiterate servant (minor roles are relentlessly cut in Zeffirelli's version), he preserves Capulet's description of Juliet's dead siblings. So although Zeffirelli is happy to have Romeo and friends unexpectedly show up at the Capulet house, he still needs his audience to know Juliet's value as the sole surviving child. Likewise, Zeffirelli greatly simplifies a number of objections to Friar John's delay by simply having Balthazar witness Juliet's funeral, hop on his horse and ride like gangbusters for Mantua, inadvertently passing the friar on the way.

In order to place Romeo and Juliet at the absolute heart of his film and show their love more as a form of generational rebellion than anything else — to celebrate their disobedience and mutual idolatry — Zeffirelli refrains from making very many other social criticisms. Although most critics would disagree, I would argue his Verona has no sense of a realistic setting. His Verona, for example, shot in a variety of locations across Italy, shows an incredibly sanitary Renaissance Italy, sterile and clean. The street scenes, the feasts, even the battles that rage between the two families are more stylized than anything else. His locations might as well have been a sound stage rather than the Italian countryside.

Like Zeffirelli, Luhrmann presents a fairly truncated version of 1.2, and also decides to omit the device of the illiterate servant and the guest list. But instead of merely cutting inexplicably to the Capulet party, Luhrmann's Romeo sees the guest list read aloud on television — perhaps this is Luhrmann sarcastically commenting that television is the new illiteracy. However, although Luhrmann preserves an explanation for a Montague presence at the Capulets' feast, he nevertheless discards Capulet's comment about his dead children. Luhrmann handles Friar John's delay in much the same way: he omits it. Instead, Luhrmann shows a courier arriving in a timely manner, but who is unable to deliver the letter directly to Romeo. For when the courier is knocking on his door, Romeo is off by himself, playing a makeshift and solitary game of baseball behind the motley collection of trailers that stands in for Mantua.

Luhrmann's vision of *Romeo and Juliet* foregrounds issues of governance but dismisses the influence of the plague, removing it entirely from the plot. Certainly, he has preserved, indeed highlighted, many features of the play's pre-millennial mood, including unrest, neglect, poor rulership, rebellion, urban decay: these are what interest Luhrmann most in *Romeo and Juliet*, but he is eager to show a world that is shaken to its core by its violence and foolishness, not by any supernatural forces, nor by any natural factors such as disease. The plague, therefore, has to go. It simply does not fit in with Luhrmann's reading.

Unlike Zeffirelli's version, however, Luhrmann's Verona is a real place, a blend of wealth and poverty, run down slums and shining buildings. Wealthy characters inhabit one realm, simple townspeople another. Luhrmann uses his locations wisely and allows them to become characters. The aforementioned trailer park, for example, which stands in for Mantua, provides an excellent reading of the loneliness, despair and isolation of exile. In Zeffirelli's version, it is impossible to see any real difference between Verona and Mantua. In the Renaissance, however, exile was a death sentence. To be cut off from kin would have been disastrous.

Of the three versions that I am considering, Madden's *Shakespeare in Love* comes closest to creating a world where the plague periodically makes itself felt in the drama. During the film's internal rehearsals for the premier of *Romeo and Juliet*, for example, the playhouses are shut down due to the plague. The film is set in 1593 — presumably in the spring — during one of the great outbreaks. The Master of Revels reopens them, not because the danger has passed, but because he wishes to have greater access to his mistress, Rosaline, a seamstress who at one point or another is also the lover of both Shakespeare and Burbage. This treatment of the plague, although recognizing it as a feature of Elizabethan life, nevertheless minimizes its importance.

Although the plague appears in *Shakespeare in Love*'s recreated and at times deliberately anachronistic Elizabethan world, the plague does not visit the internal production of *Romeo and Juliet*. *Shakespeare in Love* features a great many of *Romeo and Juliet*'s "greatest hits" — brief snippets of the play shown either in rehearsal or in the premier performance. Not too much, obviously, can be taken from the elimination of two small scenes.

Shakespeare in Love manages to shadow *Romeo and Juliet*'s brand of apocalypticism well, with the characters inhabiting a chaotic world consumed by pre-millennial angst, but full of brash predictions for the future. The film smashes its characters' hopes and dreams, but concludes by providing a vision of an even brighter future which includes functional immortality for its two protagonists.

Whereas Mark Norman and Tom Stoppard's screenplay makes light of the plague and depicts it as being an inconvenient fact of life, Medieval and Renaissance writers described the disease as an entirely different matter. To writers such as Petrarch, Boccaccio, Stowe and Dekker, the plague was a never-ending horror, a brute thing that threatened to destroy humanity:

> I observe about me dying throngs of both young and old, and nowhere is there a refuge. No haven beckons in any part of the globe, nor can any hope of longed for salvation be seen. Wherever I turn my frightened eyes, their gaze is

troubled by continual funerals: the churches groan encumbered with biers, and, without last respects, the corpses of the noble and the commoner lie in confusion alongside each other. The last hour of life comes to mind, and, obliged to recollect my misfortunes, I recall the flocks of dear ones who have departed, and the conversations of friends, the sweet faces which suddenly vanished, and the hallowed ground now insufficient for repeated burials. This is what the people of Italy bemoan, weakened by so many deaths; this is what France laments, exhausted and stripped of inhabitants; the same goes for other peoples, under whatever skies they reside [Petrarch].

As would probably be expected, *Twelfth Night* fares about as well as *Romeo and Juliet* does with regard to its subtle use of plague imagery. Of the two versions of *Twelfth Night* I will consider, Nunn's film certainly picks up on the play's overall sense of disquiet and attempts to expose *Twelfth Night's* dark and dangerous underbelly. As Nicholas Jones writes, "there are darker critical and social implications to the action than any of us — characters or viewers — might want to engage with" (8). The first example of these "darker implications" occurs at 1.2 (re-ordered by Nunn to appear slightly before 1.1), when Nunn's Captain advises Viola:

> CAPTAIN. The war between the merchants here and ours
> Too oft has given us bloody argument;
> We must not be discovered in this place.

Although Peter Holland calls Nunn's additions to Shakespeare's play "fake," the dialogue here is entirely plausible — "bloody" for example, occurs six times in the play, and "bloody argument" itself appears at 3.3.32. The effect of these invented lines, when coupled with the scene's music and the sight of dark-uniformed men on horseback while Viola and the Captain take cover in a cave, add to Viola's understanding of Illyria's inherent danger and offer a slightly better explanation of her motivation to begin cross-dressing. Dramatically, Nunn's changes to the script do not work well because the Captain no longer explains that he was "bred and born" (1.2.21) in Illyria, nor that he was in the country as little as a month prior (1.2.27); therefore, his inside information seems implausible. Curiously, Nunn's script change spares Orsino any blame for the danger by asserting that the quarrel between the two city states is between their respective "merchants." The insinuation is two-fold: one, that a merchant quarrel could result in arbitrary death sentences carried out against mere travelers; and two, that Illyria's aristocrats are powerless to stop an usurping merchant class. To accommodate this odd social construct, Nunn subtly reworks his description of Orsino. No longer is he "noble in nature as in name," but is instead shown as being an extraordinarily melancholy bachelor, seemingly self-emasculated:

CAPTAIN. And so is now, or was so very late;
    Tis said that no woman may approach his court
    For but a month ago 'twas freshly murmured
    That he did seek the love of fair Olivia.

The added line ("Tis said ...") is taken from *Love's Labor's Lost* and gives the viewer a slightly nuanced picture of Orsino as a man who is now just as shut off from the world as Olivia. Orsino, when he is introduced, inhabits a dark Victorian parlor, almost like a "putting out room" where coffins are displayed during formal wakes. As Peter Holland explains,

> The darkness of the play is palpable on screen. It is there not just in the gloomy autumnal landscape of the film's world but also in the oppressive interiors of the buildings.... It is also there in the militarism of Orsino's kingdom, where soldiers chase Antonio when he is recognized, and where the shipwrecked Viola and sailors scurry for cover when a troop of Orsino's horsemen investigate the debris of the wreck on the seashore [Holland].

Orsino, true to the Captain's rumor, indeed exists in an exclusively homosocial and militaristic space, where his attendants all stand, sober and concerned, while he reclines on a horse hair chaise. The music — not so much the food of love in this instance, but somber classical music — does not make for a happy scene.

    Nunn's film is consumed with an overwhelming sense of social danger. The setting does not so much appear to be interested in showcasing pre-millennial tension as it does with depicting a more earthy dystopia. The costumes are militaristic as if society has disintegrated to the point where order is only being mainted through the constant threat of violence. Groups of guards hover around the edges of the action. Scenes are lit with subdued lighting, dust motes hang in the air, clothes are all dark. Even the Fool is dressed in dank rags. The plot against Malvolio, despite Richard E. Grant's sparkling Sir Andrew, seems even more mean-spirited than it does in Shakespeare's original. But these are all man-made concerns. In Shakespeare's play, there is something wrong with Illyria itself, and that dis-ease becomes expressed in the social order. In Nunn's Illyria, on the other hand, the place is more like a police state, where some unknown force wishes to keep all of the inhabitants on their collective edge. Nunn, perhaps, rather than reproducing Shakespeare's brand of apocalypticism, has exaggerated it and in doing so has swung the balance too far to the side of dystopia.

    Fickman's *She's the Man* likewise presents a socially dangerous Illyria. In this analogue, Shakespeare's strange setting is transformed into the ultimate gender-segregated space — a private high school. The time is the present and the location is a vaguely romanticized upper middle class United States. In *She's the Man*, Viola is not shipwrecked in any real sense, but is denied a position on the boy's soccer team after the girl's team is cut. Just before a new school year starts, Viola purposefully trades places with her brother (who decides on a whim to take off to Europe) and assumes his identity so that she can prove her abilities to the boys at her old school. In this film, Duke Orsino's court transmutes and reduces to the size of a shared dorm room, where Viola's fear of discovery takes on a very real form. Indeed, there are several scenes in which at least the implication of a possible sexual assault is hinted at, including a narrow escape from an all male shower (this is a PG–13 film after all). There is even the occasional moment of same-sex tension and homophobic reaction — as when Duke and Viola encounter an escaped tarantula and end up jumping up and down on a dorm bed, in each other's arms.

The disquiet that resides in Shakespeare's play is picked up in the film by Ewan Leslie, Karen McCullah Lutz, and Kirsten Smith's script and transformed into a pervasive gender meltdown that spans most of the film's relationships. Of these three writers, it is Leslie's story, but Lutz and Smith formed the team responsible for writing the clever *Taming of the Shrew* analogue *10 Things I Hate About You*, as well as for writing *Legally Blonde* and *Ella Enchanted*. The most telling change the writing team made to *Twelfth Night* is in the nature of Olivia's great personal tragedy. They removed it entirely, and instead of having Olivia's reluctance to court be based on any external force, they blame her dismissal of Duke simply on the realities of teenage romance and attraction.

The message of *She's the Man*, however, is almost as bleak as Shakespeare's play. Love, in this romantic comedy, fails more often than not. Viola's parents are divorced. Her original high school sweetheart publicly humiliates her. Her best friend is subject to at least one unwanted same sex advance. Her brother's original girlfriend in the film is cruelly abused and attempts public revenge. In this film, characters are frequently criticized for their appearance, and on two occasions, the exposure of genitals is the only thing that can resolve a dramatic difficulty. It is a strange world.

Interestingly, though, no matter how easy it is to argue the relatively obvious centrality of the plague in Shakespeare's versions of *Romeo and Juliet* and *Twelfth Night*, when they are updated and their close cousins or distant analogues find their way from stage to screen, the disease vanishes, leaving neat, plague-sized holes that are quickly filled with other thematic concerns. Filmmakers, although sensing unease in the two plays, uniquely interpret the cause of the disquiet, losing, I think, an important part of Shakespeare's apocalypticism.

Twelfth Night's unexplained deaths vanish from *She's the Man*, as do all lexical indications of illness, disease and death. The point is a valid one,

Viola (Amanda Bynes, far right), attempting to impersonate a male, experiences another humiliating moment in the boy's dorm, surrounded by her crush, Duke (Channing Tatum, third from left), and their friends (Clifton MaCabe Murray, at left, and Brandon Jay McLaren) in Andy Fickman's *She's the Man* (2006) (Photofest).

as the screenwriters' previous foray into Shakespearean analogue, *10 Things I Hate About You*, picked up a great deal of dialogue and verbal cues from its source material. Likewise, in any number of *Romeo and Juliet* analogues — with the exception of Madden's film, in which its role is openly mocked — the plague often vanishes from the plotline or is replaced by less threatening community or personal forces. In Nunn's *Twelfth Night*, hints of plague become replaced by militaristic oppression.

The causalities behind these changes appear to be complex: a desire on the part of filmmakers to avoid topics that carry too much specific or too little general cultural resonance, the necessity of plot simplification due to time constraints and other limitations, and a blanket unease with genre dissonance. *Romeo and Juliet* is a tragic love story, and to many of its adaptors, the plague is not seen as an essential aspect of mood that informs characterization and influences relationships, but instead is merely seen as scenery or symbol or as an overly convenient *deus ex machina*. This, I believe, is an error. When Luhrmann fills his film with urban gang violence and societal decay, the substitution may initially seem valid, but closer inspection, I think, argues otherwise. Urban decay and gang violence are societal troubles brought on by poor governance — already one of the play's dominant themes. The plague, on the other hand, was seen in Shakespeare's time as a supernatural force, at the very least like chance or death or the movement of the stars and at the very most as evidence of the angry hand of God. Luhrmann's film is apocalyptic in that it is highly dystopic, but his reading of Shakespeare is entirely secular, whereas Shakespeare's texts at least hint at the religious. Writing of the Geneva Bible's abstract of the Book of Revelation, Chris Hassel observes, "soften the theological edge a bit, and this could be the argument of *Richard III*, so often does it parallel the play in action, structure, tone and meaning" (27). Finally, and with regard to the third point, *Twelfth Night*, after all, must remain a nominal comedy at least, and its darker elements always suffer in this pursuit.

Avoiding unpleasant or threatening content or sub-text is certainly a commonplace in filmed adaptations of historical events and texts. Many films based on Medieval or Renaissance events and texts quickly grow uneasy with unpleasant or politically incorrect subject matter, and the more cultural resonance there is between past and the present, the more frequently unpleasant themes are abandoned. For example, it is rare to see more than a half-hearted attempt to address issues of class or gender or violence in mainstream Medieval and Renaissance-themed films. In Kenneth Branagh's *Henry V*, for example, Branagh not only omits Henry's order to the English troops that "every soldier kill his prisoners" (4.6.24) but also reads Henry's grotesque threats to Harfleur as impotent but convincing bluster (3.3.78–120), whereas the history of the Hundred Years War is full of quite real massacres of civilian populations (cf. the sieges of Calais and Limoges and Edward the Black Prince's general strategy of *chevauchée).* Likewise, films as diverse as *First Knight, Robin Hood: Prince of Thieves, Tristan and Isolde* and *King Arthur* completely ignore the historical treatment of women. Indeed, even *A Knight's Tale*, a film whose purpose would appear to be an extended critique of the class system, ultimately romanticizes and surrenders to its target.

In much the same way that filmmakers appear to back away from seeking a philosophical and political fidelity to Shakespeare's texts, they likewise retreat from a certain type of apocalypticism or they misread its purpose. In the case of Nunn and Luhrmann, this misreading results in exaggeration of surface details — the drive towards the dystopic. In the case of Zeffirelli and Fickman, the apocalypticism becomes diluted and practically unrecognizable. Of course, a version of *She's the Man* in which Olivia's father and brother have recently died of AIDS presents a background world that is simply too horrific to imagine, even though that would be the closest to the world Shakespeare crafted.

For well-known political reasons — the least of which being the Elizabethan state's fragile cultural hegemony — Shakespeare had to treat his apocalypticism with a wary hand. There could be few outright prophecies of the sort that he delivers through John of Gaunt in *Richard II*. Structurally, he could only hint at the cycle of degradation, promise and expectation, denial of easy salvation, dystopia and future renewal, and certainly had to make sure that the more secular elements were not drawn into religious readings. It is this reluctance to foreground the trope in its entirety that makes its constituent elements so easy to read in an individual context — it is entirely worthwhile to consider the apocalyptic, for example, in the general physical and cultural decay of Prince Escalus's Verona, just as it is entirely reasonable to see only personal animosity in the final exchange between Malvolio and the young couples in *Twelfth Night*. It is only when these diverse elements are reassembled that Shakespeare's orthodox and somewhat old-fashioned use of the standards of apocalypticism comes into focus.

Works Cited

Barnes, Robin B. "Varieties of Apocalyptic Experience in Reformation Europe." *Journal of Interdisciplinary History* 33 (2002): 261–274.

Boccaccio, Giovanni. *The Decameron*. Trans. J.M. Rigg. London: Navarre, 1921. 3 March 2008 <http://www.stg.brown.edu/projects/decameron/engDecIndex.php>.

Brooke, Arthur. *Brooke's "Romeus And Juliet" Being The Original Of Shakespeare's "Romeo And Juliet" Newly Edited By J. J. Munro*. Ed. J.J. Munro. New York: Duffield And Company; London: Chatto & Windus, 1908. 3 March 2008 <http://www.clicknotes.com/romeo/brooke/BrookeIndex.html>.

Cox, Nick. "'Subjected Thus': Plague and Panopticism in *Richard II*." *Early Modern Literary Studies* 6.2 (2000): 1–44. 8 March 2008 <URL: http://purl.oclc.org/emls/06–2/coxrich.htm>.

Creighton, Charles. *A History of Epidemics in Britain*. Cambridge: Cambridge University Press, 1891.

Dekker, Thomas. *The Wonderful Yeare*. London: 1603. 3 March 2008 <http://uoregon.edu/%7Erbear/yeare.html>.

DiTommaso, Lorenzo. "Apocalypses and Apocalypticism in Antiquity (Part I)." *Currents in Biblical Research* 5 (2007): 235–86.

Greenblatt, Stephen. *Will in the World: How Shakespeare Became Shakespeare*. New York: Norton, 2004.

Harding, Vanessa. "Burial of the plague dead in early modern London." *Epidemic Disease in London*. Ed. J.A.I. Champion. Centre for Metropolitan History Working Papers Series, No. 1 (1993): 53–64.

Hassel, R. Chris. "Last Words and Last Things: St. John, Apocalypse, and Eschatology in *Richard III*." *Shakespeare Studies* 18 (1986): 25–40.

Holland, Peter. "The Dark Pleasures of Trevor Nunn's *Twelfth Night*." *Shakespeare* 3 (1997). 3 March 2008 <URL http://www.shakespearemag.com/spring97/12night.asp>.

Hollingsworth, Mary F., and T. H. Hollingsworth. "Plague Mortality Rates by Age and Sex in the Parish of St. Botolph's without Bishopsgate, London, 1603." *Population Studies* 25.1 (1971): 131–146.

Jones, Nicholas R. "Trevor Nunn's *Twelfth Night*: Contemporary Film and Classic British

Theatre." *Early Modern Literary Studies* 8.1 (2002): 1–38. 3 March 200 <URL: http://purl.oclc.org/emls/08–1/jonetwel.htm>.

Kerby-Fulton, Kathryn. *Reformist Apocalypticism and Piers Plowman.* Cambridge: Cambridge University Press, 1990.

Norman, Marc, and Tom Stoppard. *Shakespeare in Love.* New York: Hyperion, 1998.

Petrarca, Francesco. "Plague." *Ad Seipsum: Epistola Metrica I.* Trans. Jonathan Usher. Decameron Web. Brown University. 14 Feb. 2008 <http://www.brown.edu/ Departments/Italian_Studies/dweb/plague/perspectives/petrarca2.shtml>.

Reeves, Marjorie. "The Development of Apocalyptic Thought: Medieval Attitudes." *The Apocalypse in English Renaissance Thought and Literature.* Ed. C.A. Patrides and J. Wittreich. New York: Cornell University Press, 1984. 40–73.

Romeo and Juliet. Dir. Franco Zeffirelli. Perf. Olivia Hussey, Leonard Whiting, Milo O'Shea, Michael York, and John McEnery. Paramount, 1968.

Shakespeare in Love. Dir. John Madden. Perf. Gwyneth Paltrow, Joseph Fiennes, Geoffrey Rush, Colin Firth, Ben Affleck, and Judi Dench. Miramax, 1998.

Shakespeare, William. *The Norton Shakespeare.* Ed. Stephen Greenblatt. New York: Norton, 1997.

She's the Man. Dir. Andy Fickman. Perf. Amanda Bynes, Channing Tatum, Laura Ramsey, Vinnie Jones, and Julie Hagerty. Dreamworks, 2006.

Twelfth Night. Dir. Trevor Nunn. Perf. Helena Bonham Carter, Richard E Grant, Nigel Hawthorne, Ben Kingsley, and Imogen Stubbs. Renaissance Films, 1996.

Twigg, Graham. "Plague in London: spatial and temporal aspects of mortality." *Epidemic Disease in London.* Ed. J.A.I. Champion. Centre for Metropolitan History Working Papers Series, No. 1 (1993): 1–17.

Wentersdorf, Karl P. "Hamlet's Encounter With the Pirates." *Shakespeare Quarterly* 34 (1983): 434–440.

William Shakespeare's Romeo + Juliet. Dir. Baz Luhrmann. Perf. Leonardo DiCaprio, Claire Danes, Brian Dennehy, John Leguizamo, Pete Postlethwaite, and Paul Sorvino. Twentieth Century–Fox, 1996.

8

The Politics of Apocalypse: Interrogating Conversion in Mel Gibson's *The Passion of the Christ* and Michael Radford's *The Merchant of Venice*

ADRIAN STREETE

"His blood be on us, and on our children."   — Matthew 27.24–25

"A second Daniel, a Daniel, Jew!
Now, infidel, I have you on the hip."
— *The Merchant of Venice* 4.1.328–9

William Shakespeare lived within a period when, across much of the Christianized Western world, apocalypticism was an accepted aspect of everyday existence.[1] In late sixteenth and early seventeenth century England, it was not particularly exceptional to believe that the world was coming to an imminent end and that Christ would come to judge the living and the dead. Though it would clearly be an exaggeration to say that these views were shared by all early modern men and women, it remains the case that apocalypticism was a popular and widespread discourse that could be used to a variety of ends. Having said this, it is interesting that with some notable exceptions, scholars can still be reluctant to view Shakespeare's work through the lens of early modern apocalypticism. Whether this is due to a mistaken belief that early apocalypticism invariably connotes sectarian religious posturing, or a more general wariness in pinning Shakespeare down to a particular religious or confessional position, the relationship between Shakespeare and apocalypse is an underexplored one. This is doubly ironic given the subject of this book. For while understanding early modern apocalypse in a historical sense is still restricted to fairly specialized academic study, the relationship between modern film and apocalypse is much more widely appreciated, possessing as it does a cultural language that is easily recognizable and enduringly popular. In this chapter, therefore, I want to approach the issue of Shakespeare and apocalypse from both an historical and a cultural perspective. In examining Michael Radford's *The Merchant of Venice* via Mel Gibson's *The Passion of the Christ*, both of which were released in 2004, I want to argue that Radford's film is characterized by a failure to adequately historicize the language of the play and the religio-political framework that Shakespeare's play was participating in. So, while unlike Gibson's film, Radford's is scrupulous in addressing and framing the cultural politics that a post–Holocaust audience might bring to bear on such topics, it nevertheless lacks an awareness of the ways in which the play's early modern language transmits apocalyptic and anti–Semitic values that run contrary to the spirit in which the film was clearly conceived.

The idea of apocalypse has long offered filmmakers a rich seam of imagery and tropes. In terms of recent filmic history and in particular the period leading up to the millennial celebrations in 2000, mainstream Hollywood films such as *Independence Day* (Roland Emmerich, 1996), *The Devil's Advocate* (Taylor Hackford, 1997), *End of Days* (Peter Hyams, 1999) and *Stigmata* (Rupert Wainwright, 1999) all drew upon well defined apocalyptic commonplaces that audiences could confidently be expected to identify with. These include the idea of a general political decline which in turn is mirrored by disorder and upheaval in the natural world; the promotion of the heroic individual or small group who is/are able to gain some kind of victory in the midst of the apocalypse, even if this ultimately means death; and the presence of some supernatural figure (the devil) who stands for the metaphysical instantiation of evil or institution (usually the Catholic Church) figured as the keeper of some dark secret that must be protected at all costs. Certainly, it would be possible to argue that the reheating of such tropes by filmmakers is so common because the idea of apocalypse provides them with a convenient shorthand that does not have to be politically interrogated. Audiences are so familiar with such tropes that they merely have to be repeated in order to register at a cultural level. That said, the very fact that so many of these films trade on the stock apocalyptic idea of *revelation*, that is to say, the idea that apocalyptic events necessarily presage some secret that should not be revealed, is both significant and problematic.

As scholars of apocalypse like Norman Cohn, Marjorie Reeves and others have shown, moments of heightened apocalyptic fervor have invariably been associated with periods of social and political unrest throughout history (see Cohn and Reeves). In his book *Cosmos, Chaos and the World to Come: The Ancient Roots of Apocalyptic Faith*, Cohn offers a definition of *apocalypse* that is pertinent to this discussion. He writes,

> The Greek *apokalypsis* means "unveiling," "uncovering" — and the one feature common to all the apocalypses is that they purport to unveil to human beings secrets hitherto known only in heaven. Sometimes that secret knowledge is about the heavenly world, but chiefly it is about the destiny of this our world. Indeed, the two kinds of secret are intimately connected, for what happens on earth is perceived as reflecting what happens in heaven. If the world now stands on the brink of a total and final transformation, that is because it has been so decreed in heaven [163].

Cohn's definition is useful as it demonstrates the way in which a crucial structural function, the "uncovering" of a secret, which is common to most familiar forms of narrative including film, has a lineage that can be traced back to apocalyptic thought. It also enables us to see that the common trope of filmic apocalypticism, namely that revelatory knowledge is invariably dangerous and must be hidden at all costs, is, historically at least, a contentious one. Apocalyptic knowledge can certainly be dangerous knowledge. Historically, the one fact that nearly all apocalyptic thinkers agree upon is that revelation is not something that can be contained or hidden indefinitely by any earthly or demonic individual or institution. In this respect, perhaps it is film as *genre* that comes closest to manifesting a complementary contemporary understanding of apocalypse, predicated as it is on an inexorable process of uncovering or showing to the viewer that which they do not yet know or comprehend but which will invariably be revealed to them.[2] Apocalypse in film may often rely upon a curtailed *narrative* sense of the power of revelation, but as genre the filmic impulses of revelation are inescapable. If this definition is guilty of arrogating a degree of "theological" status and knowledge to a film and its creators, then it is probably because, as Frank Kermode has shown, most popular Western narrative forms, such as film or the novel, are structurally derived from and implicit upon the theology of revelation: "the paradigms of apocalypse continue to lie under our ways of making sense of the world" (Kermode 28). Though, at the level of narrative, film invariably relies upon absence, silence and the prohibition of dangerous knowledge, structurally it is always compelled towards some kind of revelation, even if it is partial or oblique. Indeed it is this realization that invariably makes good baddies but bad theologians out of the Catholic prelates who are the stock in trade of much apocalyptic filmmaking.

Subjecting apocalypse to a historical reading that broadens our understanding of its tropes beyond those of twentieth/twenty-first century filmic conventions begs a further question: to what extent might these conventions be complicit in other more troubling forms of political concealment? In order to answer this question, we might observe that the notion of filmic revelation demands a dedicated fidelity to history *as* revelation. It may be usefully objected that few will go to see a Hollywood film looking for a balanced reading of historical praxis, and that history as grand conspiracy is so much more entertaining than the intricacies and contradictions of history that scholars spend their careers attempting to contextualize and elucidate. Certainly it is important not to be too po-faced about such cultural productions, but it is nonetheless worth noting the degree to which this "Discovery Channel-meets-Althusser-101" approach to historical praxis has become the norm in so many "popular" approaches to history. Whether in films like *Stigmata* or *The Da Vinci Code* (2006) that rely upon spurious pseudo-historical justifications dressed up as "fact" in order to support their conclusions, or even in British history programs such as *Time-Team* and Channel Four's popular *Secret History* series, the idea that history is a mysterious concealed secret that may (or may not) be revealed to the many is so deeply ingrained in our popular consumption of history that it is broadly accepted without demur. In most of its early twenty-first century incarnations, history as revelation has become inescapably filmic in presentation and consumption.

To take one of these examples, in *Stigmata* the Catholic Church is shown to be party to a secret about a "lost" gospel. This gospel, which is inadvertently revealed by the stigmatic Frankie (Patricia Arquette), purports to attack the institutional validity of Church worship in favor of a less mediated, "personal" relationship with God, and for revealing this secret, Frankie must be destroyed. Put bluntly, the secret that the Catholic Church tries so hard to hide is a form of Protestantism. However, in order to assert this reading, it is necessary to subject the film to precisely the kind of historicized reading that it attempts to disavow. This is because *Stigmata*'s version of history as revelation relies upon the idea that history is invariably a dark secret available only to the few, waiting to be brought forth into the open for the benefit of the uninitiated. This approach to historical exegesis is based upon the idea that world history as we know it is a fraud promulgated by a select group of elite and knowledgeable individuals. These individuals are all desperately attempting to protect some dark secret that would mean a crisis in political stability of suitably apocalyptic dimensions and so a diminution or loss of their power. It thus also draws upon a partial, if popular, idea that historically, apocalyptic revelation is invariably something that can be withheld or hidden in the service of those in power. Alternative readings of apocalypse have no place in this view of history. The long association of apocalypticism and political utopianism, for example, is conveniently sidestepped in this understanding. We might well think here of Portia in *The Merchant of Venice*. Not only does she preside over the utopic space of Belmont (rendered in an especially idealized way in Radford's film), but she is also the one who withholds crucial knowledge in the trial scene. She holds on to her superior, if dubious, secret legal knowledge that Shylock may have Antonio's flesh but not his blood until the last possible second in Radford's film. Not only does this turn the tables on Shylock but it is, of course, the ultimate "revelation" of the supposed superiority of Christian law.

More seriously, what these popular "revelatory" models of history commonly neglect to engage with is the highly exclusionary politics that have traditionally underpinned such understandings. As Cohn has shown, revelation has invariably been a politically bifurcated notion. In many cases this has manifested itself as a form of revolutionary millenarianism that "draws its strength from a population living on the margin of society" and promises liberation from tyranny and oppression (Cohn, *Pursuit* 284). Many of the films mentioned above broadly conform to this paradigm. However, the promise of revelation can also be utilized to far less utopic ends. In order for the apocalypse to signify, it requires a revelation that asserts the singular triumph of one elite group. According to this apocalyptic mindset, the withholding of revelatory knowledge is simply a precursor to the revelation of true knowledge. What *is* crucial in this regard is the ultimate assertion of one group's religious, moral and social superiority at the expense of another's. As I will show, this fact is inadvertently but brutally demonstrated in Radford's film. In Cohn's words, this is "a restlessly dynamic and utterly ruthless group which, obsessed by the apocalyptic fantasy and filled with the conviction of its infallibility, set itself infinitely above the rest of humanity" (*Pursuit* 285). The very fact that this superiority is *ultimate* is what gives it its dangerous political purchase. Regardless of whether or not it intends to, Radford's *The Merchant of Venice* exposes the ruthless expression of this apocalyptic fantasy. The most painful instantiation of this fact can be best understood in the connection between apocalypticism and anti–Semitism. A full historical consideration of this relationship is beyond my present scope here. Nevertheless, I want to say something about this issue because it pertains to the two films that are the subject of the rest of this chapter, Mel Gibson's *The Passion of the Christ* and Radford's *The Merchant of Venice*.

In the case of the former, the accusation that the film is anti–Semitic has been thoroughly, and sometimes vituperatively, debated by scholars and critics (see Corley and Webb; Gracia; Beal and Linafelt). This is especially the case in relation to the blood curse or libel from Matthew 27 quoted at the start of this chapter. Notoriously, this line is spoken in Aramaic in the film by the High Priest Caiaphas but not translated in the English subtitles. Throughout the film we are presented with a negative portrayal of the Jews that draws upon long established anti–Semitic stereotypes. For example, the Jewish priests spit on and mock Jesus and the Jewish crowd beat him; individually and singularly the Jews are shown as bloodthirsty and politically volatile; lastly, the Jews are frequently shot with the Devil in their midst. Gibson also draws heavily on *The Dolorous Passion of Our Lord Jesus Christ*, an early nineteenth century text that recounts the visions of a German mystic and nun, Anne Catherine Emmerich, and which also "reveals a clear anti–Semitic strain throughout" (Webb 172). A summation of one important strand of thinking on this issue is offered by the biblical scholar Paula Fredriksen[3]:

> So is Mel Gibson an anti–Semite, and is the film anti–Semitic? My response is: who cares? The only thing that matters is that the film is inflammatory and that its depiction of Jewish villainy — exaggerated well beyond what is in the Gospels and violating what historical knowledge we have of early-first-century Judea — will give aid and comfort to anti–Semites everywhere [97].

This piece was, however, written before Gibson was arrested in July 2006 for allegedly making anti–Semitic remarks to a police officer whilst being arrested for drunk driving. His alleged comment, "The Jews are responsible for all the wars in the world" (qtd. in Gillan)[4], would seem to align him with the views of his father Hutton Gibson, an avowed ultra Conservative Catholic and Holocaust denier (see Perry and Schweitzer 16). In any case, the paranoid mindset that this comment reveals is in keeping with the "history as dark secret" paradigm outlined above.

As the distinguished religious scholar Richard L. Rubenstein has observed, the elder Gibson holds a view of history that is unapologetically contra the conclusions of the Second Vatican Council.[5] This Council, *Nostra Aetate*, was held in 1965. Its initiator was Pope John XXIII and it was ratified by Pope Paul VI. Although far from being the beacon of pro–Semitic enlightenment claimed by some Catholic apologists, it was still a landmark declaration, affirming as it did that the Jews could not be collectively held responsible for Christ's death. Hutton Gibson's view of history does not square with this promulgation, and indeed his opposition to *Nostra Aetate* is necessary in order for him to adhere to a model we already have some familiarity with. In Rubenstein's words, "According to Hutton Gibson, the alleged destruction of the church by the post–Vatican II popes is a sign of the apocalypse. As soon as the destruction is complete, the world will end" (Rubenstein 114). In the Gibson view of world history, the revelation that the end of the world brings will also reveal those who cleave to the "true" faith and their triumph over those whom Gibson pére calls "heretics" (qtd. in Rubenstein 114).

In order to properly understand this view of world history, we need to see it in terms of a strain of apocalyptic anti–Semitism that characterizes much Western thought on the matter in the period leading up to *Nostra Aetate*. This is necessary since, as Mary C. Boys observes, the "reason that so many Christians are insensitive to the potential for anti–Semitism in the wake of the film [*The Passion of the Christ*] is the dominance of fundamentalist readings of Scripture in the public domain" (13). Such readings derive from a worryingly literalist interpretation, reaffirmed throughout Gibson's film, of the complicity of the Jews in Jesus's death. In his book *Christ Killers: The Jews and the Passion from the Bible to the Big Screen*, the historian Jeremy Cohen has written of "the extent to which the Western mentality had internalized the Christ-killer myth. The 'fact' of the Jews' guilt in the Passion story did not require a second thought" (135). Shakespeare's *The Merchant of Venice* is involved in a complex negotiation with this "fact": Gibson's film takes this "fact" as read. As we have seen, the Second Vatican Council specifically rejected this interpretation, but as fundamentalists like the Gibsons demonstrate, such views are not easily countered. This is important because, as the religious historian Marjorie Reeves has demonstrated, this anti–Semitic ideology is so deeply intertwined with the interpretation and

Jesus (James Caviezel) receives help carrying the cross from Simon of Cyrene (Jarreth Merz) as Roman soldiers mock and drive the son of God toward his crucifixion in Mel Gibson's *The Passion of the Christ* (2004) (Photofest).

consumption of the biblical book of Revelation, an association that persisted into the twentieth century. Reeves notes that during the medieval and early modern periods it was a commonly held tenet of apocalyptic ideology that the Second Coming would be presaged by a time that "follows the usual lines, with the conversion of the Jews, conquest and conversion of the infidels, and the gathering of all the world into one flock under one shepherd by the Angelic Pope" (Reeves 237). The medieval/early modern connection is not as far fetched as it may seem. Gibson has said that his cinematography was influenced by Caravaggio and Piero Della Francesca, and a number of scholars have drawn attention to various medieval/early modern Passion-inspired antecedents that inform the film's *mise-en-scène* (see Goa; Plate 85–136). The difference between these pre-modern ideas and those intimated in Gibson's film is that the former hold out the possibility that the Jews may be converted: the latter does not. I therefore suggest that *The Passion of the Christ* is best understood as a medieval/early modern apocalypse concerned primarily with revealing the "truth" of Gibson's brand of conservative Catholicism to the exclusion of all other faiths.[6] As Susannah Heschel observes,

> While Gibson might hope that the film will inspire its viewers to convert to Christianity, the film's primary goal is something different: to reveal those in its audience who are saved and who are not. The film is precursor to the "rapture," the instantaneous translation into heaven of saved Christians that precedes the Second Coming, according to premillennial dispensationalists [Heschel 107].

Indeed, *The Passion of the Christ* was made by a man who has said, "There is no salvation for those outside the Church" (qtd. in Crossan 18). It thus seems clear that the apocalyptic is merely a staging frame for a deeply worrying politics of religious superiority that is exclusionary and deeply anti–Semitic in orientation.

This last point brings me to Michael Radford's *The Merchant of Venice*. Radford's film has not received anything like the same amount of scholarly attention as Gibson's. It may be the case that the furor surrounding *The Passion of the Christ* has deflected attention away from a film that might otherwise have garnered more scrutiny. Whatever the case, it is surely of some interest that Radford's film, which as I have said was released in the same year as Gibson's, is also one that deals with anti–Semitism and the politics of religious conversion. Undoubtedly, the aims and rationale for Radford's film are markedly different from those of Gibson's and I want to state from the outset that I do not believe Radford's *The Merchant of Venice* to be a consciously anti–Semitic film. Indeed, Radford goes out of his way to offer his viewers a contextualized setting within which Venetian anti–Semitism can be understood. This takes the form of what Samuel Crowl calls a "historicist-inspired scroll ... providing details of anti–Semitism and usury and sumptuary laws in Renaissance Venice" (Crowl 113), as well as a non–Shakespearean "Prologue" that shows an anti–Semitic sermon being given, a Jew being pitched into the canal, the Torah being burnt and Shylock (Al Pacino) being spat upon by Antonio (Jeremy Irons). Nevertheless, even if Radford's film is scrupulous in contextualizing the anti–Semitic content of Shakespeare's play for a post–Holocaust audience, and even if it avoids some of the more virulent anti–Semitic language and imagery used in the play, I want to argue that the problematic and apocalyptic religious politics of Shakespeare's play cannot be bypassed so easily.

In a recent essay on Radford's film, Mark Thornton Burnett has argued that "*The Merchant of Venice* as a film is less anti–Semitic as it is about anti–Semitism, a cinematic work that is distinctive for attempting to pursue — and withdraw from — the implications of its field of ideological production" (88–89). I agree with this assessment, but Burnett's conclusion that the film aspires "towards a future in which the terrors and traumas of the past can begin to find a healed relation with present requirements and realities" (106) seems overly optimistic to me. Without eviscerating the play entirely of its religio-political framework, it remains the case that Radford's *The Merchant of Venice* dramatizes the forced conversion of a Jew and the triumph of an elite group of Christians over him. Moreover, despite the film's attempt, if not to avoid, then at least to historically frame the anti–Semitism that characterizes its source, anti–Semitism remains as an indelible trace throughout the film. Indeed, given this, I am not sure that it would be possible to present a version of this play that is *not* anti–Semitic, or at least not a version that would be recognizably "Shakespearean." In particular, the film fails to confront the fact that throughout the play, Shylock's eventual conversion is repeatedly understood in the context of an apocalyptic framework, one that is uncannily similar to the politics underpinning Gibson's film. Indeed, it is *The Merchant of Venice*'s inability to adequately historicize the political and religious implications of the apocalyptic language and imagery of Shakespeare's play that is its greatest failing. The irony is that a film that attempts to establish a historically sensitive context for its exploration of anti–Semitism does not understand that anti–Semitic implications are written into the very fabric of the play's language and imagery. In order to prove this point, I want to look in some detail at the trial scene in Radford's *The Merchant of Venice*.

Like the rest of the film, the trial scene removes some of the racially charged and anti–Semitic language that characterizes this scene in the play. This is particularly the case with regard to the Duke (Anton Rogers). His comment to Antonio in the play that Shylock is a "stony adversary, an inhuman wretch" (4.1.3)[7] and his reference to "stubborn Turks and Tartars never trained / To offices of tender courtesy" (4.1.31–32) are both excised. On one level, this helps to construct the Duke as a recognizably modern and appropriately impartial figure of justice, and Rogers's measured RSC tones and understated performance add to this general intention. That said, it is clear that the Duke of the play views Jews and other non–Christians in much the same way as Antonio, Bassanio and the other Christians do. The fact that the jibes against Shylock by Gratiano (Kris Marshall) "O, be thou damned, inexorable dog" (4.1.127), "cursed Jew" (presumably changed from the play's "currish Jew," 4.1.287) and Bassanio's (Joseph Fiennes) "cruel devil" (4.1.212) are not cut from the film is all the more strange. Some anti–Semitic lines are cut; others are left in. Why? Is it to give a little local and historical "color" to the scene? Or is it because the scriptwriters did not perceive the anti–Semitic locus of some of these non-excised lines? In any case, the point is that the comments of the Duke, Gratiano and Bassanio are *all* part of the same anti–Semitic discourse that views Jews not only as heathens but also as demonic anti–Christian figures.

For an audience watching this film in a multiplex, such language could easily be assumed to represent unpleasant but fairly standard "historical" slurs that are justified in light of Shylock's construction as the filmic "baddie." But what this reading, like the film, fails to appreciate is that such discourses have an apocalyptic resonance that has a long and terrible history. For example, Norman Cohn outlines a common medieval opinion that persisted into Shakespeare's day, when "[i]t was believed that in preparation for the final struggle Jews held secret, grotesque tournaments at which, as soldiers of Antichrist, they practiced stabbing" (*Pursuit* 78). Such views contextualize Shylock's desire for Antonio's flesh. Moreover, Cohn notes that "[d]ramas were written showing how the Jewish demons would help Antichrist to conquer the world until, on the eve of the Second coming ... Antichrist and Jews would be annihilated together amidst the rejoicings of the Christians" (*Pursuit* 78–79). The near triumph of the demonic Jew, Shylock, is well in keeping with this strain of apocalyptic anti–Semitism outlined by Cohn. Again, my point is not that Radford's film consciously sets out to make capital from such reactionary discourses, but that in its selective cutting of "obvious" racially charged anti–Semitic language, it fails to comprehend the way in which nearly all of the insults made against Shylock in the trial can be traced back to this cankered root.

The fact that the trial scene dramatizes a clash between the religious ideology of gentile and Jew represented in the clash between the legalism of the Old Law and the mercy of the New is, of course, a staple in scholarly commentary on the play (Lewalski). But the only time that the film hints at

Al Pacino as Shylock surrounded by his Christian enemies during the trial scene in Michael Radford's *Merchant of Venice* (2004) (Photofest).

this important historical and contextual framework is in the opening exchange between the Duke and Shylock. When the Duke declares, "We all expect a gentle answer" (4.1.33), the pun on "gentle/gentile" that the play makes such crucial use of throughout is affirmed in the line "To have the due and forfeit of my bond" (4.1.36). Here, Pacino finds a brilliant if unexpected pun on "due/Jew" rendering the antagonists' competing notions of justice open to view. The trial itself takes place in a court room where, as Burnett rightly notes, Shylock is "encircled, embattled and spat upon" and "appears an unlikely prospect for the execution of a citizen's rights" (99). In this respect, this scene interestingly mirrors Jesus's trial in *The Passion of the Christ* before the Jewish leaders and then in front of Pontius Pilate. However, there is an important difference. Gibson's film depicts a decidedly non–Semitic looking Christ being mocked, spat upon and beaten by Jews. The point here is not simply that Jesus does not share the Semitic identity of the other Jews, but that in representing Christ as a "muscular, white body," Gibson implicitly constructs him as an uncircumcised gentile (Krondorfer 19). This is important since, as James Shapiro has shown, uncircumcision "was the undoing of the seemingly irreversible physical act that had been accomplished through the observance of Jewish law" (129). To put it another way, uncircumcision has traditionally been understood in Western thought as marking a conversion from Judaism to Christianity. Certainly this makes sense in terms of *The Passion of the Christ*'s politics: Jesus was never really a

Jew to begin with. What is fascinating is that although an analogous ideology is in operation in Shakespeare's play, it is clumsily but only partially excised from Radford's film version.

For example, Antonio's admission to Bassanio that he is "a tainted wether of the flock, / Meetest for death" (4.1.113–114) is cut in the trial scene. In this line, the "tainted wether" or castrated ram is an apt image considering Shylock's impending exaction of the bond from Antonio. A psychoanalytically inclined critic might observe that the threat of castration implied here is linked to the nullifying of Antonio and Bassanio's homoerotic relationship through the institution of marriage. But the theologically inclined critic will point out that in his ritualized "murder" of Antonio, the threat of castration that Shylock represents can also be read as a threat to circumcize Antonio, that is to say convert him from Christian to Jew. As Lisa Freinkel has observed, "the conversion is one of the few plot elements of the trial scene that is entirely Shakespeare's own" (135). Structurally, therefore, the dual threat of Christian becoming Jew then Jew becoming Christian is central to the trial scene. In cutting Antonio's lines, the film's attempts to render him a stoical hero who is prepared to sacrifice his life for (his) young love. But in so doing, it vitiates the play's admittedly fraught attempt to contextualize the politics of Jewish conversion by raising the threat of Christian uncircumcision.

The issue is further complicated by the fact that the resolutely apocalyptic language associated with Shylock's failed exaction of the bond and his subsequent conversion remains integral to the film's trial scene. Admittedly this scene is rendered with some considerable power, largely due to Pacino's extraordinary performance. His attempts to take the money and run after Portia/Balthasar's judgment manage to combine pathos and fury in equal measure. And his final humiliation as he is forced to his knees to beg mercy, together with his silent weeping as the sentence is passed, are so compelling that they almost deflect attention away from what is being said. However, the film retains both Shylock's assertion that Balthasar is "A Daniel come to judgment, yea, a Daniel!" (4.1.218) as well as Gratiano's triumphal "A second Daniel, a Daniel, Jew" (4.1.335) after Shylock's humiliation. Once again, the application of a historicized reading exposes the deeply problematic theology that contextualizes these lines. As the *Norton Shakespeare* notes, Shylock's words may be intended to invoke the case of Daniel in the Apocrypha who manages to save Susanna from accusations of unchasteness (4.1.218). That said, Gratiano's reference to a "*second* Daniel" should give us pause. This is explicitly apocalyptic language that triumphs over Shylock's first Daniel both morally and exegetically. As Shapiro demonstrates, "In scores of sermons and tracts produced in the late sixteenth century, Daniel called to mind first and foremost the Jewish prophet who foresaw the final judgement, an event precipitated by the conversion of the Jews" (133). The overtones of Gratiano's references are clear: Shylock's conversion is an event that presages the Second Coming. The fact that Shylock is enjoined to "presently become a Christian" (4.1.382) but also to sign all his goods over to his "son, Lorenzo, and his daughter" (4.1.385) is a double punishment. Not only will he become a Christian, a fact highlighted in a shot showing Shylock barred from the Synagogue for prayers, he will also face the ignominy of a converted daughter, a fact that the film ambiguously closes with. As Jessica, who has been shown as an increasingly marginalized figure, looks out over Belmont, she is shown fingering her Father's ring. Will she remain a convert or will she reclaim her Semitic heritage? As viewers we are left guessing, but we can be in no doubt as to the potential significance of her decision.

Unlike *The Passion of the Christ*, Michael Radford's *The Merchant of Venice* does not attempt to valorize the politics of apocalyptic conversion that it explores. It makes a serious and, I believe, sincere effort to place the deeply troubling play that forms its basis within a framework that explicates its various excesses. Nevertheless, as I have also argued, this historicist framing is invariably circumscribed by the much larger historical constellations that the play participates in. Lisa Freinkel has written that

> The traditional view of anti–Semitism pivots on the question of conversion, radically distinguishing between pre-modern and modern attitudes on the basis of an essentialism that only becomes available in the nineteenth century and denies the possible redemption of the Jews [125].

But although Gibson's film consciously participates in the modern myth and Radford's unconsciously affirms the pre-modern myth, my point is that neither reading of history provides a politically edifying locus for filmic consumption, or indeed a basis for Judeo-Christian dialogue. The broader point is that both films act as uncanny commentaries on each other, evincing both the spoken and the unspoken discourses of anti–Semitic violence that underpin Western apocalyptic thought and that continue to resonate today. The fact that such discourses are still, for whatever reason, being translated into capital by the filmic industry of late modernity should give us pause to consider the ways in which our supposedly post-secular age continues to trade on such politically and morally dubious legacies.

Notes

1. I am grateful to Carolyn Jess-Cooke, Melissa Croteau and Ramona Wray for helpful comments on this paper.
2. This is not to say that filmic revelation always reveals the truth or the secret in all its fullness. Revelation can itself be partial, fragmentary or elliptical. For example, the

endings of Martin Scorsese's *Taxi Driver* (1976) and Quentin Tarantino's *Pulp Fiction* (1994) each rely upon an oblique and ambiguous sense of revelation that leaves the viewer with an interpretive puzzle.

3. Fredriksen was part of an ecumenical group of scholars asked by the United States Conference of Catholic Bishops to review the script of *The Passion of the Christ*. Their criticisms of the film led to a number of attacks on the committee members by the religious right.

4. In true Hollywood style, a few days later Gibson checked into rehab and has since conducted a slick PR campaign to re-ingratiate himself with the public. The campaign obviously worked as his next film, the aptly named *Apocalypto*, was a critical and commercial success.

5. On Vatican II, see chapter 8 of Jeremy Cohen, *Christ Killers: The Jews and the Passion from the Bible to the Big Screen* (Oxford: Oxford University Press, 2007).

6. In a study of American audience responses to the film, Robert H. Woods, Michael C. Jindra and Jason D. Baker have shown that "[t]he main audience for Christian media ... in all forms is the already 'saved' or 'born again'" ("The Audience Responds to *The Passion of the Christ*" in Corley and Webb [eds.], *Jesus and Mel Gibson's* The Passion of the Christ), 165. Other scholars, like Paula Fredriksen, have shown the ways in which the film has been used by extreme Christian groups "as a tool of evangelization" (see Fredriksen, "No Pain, No Gain?" in Beal and Linafelt [eds.], *Mel Gibson's Bible*), 98. It is also worth noting the amount of "conversions" that are shown in the film. These range from the thief on the cross to Claudia, Pilate's wife, to the centurion at the foot of the cross.

7. All references are to *The Merchant of Venice* in *The Norton Shakespeare*, ed. Stephen Greenblatt et al. (New York and London: Norton, 1997).

Works Cited

Beal, Timothy K., and Tod Linafelt, eds. *Mel Gibson's Bible: Religion, Popular Culture, and The Passion of the Christ*. Chicago and London: The University of Chicago Press, 2006.

Boys, Mary C. "'I Didn't See Any Anti-Semitism': Why Many Christians Don't Have a Problem with *The Passion of the Christ*." *Cross Currents* 54.1 (2004): 8–15.

Burnett, Mark Thornton. *Filming Shakespeare in the Global Marketplace*. Basingstoke: Palgrave Macmillan, 2007.

Cohen, Jeremy. *Christ Killers: The Jews and the Passion from the Bible to the Big Screen* Oxford: Oxford University Press, 2007.

Cohn, Norman. *Cosmos, Chaos and the World to Come: The Ancient Roots of Apocalyptic Faith*. New Haven and London: Yale University Press, 1999.

_____. *The Pursuit of the Millennium: Revolutionary Millenarians and Mystical Anarchists of the Middle Ages*. London: Temple Smith, 1970.

Corley, Kathleen E., and Robert L. Webb, eds. *Jesus and Mel Gibson's* The Passion of the Christ: *The Film, The Gospels and the Claims of History*. London and New York: Continuum, 2004.

Crossan, John Dominic. "Hymn to a Savage God." Corley and Webb 8–27.

Crowl, Samuel. "Looking for Shylock: Stephen Greenblatt, Michael Radford and Al Pacino." Ed. Mark Thornton Burnett and Ramona Wray. *Screening Shakespeare in the Twenty-First Century*. Edinburgh: Edinburgh University Press, 2006. 13–26.

Fredriksen, Paula. "No Pain, No Gain?" Beal and Linafelt 91–98.

Freinkel, Lisa. "*The Merchant of Venice*: 'Modern' Anti-Semitism and the Veil of Allegory." *Shakespeare and Modernity: Early Modern to Millennium*. Ed. Hugh Grady. London and New York: Routledge, 2000. 122–41.

Gillan, Audrey. "Mel Gibson Apologizes for Anti-Semitic Abuse." *The Guardian* 31 July 2006: 7. 12 Jan. 2008 <http://www.guardian.co.uk/world/2006/jul/31/arts.usa>.

Goa, David J. "*The Passion*, Classical Art and Representation." Corley and Webb 151–159.

Gracia, Jorge J.E., ed. *Mel Gibson's Passion and Philosophy: The Cross, the Questions, the Controversy.* Chicago: Open Court, 2004.

Heschel, Susannah. "Christ's Passion: Homoeroticism and the Origins of Christianity." Beal and Linafelt 99–108.

Kermode, Frank. *The Sense of an Ending: Studies in the Theory of Fiction.* New York and Oxford: Oxford University Press, 1967.

Krondorfer, Bjorn. "Mel Gibson's Alter Ego: A Male Passion for Violence." *Cross Currents* 54.1 (2004): 16–21.

Lewalski, Barbara. "Biblical Allusion and Allegory in *The Merchant of Venice.*" *Shakespeare Quarterly* 13 (1962): 327–343.

Perry, Marvin, and Frederick M. Schweitzer. "The Medieval Passion Play Revisited." *Re-Viewing the Passion: Mel Gibson's Film and its Critics.* Ed. S. Brent Plate. Basingstoke: Palgrave Macmillan, 2004. 3–20.

Reeves, Marjorie. *The Influence of Prophecy in the Later Middle Ages: A Study in Joachimism.* Oxford: Clarendon Press, 1969.

Rubenstein, Richard L. "Mel Gibson's Passion." Beal and Linafelt 109–20.

Shapiro, James. *Shakespeare and the Jews.* New York: Columbia University Press, 1996.

Webb, Robert L. "*The Passion* and the Influence of Emmerich's *The Dolorous Passion of Our Lord Jesus Christ.*" Corley and Webb 160–72.

9

Disney's "War Efforts": *The Lion King* and *Education for Death*; or, Shakespeare Made Easy for Your Apocalyptic Convenience[1]

ALFREDO MICHEL MODENESSI*

> ... circumstances are incalculable in the manner in which they come about, even if apocalyptically or politically foreseen, and the identity of the vital individuals and objects is hidden by their humble or frivolous role in an habitual set of circumstances.
> — Nadine Gordimer, *July's People*

"...if I know the letters and the language"

More than twenty years ago, Stanley Cavell wondered why film "is *not* ... a necessary subject of speculation to any humanist writer and scholar to whom art and America and his or her past is of interest" (107). Today, the experience of cinema not only constitutes a worldwide "habitual set of circumstances" but has become a privileged site for speculation and (of no less importance) investment — economical, of course, but also inescapably intellectual and political. Concomitantly, Shakespeare has become a site for multiple investments with equally variegated aims. Yet, despite the justified variety of approaches problematizing the received understanding of Shakespeare, it is hard not to share in the opinion that "bardolatry is alive and well — perhaps nowhere more so than in film" (Daileader 184–185). Shakespeare's resurgence and abiding presence in cinema since the late 1980s, commercially successful or not, testifies to an interest that can hardly be thought

Para Sarah, siempre.

181

to stem from a desire to challenge his prestige on the part of cinema artists, notwithstanding how much of a challenge academics may spot and discuss in a given product. Often enough Shakespeare films carry an implicit avowal of quality to general audiences (although sometimes foiled by executive caution, as when his name is carefully discredited for marketing). This does not mean, of course, that filmmakers do not engage Shakespeare in critical dialogue, especially by exploring his adaptability — suffice it to see how some make him meet their own apocalyptic visions, as this collection makes clear.

My own take on the "apocalyptic" vein of Shakespeare on film, then, concerns issues only tangentially related to the dramatist and more directly to his fame, implicit in the use that a giant entertainment corporation has made of "Shakespearean" materials to market a vastly successful animated film containing an "end-of-the-(good)-world" narrative. This essay frames "Apocalypse" as a convenient construction within an ideological system whose legitimacy depends on the sustainability of the rhetoric of threat against the standards of western "freedom" that have become "global" currency since the fall of the "curtain" and the rise of the "cultural wars." In other words, Apocalypse is understood here as a politically invested term in a scenario of societal-cognitive deprivation necessitating an expedient outlet that often takes the form of paranoia. This scenario is characteristic of democratic processes in which "the majority is ... called to decide, while, at the same time, receiving the message that they are in no position effectively to decide.... The recourse to 'conspiracy theories' is a desperate way out of this deadlock" (Žižek 219). Disney's *The Lion King* (1994, dir. Roger Allers and Rob Minkoff) "happily" solves the threat of "Apocalypse" through a technically faultless, sanitizing discourse of "universal" reach whereby the "fair" and the "foul" in "The Circle of Life" are pristinely re-turned to their "natural places" after a period of chaos — a perfect proposition, indeed, save for some trifles herein addressed.

To skew the use of absolute terms to approach this film, Foucault's notion of the *episteme* may be useful: "the total set of relations that unite, at a given period, the discursive practices that give rise to epistemological figures, sciences, and possibly formalised systems" (qtd. in Fuery 148). Thus,

> Foucault's point about epistemes not being knowledge, but rather primary forces and processes in the formation of knowledges (at a particular point in time, to a particular group), corresponds to the idea at hand here. The cinematic episteme is not a unit of meaning, or a specific interpretation of a film (or elements within a film).... Things such as generic conventions, intertextuality-transposition, ... the historical positioning of the film ... are all part of the formations of epistemes.... It is precisely this fluidity that marks the action of

cinematic epistemes, and offers one explanation as to why films shift in their status of meaning [Fuery 148–49].

This viewpoint enables screening from a dynamic perspective whereby energies inside and outside a film may be foregrounded and framed within a limited interpretive field. The perspective remains viable and legitimate insofar as it is avowedly partial yet objective. Granted, the stance may — perhaps had better — be as suspect as the premise of the film under scrutiny, but it enjoys the advantage of acknowledgment. Approaching *The Lion King* thus entails identifying its use of "apocalyptic" materials in the manner described (and its recourse to Shakespeare) as an investment in the reinforcement of a specifically American construction of conservative identity: the kind of "repetition and promotion (making the scenario seem natural, morally correct, or in accordance with "advanced" tastes and attitudes) [whereby] narrative paradigm scenarios influence our emotional lives [so that] our responses to films ... can function to prescribe and proscribe thought, feeling, behaviour, and values" (Plantinga 158). Bearing in mind Cavell's precisions about "art and America," to narrow the field, first I wish to address an earlier film embedded in a decidedly American "set of circumstances."

"Who is here so rude that would not be a Roman?"

Joseph Mankiewicz's *Julius Caesar* (1953) was made and released in post-war U.S.A. inside an atmosphere of suspicion, fear, menace, and sometimes virtual or actual deprivation of fundamental freedoms for political causes. Artists and thinkers were particularly affected, and Mankiewicz brought the threat of foreclosure on the liberal mind very much to bear on his filming, especially by making Brutus — as played by James Mason perpetually shot in careful close-ups — a "classic conscientious liberal trapped between his pure ideals and dirty politics" (Crowl 150). The play has notably been an American favorite for ages; many see in Brutus a paladin of republican ideals and a paradigm of individual integrity. Not everyone partakes of these versions of Brutus, of course.[2] But why should a 1953 Hollywood picture of a 1599 play that in 2008 retains an unshakable place in every American teenager's English textbook provide other than a black and white *Portrait of a High-Minded Victim*? Never really wrong, committed to the "good of Rome"—although whatever he means by "Rome" is unfathomable — Mason's Brutus remains a "true Roman" to his last act of righteous self-offering: an undefiled idealist, clear of heart and clean of hands, caught in a shadowy net of villainy below his moral stature, yet spiritually above a resentful crew of butchers, with the support of a "true and honorable wife" who, in Mankiewicz's scenario, would never try anything too sharp on her thigh.

Despite Mankiewicz's and producer John Houseman's outspoken intentions (see Crowl 149), their film can be considered "an antifascist production" (Burt, "Shakespeare and the Holocaust" 313) only by the grace of labeling. Signifying politics and history through a performing art demands politically defined didactics more than efficiently emotional and decorative skills. The 1953 *Julius Caesar* is insufficiently nuanced regarding historical and social matters to address the issue of fascism because Mankiewicz cut straight from close-reading to close-up, shunning a more *relational* approach to the material of *Julius Caesar*. Should one note that the film never suggests that after Brutus's death Strato will remain a "bondman," re-negotiated to Octavius, when his being one is not even hinted at? — i.e., that Shakespeare's interest in master-servant relations went almost entirely disregarded? Or that the last scene of act three was cut — a delightfully black comedy of mistaken *social* roles and identities ending in lynching — although Mankiewicz carefully scripted and even shot it "including Antony's indifference as a 'strong curtain'"? (Jorgens 103). Or that nearly every role was flattened out by the reduction of almost all *contradictions* to mere *oppositions*?

Mankiewicz probably selected *Julius Caesar* "for its parallels not with pre-war Europe, but with post-war America" (Crowl 149). His film offers, then, a melodramatic take on the heroics of the individual. At its climax, Strato, sword in hand, faces the wind to the epic score of Miklos Rozsa, ready to defend the "poor remains" of his "sometime master" against what ravishing force may come — interestingly, from the right side of the frame. The film did not actualize a complex reading of the main part's political shortsightedness and shortcomings in combination with other characters' contributions to a play of *power*. Mankiewicz's *Julius Caesar* is *not* about Brutus as Portia's putative husband, Cassius's brother-*and*-rider, sleepless Lucius's sleepless master, or Caesar's "[twin] evil spirit"; in sum, it does *not* treat Brutus's ideals as a one-man dream-show of misapplied priesthood. Instead, it portrays Brutus as "Caesar's Angel" and Antony's vilely defeated market-rival. Who *would not* be "such a Roman"?

I would not — although under the spell of Brutus' noble and inspiring (read sincerely motivational) speeches not many are expected to disagree with him until the end of 4.2. My dissension notwithstanding, I would not ask the film to be anything but what it is. Mankiewicz's *Julius Caesar* efficiently tells the story of a well-meaning man who wished everyone a world too good to imagine any other way than his, found himself wrong and wronged, and "grievously answered" for it, howbeit that, unlike Brutus, most such people seldom sully their hands with "vile trash"— or die heroically.

Fifty-five years later, in a world haunted by apocalyptic shadows that are less the outcome of "metaphysical aid" than of imperial greed and gullibility, Mankiewicz's film remains self-explanatory about self-construed ethical, cultural, and manifestly desti-national ideals proving increasingly duplicitous. His version of *Julius Caesar* is about being a "true Roman" among barbarians who will not yield to what is best for them while vile un–Romans exploit their needs and circumstances. More specifically, this 1953 film epitomizes the "American political anxieties about an internal enemy" (N. Taylor 266). But the best thing about Mankiewicz's film *now* is that, like *then*, it advances somewhat naive premises without trying to mask their ideological flatness as a fable of "timeless and universal values" purportedly meant to entertain children. That is Disney's business.

"Thus will I save my credit in the shoot"

Many citations and — at times remote — evidences of "inspiration" from Shakespeare in films and filmic by-products have been extensively documented and discussed in recent years. Generally looking to surf the high tide of the bard's "shrinking reputation" (cf. Gary Taylor), such appropriations of Shakespeare at best have something to offer for cultural study; at worst, they are opportunistically conservative and corporate-friendly, leading the path to the temples of ideological simplification that many movie-houses have become in our "apocalyptic times" — usually so called by people who have worked very hard to bring *Apocalypse Live* to a theater near you or to your favorite channel.

The "Disneyfication" of Shakespeare should indeed be counted among the things that ally him "with the interests of corporate media" (Lanier, "Shakescorp Noir" 166). For instance, the Disney executives, writers and staff who chronicle the genesis of *The Lion King* in the "special features" of its 2004 DVD release pay due reverence to Shakespeare and acknowledge the input they (sought to?) find in his work. The authority of Shakespeare in *The Lion King*, fully exploited for prestigious marketing, is not the only one invoked, however. Their list begins with "religious epic quality" and "Joseph and the Bible" — with talk of the title character's dead father resembling "God speaking from a Burning Bush" — and eventually, and casually, includes anything from Bambi to Bettelheim and Campbell. In short, its makers define the film as belonging in "the realm of archetypes," as an epic of self-redemption based on undying "human essentials." Still, their more famous and promptly cited "debt" is, of course, to *Hamlet,* even if whatever *Hamlet* there is in *The Lion King* owes more to the *Reduced Shakespeare Company* than to the *Cliffs Notes.* In fact, they acknowledge that Scar, the villain of the film, was not originally designed to be a member of the royal family, but then, Disney people say, they realized that "you make him a brother, and all of a sudden you've got *Hamlet!*"[3]

Also roughly inspired by Osamu Tezuka's series *Kimba the White Lion*, *The Lion King* revolves around Simba, a feline royal heir who leaves his prideland still a cub after his dastardly uncle Scar murders his majestic father Mufasa. Simba grows up in the wild (feeding on insects in the company of two funny loafers: Timon and Pumbaa), talks with his father's ghost, and returns to vanquish the usurper. That is about all of the first-hand anecdotal resemblance between *The Lion King* and Shakespeare's play, and likely what made reviewers jump and shout "*Hamlet!*" like the Disney writing and marketing divisions — only backwards. But script materials that at first glance seem obviously linked to a Shakespearean source usually derive more from broad association than from rigorous analogy. For instance, the Disney writers do not discuss the conversation between Simba and Mufasa's ghost — located late in their plot — as a parallel to Hamlet's early and very conflictive talk with his father's "shadow" but as *their version* of the "to be or not to be" speech; *i.e.* as a solution to a need strictly of their own: the inclusion of an epiphany whereby Simba decides to confront his past and enemy, regardless of cumbersome nuances actually stemming from Shakespeare's playtext. Disney writers stand to Disney reason.

All additional bits of "shake-spiration" in the film — the Polonius-like verbosity of Zazu; the bug-eating sidekicks Pumbaa and Timon being a sort of split Falstaff to Simba's Hal-in-the-wild; and the abundant traces of Richard III and Macbeth in the villainous Scar — belong in the pile of snatch-and-paste materials that all efficient poachers must keep in their drawers to be writing for the powerhouse of dreams. The "Shakespearean" origins of such materials are in turn publicized to claim the "high-culture" legitimacy that The Bard usually affords.[4] In other words, should one not take literally such declarations of dependence on Shakespeare (generally emerging *post-facto*) all of the above would belong in a circular pattern where bits of plots, characters and lines surely but not exclusively informing a Shakespeare text partake in the making of a serial product, are later recognized as *found* in Shakespeare as a matter of cultural course, and eventually re-inscribed as "Shakespearean," mostly to legitimize and promote these effective industrial products as "high-minded and universal." *The Lion King* shares a profile with Disney adaptations before and since: conventional high-quality entertainment with ideologically conservative cleanliness and a whiff of "Big Literature." To the DisneyMachine, then, "Shakespeare" means leftovers of bardolatry freely circulating in ready-to-use packages.

How do Shakespeare scholars tune in? As far as spotting "shakesploitation," Richard Finkelstein makes an interesting case. He examines Disney's *The Little Mermaid* (1989, dir. Ron Clements and John Musker) and *The Lion King*, rightly arguing that both use Shakespeare to authorize "essentialist, puritan models of development" (183). His thorough analysis of *The Little Mermaid* as *The Tempest*-in-(counter)drag, however, ultimately reads as if he were not trying to assess how much Shakespeare was sucked into the film, but rather how much Shakespeare can be pushed into a critique of it (like playing "Six degrees of William Shakespeare"), although his take on the film's ideological agenda would work well without that. On the other hand, his reading of *The Lion King* may be undermined by an opposite case of *under*spotting. After showing how the film relates to the *Henriad*, Finkelstein examines the carefree Timon not only as Simba's "Falstaff"—and as a dubious derivative of *Timon of Athens*, given his "misanthropy" (187)—but also as a character "signifying gayness" (188) because Nathan Lane, Timon's voice, is an actor well known for playing campy gay roles. This may to some extent warrant the affirmation, indeed, but Finkelstein leaves Pumbaa, Timon's inseparable partner in "falstaff-ness," out of his *Henriad* equation— a nothing campy warthog, whose own "misanthropy" (rather, "outcast state") derives from being thick-headed and unbearably flatulent, traits more likely to arouse conventional associations with "manliness" than with "gayness." Pumbaa's objective existence at the very least begs the question whether the category "homosocial" or some such could not have offered room for an ampler and at once sharper take on the presumably Shakespearean input to the relationship between Simba-Hal and Timon/Pumbaa-Falstaff. Leaving the hog out of the picture suggests that the critic has adjusted the film to his point instead of making a point on the film—legitimately selective as it may be. Finkelstein's persuasive illustrations of how Disney co-opts commonplaces of "high-culture" are weakened by the over/underspotting of issues presumably relating to Shakespeare in which criticism would apply without resorting to The Bard for *counter*-legitimization of items that often appear in Disney's conservatively biased agendas. Shakespeare scholarship might better, perhaps, *detach* the still valuable playwright from facile appropriation as a marketing ploy. Disney's backward approaches to almost every subject nearly always owe more to Disney's own conservative tradition than to external sources, no matter how heavily manipulated.

Shakespearean bits (turns of phrase, allusions, rough quotations) directly informing the script of *The Lion King* can of course be pointed out, but most pertain to *Richard III* rather than to *Hamlet*. Thus, it may be more accurate to say that *The Lion King* overtly resorts to *Hamlet* commonplaces, and to sundry other Shakespeare-related commonplaces, as "plugging" devices, and covertly to the canonized notion of "Shakespeare" as a strongly manipulated "intertext" inasmuch as it epitomizes complex literature to be perceived as "highly respectable" and "truth-bearing." As Arthur L. Little reminds us, "*The Lion King* is very much a popular (a mass) treatise on the social and political philosophy of place — of existence — of self, and *Hamlet* emerges as the text which the proper Disney viewer both needs to remember and reinvent" (10–11). What does this film want us to "remember and reinvent" as "truly" connnected with Shakespeare? That is the question, yes. Little provides a good deal of the answer:

> *The Lion King* is an indulgence in a nostalgic imperialism and colonialism right here at home. If the American ... white heterosexual self has become so lost, so displaced — so forgotten — because his natural world has become so mired in multiculturalism, ... then what Disney proposes to do is remember the invention of that deeply *rooted* cultural self ... not the way multiculturalists are demanding [that] U.S. citizens re-remember, ... but by simply holding a mirror up to [it] [12].

There is plenty of Disney's "home" prejudice in *The Lion King*, indeed. Its (in)famous reinforcement of racial and social stereotypes through formulaic voices and visuals is but an obvious instance. The notorious casting of Whoopi Goldberg as one of the hyenas and her use of "ghetto-speak" in contrast to the supposedly "racially unmarked" voice of James Earl Jones's Mufasa (Burt, "Slammin' Shakespeare" 222)[5] was and can still be rightly called an instance of worn-out condescension and commonplaceness faintly concealed as "sheer fun" and "color-blind" casting — not to mention that the other speaking hyena part was given to Cheech Marín, who also played it with an "uneducated" ethnic inflection, in his case Mexican-American. On the opposite side, the subtly effeminate, British-accented and Shakespeare-allusive Scar of *The Lion King* (Jeremy Irons) fits Harriet Hawkins's view that in popular entertainment interest in intellectual matters makes characters look "as either a sissy (by implication homosexual), an ineffectual intellectual (a wishy-washy liberal), ... or a sinister, un–American villain" (13), and confirms what Douglas Lanier has noted: "The act of citing Shakespeare [has been] a conventional mark of the Other, the sign of a character's deviation from the bourgeois norm" (*Shakespeare* 66). Whether African, Mexican or British — and hence dangerously "educated" — these characters are paradigms of everything "un–Disney." What is "pro–Disney"?

In *The Lion King* positive power is signified as raw, "manly" strength. The first time the hyenas see the lanky and effeminate Scar they are relieved that despite also being a lion, and a royal at that, he is not "somebody important, like Mufasa," whose name alone makes these "natural" idiots shudder: "now, that's power!" Conversely, to them Scar is an "old pal" who even brings food from time to time — a big license regarding "the circle of (real) life" that confirms not only their abjection but also their awareness that lions, including the un-lionish Scar, are still to be regarded as "naturally" supreme. Irons's voice and inflections stand in sharp contrast to Jones's "heroic" rendering of Mufasa: the gaunt, sometime RSC player delivers a depraved, decadent Old World counterpart to the New World's robust character, who is just as deeply voiced but "noble" and physically imposing — as is his likewise muscular but distinctly white- and thin-voiced heir Simba (Matthew Broderick). These contrasts are sufficiently meaningful to invite construction as a complex reversal of the multi-layered correlation between the Old Vic veteran Mason as "clean" Brutus and the American method-actor Brando as "dirty" Antony in Mankiewicz's *Julius Caesar.* If we add to these the also well-noted simplistic equation of the Lion's rule in this Disney-Wonder-Land of an Africa-without-Africans to the rule of "Natural Order" in "The Circle of Life," as well as some fitting visuals — e.g., the black mane of the Usurper in contrast with the golden ones of the rightful King and Cub; or Scar's queer gestures and turns of phrase equally contrasting with the "masculine" depictions of Simba and Mufasa — a recognizably "white-heterosexual"-biased picture will be in need of nothing but the right décor.

"The readiness is all," however, for all these in-built ideological trappings can also serve more specific, timely ends. Given the re-release of *The Lion King* on DVD ten years after its première — which in turn occurred three years after "Desert Storm"— not only the notorious features above demand to be stressed but, perhaps more importantly, these elements and others of their kind should be considered in more than "home" (i.e., American) terms when the notion that Apocalypse is approaching has been so efficiently spread not only as a source of mythical fear within the U.S.A., but also as a close threat, or even a real experience, anywhere American conflicts are re-located outside their borders. The release of *The Lion King* on DVD took place in the present scenario of "cultural" wars; furthermore, it was just as interestingly followed by a DVD collection of significant Disney "War Effort" films (2004) — among them the legendary short *Education for Death* (Clyde Geronimi, 1943). Comparing that short with the key musical sequence "Be Prepared" in *The Lion King*—where in brilliantly apocalyptic fashion wicked Scar persuades the ill-bred hyenas to help him murder kingly Mufasa — may provide timely reminders of what Disney movies can often signify within and without their home limits. What do the warring brothers and despicable carrion-eaters represent in a tale of animals reportedly seeking to convey "timeless human essentials" through the worldwide power of distribution afforded by BuenaVista Inc.?

"... fashion your demeanor to my looks,
Or I will beat this method in your sconce"

Based on Gregor Ziemer's book *Education for Death: The Making of a Nazi*, issued also in 1943, Disney's *Education for Death* is an unusually grim ten-minute animated film. According to legend, at some point it was even "banned" at Disney's studios, never again to be released, although it ended up re-appearing on DVD the same year as *The Lion King*. In *Education for Death*, Hans, a German boy, learns the hard way to be a "good" Nazi. At starting, didactic, documentary-style sequences show Nazism to be the opposite of Democracy. One is a parody of *Sleeping Beauty*: a "distortion of the tale," according to Art Smith's voice — a popular announcer in the 1940s who might as well have been referring to Disney's own version of that story. The parody is underscored by an equally mocking arrangement of Wagner's ubiquitous "Ride of the Valkyries." Germany, the title princess, is an elephantine, beer-drinking opera singer; Democracy is a wicked witch straight from *Snow-White*; and the gallant prince to the rescue is Hitler himself. Later, an imposing, expressionistic long shadow threatens to take Hans away from home if his health does not improve or his mother continues to pamper him. Next, we see the boy at school, learning the hard way that the fox *must* eat the weak, cowardly, and hateful rabbit: "Germany will rule the world; all will be her slaves." These three sequences of *Education for Death* make points that are significantly also made in *The Lion King*, the more salient being a stress on the "natural" supremacy of the strong, a point expressly denounced as part of Nazi ideology in the former film, but not exactly characterized as fascist in the latter.

Yet, the most relevant and powerful connections between *The Lion King* and *Education for Death* belong in the musical number "Be Prepared" of the feature film and the closing sequence of the short. After his lesson, Hans begins a long and relentless march towards his "Aryan" destiny as one of Hitler's faithful. Through effectively paced dissolves, he seamlessly grows into a young Nazi, then a soldier in an apparently endless company of equally patriotic youngsters, and finally becomes a tomb in a massive graveyard. Prior to this, however, we see a number of similarly disturbing images flash in tight keeping with the music against an ominous fire-red background: fanatical Nazis bearing torches; a pile of books ready to be burnt and burning (Shakespeare unincluded); a Bible becoming a volume of *Mein Kampf*; a crucifix turning into a sword decorated with a swastika; the smashing of a stained-glass church window — all these explode before our eyes leading to an upsurge of martial music that continues to accompany Germany's best as they goose-step their way to the grave while the narrator's voice delivers the moral of the story: Hans and all the youth of Germany will die for the wrong cause.

Fittingly entitled after the Boy Scouts' motto, *The Lion King's* musical number "Be Prepared" resembles *Education for Death* mostly through stylistic allusiveness. The design of the earlier picture expressly combines traditional Disney techniques with some of Leni Riefenstahl's characteristic framings, sharp angles, high contrasts, deep fields, uses of monumental architecture and symmetries, and so forth. "Be Prepared," in turn, seems to recycle similar takes of Riefenstahl's *Triumph of the Will* (1934), especially while combining goose-stepping troops and grandiloquent sceneries. In both films, the marching also seems to bear traces of Oskar Fischinger's designs for the 1934 *Muratti* ads, intimating that his stint with Disney, howbeit brief, had lasting effects.[6] The background for the closing sequence of *Education for Death* is pervasively red from torches and other sources of fire, while "Be Prepared" displays suggestions of flames and lava about to break loose from under the ground of the already underground cave — both sequences relish in hellish atmosphere. Timing is very similar: for example, the break into the march in either case occurs upon conspicuous musical cues that propel action in an unflinching climb towards climax. Although many details in common could be merely coincidental, one suggests that the correlation is not entirely unwitting. In *Education for Death*, as Hans marches and becomes a soldier, a full side shot of his body zooms into a profile close-up as the announcer chronicles his transformation: he will see, hear and do what the party tells him. With each phrase a new element is added to Hans's head and headgear: eye-blinders, a muzzle, and a spiked collar and chain. He is visually transformed into an animal — a dog, to be precise. The resemblance is such that the now canine profile of Hans may legitimately be argued to have played a major part in the final design of the marching hyenas' faces for *The Lion King*.

The transfer of these images from the 1943 short into its 1994 "clone," "Be Prepared," and the digital recycling of both on DVD in 2004, do not seem to want present significance. Literally, on top of locating Scar and his *Wehrmacht* of hyenas in a Nazi-like scenario, at its end, instead of a swastika or another similarly fascist sign, "Be Prepared" features a conspicuous crescent moon, the unmistakable symbol of Islam, presiding over the fiery rise of Scar(e) to the top of his rocky throne of blood and iniquity. The slow but certain, and terrifying, elevation of Scar to the top of a night-clad mountain with the half-moon on top is effected as a transformation akin to those found in *Education for Death* when a crucifix becomes a sword decorated with a swastika or a Bible turns into a copy of *Mein Kampf*. To boot, the crescent moon later presides over Scar's Claudius-like speech of acceptance of the throne, in which he very significantly announces "the dawn of a new era in which lion and hyena come together in a great and glorious future," with the hysterical laughter of his canine paratroopers providing an exclamation point. The blatantly foul difference is that now the sign deliberately associated with images and sounds meant to bring about fear and repudiation is neither openly defined nor outspokenly identified by a voiceover in an avowedly propagandistic short as overtly inimical to a specific (non-)choice of lifestyle, but merely "casually" or "conventionally" displayed in a film "apt for all ages" to accompany the murderous plans of a "naturally evil," apocalypse-bringing leader and his followers: "subtle" moves likely to have significant impact among vulnerable and unaware audiences — particularly children.

Already "scary" back in 1994, in 2004 and today these images re-fashion the evil and purportedly Shakespearean traitor Scar (frankly the most interesting character in *The Lion King*) as relating directly to one of the sacred icons of a very identifiable culture; also, it pointedly re-effects an unfair, covert, and blanketing mis-definition of Islam as *Clear and Present Danger*, in unsurprising contradiction to Disney's outspoken aim at making a "timeless and universal" epic. Worse still, Scar may have been originally, perhaps unwittingly, designed with ominous images of the Ayatolla Khomeini in mind. The gaunt figure shot from an upward angle, often overlooking a cliff in black robes; the lean and stern face with graying or white-streaked beard framed by a black turban, whether in photographic or cartoon depictions; the yellowish evil eyes; the signs of death often surrounding him; even direct equations of the Iranian villain with Hitler, or hilarious depictions of him as a half-moon-shaped vampire — all these may be found among the thousand images of the Evil Ayatolla that pervaded the American imagination from the late 1970s through the administrations of Reagan and Bush I.[7] Some of these images, or remnants of them, may have *timely* re-emerged in 1994 to inspire the design of Scar.[8] I would qualify a reminder that "Be Prepared" deplorably is linked more to Islam than to Shakespeare as "timely" because both the 1994 theatrical release and the 2004 DVD of *The Lion King* coincide with times when the Bushes of the (south)West waged Holy War against "malignant and turban'd" people, and also because some Shakespeareans — e.g., Burt ("Shakespeare and the Holocaust") and Lehmann — have rightly reflected that the reading of Shakespeare on film cannot be the same after 9/11— *nor*, if I may add, after *its causes and consequences.*

Similarly sharp overtones of "global" reach concerning social order may also be spotted in *The Lion King*'s "Be Prepared." Apart from their representation as thick-headed Black, Chicano, and/or Nazi-Islamic minorities, the hyenas are marked as hunger-driven and good for nothing but to destroy each other. They are "danglin' at the bottom of the food-chain [of being?]," capable of eating their own legs, little more than *lumpen* chow for the ambitions of the decadently European, much smarter and refined Scar. This becomes emphatic in the Broadway version of "Be Prepared," which Scar introduces thus:

> I never thought hyenas essential,
> they're crude and unspeakably plain.
> But maybe they've a glimmer of potential,
> if allied to my vision and brain.

These additional lines not only (counter)supplement Disney fantasies about the "Circle of Life" with blunt truths of well-known colonial assumptions, but are also thoroughly consistent with other new lyrics and tunes by Tim Rice and Elton John for the Broadway show. Therein, Scar and the hyenas were "fleshed out" by means of two new numbers that epitomize what Disney perceives as the worst signs of irredeemable vileness. The first, "Chow Down," is a (not really) "heavy metal" piece — the only one of its kind in the musical and the only one expressly written for *The Lumpenband* of hyenas — which inextricably links their bottomless hunger and abjectness to a likewise despicable enjoyment of that 2/4 electric guitar, bass and drum noise otherwise known as "rock music." The second, "The Madness of King Scar" — a solid number in which Scar becomes even more allusive to Shakespeare — perfects the hyenas' ignominy as they beg for "a fix of flesh" to ease their "needs." Thus, as if to supplement their original (vocalized) anti-social marginality, Scar's Broadway warriors of the crescent moon are tellingly scripted as rock-consuming junkies.

And just as one thinks the catalogue cannot go on, Sir Elton's original score for "Be Prepared" complicates prejudice further by expropriating specifically Latin-American rhythms to adorn Sir Tim's flawlessly clever lyrics for carnivalesque effects. In either its filmic or its Broadway version, *The Lion King*'s "Be prepared" grows subtly and ends wildly to the beat of a "*bery exotic*" — typically reductive — mix of your basic "*conga*" with bits of "*rumba*" and "*candombe*" as if to accessorize Scar's closing statements in aggressive "Banana Republic-ruler" fashion[9]:

> So prepare for the coup of a century,
> be prepared for the murkiest scam.
> Meticulous planning,
> tenacity spanning
> decades of denial,
> is simply why I'll

be King undisputed,
respected, saluted,
and seen for the wonder I am.
Yes, my teeth and ambitions are bared.
Be prepared!

Thus, the villain and his maladjusted "un–American" horde — now, all things considered, made of hungry minority Nazi-Islamic rocker junkies with a zest for "*salsa*"[10] — are finally shown to rejoice in the thought of a future "*vida loca*" of crescent moons against dark blue skies, red fire, black destruction — "strange images of death." Clearly, the ultimate warning in the song is not so much directed to the hyenas as to all good Scouts beholding the scene, alerting them to the threats involved in lifestyles outside the *right* norms, regardless of age — but not of ideological bias. Who could ask for anything more "timeless and universal"? Whether on stage or screen, musical numbers are designed to obtain definitive characterological and thematic effects. "Be Prepared" can be categorically highlighted for illustration.

Despite the potential dismissal of these things as just another sampler of uselessly — and avowedly — paranoiac reactions, to date I am not aware that such casting, vocal, visual, and musical practices have ceased to effectively contribute to the dissemination of prejudicial stereotypes and commonplaces through theatre or film, especially among children.[11] Of particular significance to studies of Shakespeare appropriation, however, is the fact that the facile correlation of *The Lion King* with *Hamlet* is now currency, often cited and positively regarded — notoriously even by those who are the objects of its prejudiced subtexts. This alone efficiently illustrates how "the main historical activity remaining to [an] underlying [culture] is to misconstrue the effects of imperialism as their own cultural traditions" (Sahlins 477). These practices of Shakespeare appropriation, then, demand to be specifically ear-marked as at best oversimplifying Shakespeare and, at worst, inscribing his work in a list of texts "appropriate" for the *(re)Education of a Lion King for Death* — or something to that effect. The actually slight but effectively marketed and even glorified connection between *Hamlet* and *The Lion King* makes Shakespeare unfairly complicit with the patronizing, conservative, and prejudice-promoting fictions of Disney. If such fictions prove extremely efficient in their own terms and in all spheres it is because the DisneyMachine knows well how and when to mock certain things that *others* think respectable — or at least *theirs* to mock. But the DisneyMachine can be made mock of as well. The recent DVD releases of these "war efforts," whether originally dated 1994 or 1943, may be a good place to start.

Notes

1. A draft of this paper was presented at the seminar "Apocalyptic Shakespeares," 32nd meeting of the Shakespeare Association of America, New Orleans, April 2004, and another at the 31st International Shakespeare Conference, Stratford-on-Avon, July 2004; an earlier version was printed in *Ilha do desterro* 49 (2005): 397–415. My gratitude to the Modern American School of Mexico City and Jose Roberto O'Shea.

2. To illustrate, some of my own rough notes for a Mexican production: "'Peace, ho! Brutus speaks.' And except for (mis)placing fatal blows in the bodies of his 'best lover[s]' (i.e., Caesar and himself), he does little else. Worse, he seldom listens. 'With himself at war,' this self-appointed hero suffers from, and dies of, self-deception. Brutus's disease would be harmless were it not for his honorably gilt but politico-logical-faulty efforts at spreading it among friends, flatterers, countrymen, bondmen, and gullible audiences. However, just as he seems to have talked the populace into sharing his grandiloquent sanitizing of assassination as sacrifice, shrewd counter-spin doctor Antony performs a self-serving damage-control operation and turns the masses' attention from Brutus' sophistry to the 'savage spectacle' of a 'bleeding piece of earth' with promises of mutiny and revenge, plus a persuasive 75 dracmas apiece. No need to ask who is the more politically savvy here."

3. This is probably why Scar's rhetoric after killing his brother ("... it is with a heavy heart that I assume the throne") echoes that of Claudius's first speech in *Hamlet*.

4. Disney's *The Jungle Book* (1967, dir. Wolfgang Reitherman), requiring little else than its source for legitimization, looks closer to the *Henriad* than to Kipling in its depiction of a "boys-only" relationship between Mowgli (Hal) and Baloo (Falstaff) ending in separation. In this case, the Disney staff seems to have "shakespearized" Kipling, thereby simplifying *both* authors. Still, this apparent recourse to Shakespeare has not been cited to merchandize *The Jungle Book*— or its sequel *The Jungle Book 2* (2003, dir. Steve Trenbirth). Evidently, *Hamlet* is taken to ring a stronger note of "greatness" with the unaware consumer than a simple Harry or Jack ever could.

5. Can Jones's voice ever be thought of as "unmarked"? Not only is he among the foremost African-American actors, with a history of Shakespeare roles, but one of the most memorable *villain* voices ever: Darth Vader's.

6. Fischinger was censured by the Nazis in 1936 as a "degenerate." His most recognizable contribution to Disney is the disturbing "Sorcerer's Apprentice" sequence in *Fantasia*— a derivative of his parodic "goose-stepping" Muratti ads.

7. A web-search of "Khomeini images" will render more than a hundred thousand results, many of them American menacing or parodic portraits.

8. Scar's supervising animator was the talented Andreas Deja.

9. Many recognizably Latin-American musical genres have an African origin, of course.

10. Or for *tango*, as is evidenced by a song in the Broadway version ("The Madness of King Scar"), in which the villain grows momentarily "Argentine" and woos Nala to the beat of that stereotyped "music of seduction."

11. Cf. Disney's *The Jungle Book* again, which is incredibly more prejudiced than Kipling's original in its "funny" rendition of King Louie and his Band of Apes by means of black accents and jazz. Moreover, in the Spanish dubbing of the film, Louie's voice went to an entertainer well-known for his impression of Louis Armstrong, which he put to use with an equally prejudiced "black Cuban" ring. Curiously, too, in an album recovering the otherwise enjoyable, Oscar-winning *Jungle Book* music, featuring big time pop artists like Sting, the song in question, "I wanna be [human] like you," was performed by the Chicano band *Los Lobos*.

Works Cited

Burt, Richard. "Shakespeare and the Holocaust: Julie Taymor's *Titus* is Beautiful, or Shakesploi Meets (the) Camp." *Shakespeare after Mass Media.* Ed. Richard Burt. New York: Palgrave, 2002. 295–330.

_____. "Slammin' Shakespeare in Acc(id)ents Yet Unknown: Liveness, Cinem(edi)a, and Racial Dis-integration." *Shakespeare Quarterly* 53 (2002): 201–226.

Cavell, Stanley. "What (Good) Is a Film Museum? What is a Film Culture?" *Cavell on Film.* Ed. William Rothman. Albany: State University of New York Press, 2005. 107–14.

Crowl, Samuel. "A World Elsewhere: the Roman Plays on Film and Television." *Shakespeare and the Moving Image.* Ed. Anthony Davies and Stanley Wells. Cambridge: Cambridge University Press, 1994. 146–62.

Daileader, Celia. "Nude Shakespeare in Film and Nineties Popular Feminism." *Shakespeare and Sexuality.* Ed. Catherine Alexander and Stanley Wells. Cambridge: Cambridge University Press, 2001. 183–200.

Finkelstein, Richard. "Disney Cites Shakespeare: The Limits of Appropriation." *Shakespeare and Appropriation.* Ed. Christy Desmet and Robert Sawyer. London and New York: Routledge, 1999. 179–96.

Fuery, Patrick. *New Developments in Film Theory.* London: MacMillan, 2000.

Hawkins, Harriet. *Classics and Trash: Traditions and Taboos in High Literature and Popular Modern Genres.* Toronto: University of Toronto Press, 1990.

Jorgens, Jack. *Shakespeare on Film.* Bloomington: Indiana University Press, 1977.

Lanier, Douglas. *Shakespeare and Modern Popular Culture.* Oxford: Oxford University Press, 2002.

_____. "Shakescorp Noir." *Shakespeare Quarterly* 53 (2002): 157–180.

Lehmann, Courtney. "Crouching Tiger, Hidden Agenda: How Shakespeare and the Renaissance Are Taking the Rage out of Feminism." *Shakespeare Quarterly* 53 (2002): 260–279.

Little, Arthur L. "Remembering the American Self: *Hamlet*, Africa, and Disney's *The Lion King*." Unpublished paper presented at the seminar "Apocalyptic Shakespeares," 32nd Meeting of the Shakespeare Association of America, 2004.

Plantinga, Carl. "Spectator Emotion and Ideological Film Criticism." *The Philosophy of Film: Introductory Text and Readings.* Ed. Thomas E. Wartenberg and Angela Curran. Oxford: Blackwell Publishing, 2005. 148–59.

Sahlins, Marshall. *Culture in Practice.* New York: Zone Books, 2000.

Shakespeare, William. *The Riverside Shakespeare.* Boston: Houghton Mifflin, 1974.

Taylor, Gary. "Afterword: The Incredibly Shrinking Bard." *Shakespeare and Appropriation.* Ed. Christy Desmet and Robert Sawyer. London and New York: Routledge, 1999. 197–205.

Taylor, Neil. "National and Racial Stereotypes in Shakespeare Films." *The Cambridge Companion to Shakespeare on Film.* Ed. Russell Jackson. Cambridge: Cambridge University Press, 2000. 261–73.

Žižek, Slavoj. *Enjoy Your Symptom!* 2nd ed. New York and London: Routledge, 2001.

10

Four Funerals and a Bedding: Freud and the Post-Apocalyptic Apocalypse of Jean-Luc Godard's *King Lear*

ANTHONY R. GUNERATNE

And I saw when the Lamb opened one of the seals, and I heard, as it were the noise of thunder, one of the four beasts saying, "Come and see." And I saw, and behold a white horse: and he that sat on him had a bow; and a crown was given unto him: and he went forth conquering, and to conquer…. And when he had opened the fourth seal, I heard the voice of the fourth beast say, "Come and see." And I looked and behold a pale horse: and his name that sat on him was Death, and Hell followed with him. And power was given unto them over the fourth part of the earth, to kill with sword, and with hunger, and with death, and with the beasts of the earth.

—*Revelation* 6.1–2, 7–8

Signor Freud and Herr Mor*elli*; or, From *Moses* to *Signorelli*

For a brief moment early in 1938, when the Catholic Church seemed the only hope remaining to Vienna's Jewish community in its effort to stave off the depredations of the Nazis, Sigmund Freud exercised an uncharacteristic restraint in delaying the publication of the third and final part of *Moses and Monotheism*. By June, in exile in London, he would append two prefatory notes to this final installment, the first explaining the cause of his (magnanimous) hesitancy, and the second noting that the church's protection proved all too fragile in the face of "the German invasion."[1] Freud then proceeds to elaborate on his initial historical account of Moses, citing a succession of authorities to demonstrate that the man we suppose to have led the Israelites out of Egypt was, in fact, an Egyptian who introduced the cult of Aton to an unruly Semitic people and that he was subsequently killed by them in a rebellion only to have elements of his religion reappear in later history so that the worship of the God who succeeded him, Jahve, gradually reassumed the forms of practice he had introduced.[2]

As is also true of his late speculations about the authorship of Shakespeare's plays, Freud's twilight account of the Mosaic tradition has frequently been regarded as an eccentricity, even a deliberate provocation. The figure of Moses had, however, occupied a central place in his thinking for many years. Peter Gay, for one, argues that it was Michelangelo's monumental sculpture of Moses for Pope Julius II's tomb that had enabled the classically-inclined Freud to overcome his reluctance to confront Rome, a city that he often spoke of with reverence but stopped short of visiting on numerous Italian journeys. "My longing for Rome is deeply neurotic," he wrote to his associate and confidant Wilhelm Fliess, "[and] connected with my schoolboy enthusiasm for the Semitic hero Hannibal" (Freud, *Complete Letters* 132). Already an ardent collector of Egyptian, Greek and Roman antiquities, he suggested that his desire for the conquest of Rome cloaked other "longed-for wishes"; but rather than marching a host of elephants to the Eternal City he proposed holding a congress of psychoanalysts there, having on earlier occasions approached as near as Orvieto and (like Hannibal) Lake Trasimeno as he hovered around his prize (Freud, *Complete Letters* 132).[3]

Something extraordinary appears to have occurred on the first of his Italian journeys, which culminated in his visit to Orvieto, a transformative event that proved to be a turning point in his conception of psychoanalysis and that probably reveals at least one of the anxieties that awaited him in Rome. Not long after detailing his Italian itinerary to Fliess (Orvieto being the last stop), and still in Italy, Freud dispatched the celebrated letter of 21 September 1897 in which he announced that he had rejected his previous theories of childhood neuroses, a declaration that was the prelude to commencing an exhaustive and fruitful self-analysis.[4] Within months, he also published a detailed account of his unwitting repression of the name of the painter of the frescoes of the Four Last Things in the city's cathedral, Luca Signorelli. Included in his collection devoted to common errors of memory and slips of the tongue, *The Psychopathology of Everyday Life*, the essay on Signorelli (originally written in 1898) begins with an account of his journey from Ragusa to "a place in Herzegovina" in the company of a lawyer from Berlin. He wonders why he misremembers the name in conversation, substituting first Botticelli and then Boltraffio for Signorelli. When, in hindsight, the series of associations becomes clear to him, he goes so far as to provide a visual illustration of the mechanisms of substitution of various portions of words that resulted in the process he refers to as paramnesia "motivated by repression" (9–17).

If we take Freud's recognition that his unconscious has cleaved "Signor" and "-elli" apart, and thus initiated a chain reaction of likely substitutions — the "-elli" giving rise to an association with Bottic-elli, the "Signor-" being occluded by its association with the Her[r], in Her-zegovina, and so on — then we might discern another series of repressions at work. Freud's apparently confident reattribution of the Last Judgment to Signorelli is largely but not entirely correct. Fra Angelico and his assistants, among them Benozzo Gozzoli, began work on some of the vaulting as early as 1447, and Perugino was later (unsuccessfully) offered a contract to complete the more extensive panels. Signorelli replaced him, possibly at his recommendation, and submitted an innovative design that made a hitherto unprecedented use of pillar-and-arch supported wall surfaces, completing his commission in a mere three years between 1500 and 1503. Thus Freud may have heard more than one name associated with the fresco cycle, selectively misremembering only the artist most closely associated with the project.[5] A still more imposing figure may hover in the background. In recounting his solution of the problem of misremembered names to Fliess, Freud describes Signorelli as "the renowned painter who did the Last Judgment in Orvieto, the greatest *I have seen so far*" (my italics).[6] The greater Last Judgment to which he alludes is undoubtedly that of Michelangelo in the Sistine Chapel, which was just as profoundly influenced by Dante and no less sanguine in consigning unbelievers (among whom Freud vociferously included himself) to perdition. Avoiding — one might even argue escaping — Michelangelo's damning fresco, therefore, he turned to the statue of Moses, a defense mechanism stemming from his insistence that Michelangelo defied scriptural authority to impose his own reading upon the character of Julius's favorite Old Testament prophet. Freud saw the statue on his first visit to Rome in 1901 and on every subsequent visit, making daily excursions to the church of San Pietro in Vincoli where he sketched it and contemplated it for nearly three weeks in 1913. By then he already felt himself beleaguered by C.G. Jung and other dissident psychoanalysts, and he may very well have seen his own portrait in Michelangelo's larger-than-life marble colossus to which he ascribed a superlative restraint uncharacteristic of the volatile figure chronicled in *Exodus*.[7] It is quite plausible that Freud even embedded a clue as to the intensity of his identification in his essay on the statue. In the introductory remarks to his minute analysis of the positioning of Moses's right index finger, he recounts the method by which a certain art connoisseur, adopting the pseudonym of Ivan Lermolieff, had reattributed paintings in major galleries by rejecting general impressions and concentrating on minor details such as earlobes and fingernails. "It seems to me," says Freud, "that his method of inquiry is closely related to the technique of psycho-analysis [in that it, too, divines] secret and concealed things from despised or unnoticed features, from the rubbish-heap, as it were, of our observations" ("Moses" 133–34). He reveals the true identity of the connoisseur-detective as Morelli, a name that his own treatment of memory in his earlier work on Signorelli suggests an inescapable connection with, especially in light of his preoccupation with the derivation of Moses's name (Mose, Mosche, Moshe).[8]

* * *

I begin with this extended, characteristically Freud-like introduction not in order to furnish some historical background for a discussion of representations of the Last Judgment, but instead to show the extent to which Jean-Luc Godard's *King Lear* (1987)—ostensibly a cinematic adaptation of Shakespeare's play—participates in the discourse of psychoanalysis.[9] Just as Freud views lapses of memory in the light of repressed trauma, trauma he actually displaces to Herzegovina (while, in fact, being that engendered by Signorelli's literal vision of the enthroned Christ's condemnation of the damned and elevation of the blessed), Godard's work emerges from a similarly obfuscated, but no less traumatic confrontation with imminent apocalypse, in his case as a metaphor of a modern, technological holocaust, his film having been conceived in the immediate aftermath of the Chernobyl meltdown. Words fail both Freud and Godard, in Freud's case those he had stocked in his mind, in Godard's those lodged in a collective memory of the sanctified *oeuvre* of Shakespeare, the Moses of modern psychological drama. The film, indeed, is less a cinematic narrative than a filmic essay on remembering, the recovery of words being predicated on the potentialities of unlocking repressed memory. A meditation, likewise, on the function of words in different artistic media, a forthright polemic on the relationship of words and images, at times even an abstruse and recondite analysis of diverse kinds of images, *King Lear* deploys the conceit of a world recovering from nuclear catastrophe—one in the midst of rediscovering its technological capabilities and artistic heritage in a jumbled but instructive progression— to comment on the role of art in the shaping of history. As if in confirmation of Jacques Derrida's notion of arche-writing, for instance, language reemerges as a system of signs that presupposes a textual trace: the sub–Promethean rediscovery of fire occurs at the expense of crumpled pages of Shakespeare, put to service as kindling, even as the lineal descendant charged with reconstructing his vanished works (William Shakespeare V, played by theater director Peter Sellars) stays true to the notion of a Shakespeare who lives not through the written but the spoken word. Sellars's presence is no reassurance, however, serving only to undermine the notion that an act of recollection — that capacity of mind Freud found so fragile and malleable — could pluck lost lines from his DNA, a notion Godard further derides in his self-flagellation as Professor Pluggy, the speech-impaired mutant inventor who initially assumes the role of Lear's Fool and who reinvents cinema as a vehicle of special effects.[10]

Shakespeare, thus, stands for civilization and its discontents. Freud turns to him often, having enough in mind to misquote regularly, yet consistently using passages from the plays as the supreme example of his conviction that artists, by illustrating the frailties of the personages they represented, intuitively anticipated the discoveries of psychoanalysis.[11] Godard's frequent deformations of the text of *Lear* follow a parallel trajectory, if in his case with the purpose of demonstrating that adaptation inescapably veers dangerously close to such associated concepts as citation, allusion, quotation, and plagiarism. Inevitably, Shakespeare is Oedipally overthrown by the act of interpretation. The cult associated with his textual traces makes him a figure that exactly parallels Freud's historical Moses, the Bard's laws being the foundation of the English theatrical tradition. Hence, adaptation, the most anxiety-provoking of forms of influence (to paraphrase Harold Bloom), necessitates the patricide of a punitive father; just as Freud has Moses slain, Godard has to give Shakespeare's son's son's son's sons in order to traduce his memory.

The recovery of Shakespeare, therefore, follows precisely the pattern of development Freud ascribed to all religious observance: indeed, in a 1935 letter to Lou Andréas Salomé, Freud described the recrudescence of Atonism among the Jews as an inevitable temporal progression, the "return of the repressed."[12] The burning of Shakespeare's texts in the hellfire of Chernobyl, and the metaphor of rediscovery as "rekindling," is but repression given material and symbolic form, and Shakespeare's eventual rediscovery as the author behind Godard's *King Lear* recapitulates the history of Freud's discovery of the trajectories of male anxieties. Perhaps the deepest layer of connection, however, is that both Freud and Godard identify with the objects of their analysis, Freud as the hunted, Mosaic progenitor of psychoanalysis, and Godard as the self-appointed dramaturge of the French New Wave betrayed into the hands of commercial cinema. It is a conceit that — like Freud's retrospection in London — stems from a particular conjunction of historical forces; one that finds its most ample expression in the film's prolonged meditation on the notion of authorship.

Deaths of the Author

The narrative to which Godard alludes in attempting to recuperate *King Lear* appears, superficially, to be self-evident. In order that Shakespeare can assume cult status, his followers have to affix particular meanings to him, to mummify him in order that he may be resurrected following the traditional pattern of the return of the repressed. Since Moses's fate parallels Aton's, then Godard's must parallel Freud's. Peter Donaldson, perhaps the first critic of cinematic adaptations of Shakespeare's plays to grant sustained attention to the relationship of concepts of film authorship to Freud's theories, has pointed out that Godard self-consciously critiques the idea of giving birth to a film, an approach to cinematic paternity that once served as a central tenet of the *politique des auteurs* that he and his fellow critics in the film journal *Cahiers du Cinéma* promulgated.[13] Indeed, for Donaldson, Godard's film restates the imperatives of patriarchy precisely by standing for a disavowed child, Edgar, "trifling with despair, toying with madness, disguising itself, enacting redemption in burlesque, cognizant of its diminishment, deeply injured, quirkily loyal, [and yet capable of establishing a] sudden, intimate connection to its parent while dissembling its filial relationship" (189–90).[14] So it can hardly be a matter of surprise that when Godard's grizzled, scarcely comprehensible Professor Pluggy succeeds in reinventing the lost art of cinema and stages a trial screening, he attempts futilely to explain this re-birth to a self-important reporter from the proverbial *New York Times*. With timing so fortuitous as to preclude mere coincidence, a French-speaking guest arrives, one Professor Kozintsev from Leningrad, who pointedly ignores the reporter. As the film within the film plays, the voice of the actor who took the part of Lear in Kozintsev's 1970 *Korol Lir*, itself a characteristically Russian allegory of the futility of cults of personality, begins his quiet monologue with the word "Cordelia," and Donaldson deduces that the film being projected must be the scene of division from Kozintsev's film (209–10).[15] As the projected film is about to play, {NO THING}, an intertitle repeated no fewer than seven times in the course of *King Lear* (and uttered even more often as dialogue), appears on the screen.

If that {NO THING}, a stark white text on a black ground, can be treated as a cinematic signifier, then Godard clearly contrives to pit the written and printed word (the newsprint in the *New York Times*) against the spoken one (Kozintsev's Lear's theatrical-cinematic prompting). The visualized {NO THING}, in this context, draws attention to the representational nature of cinema, the fact that projected images are insubstantial, cinema itself being what Christian Metz called the "imaginary signifier." It is this word's recontextualization that, in fact, authorizes the pretense of Shakespeare's authorial disappearance: the printed Shakespeare can be no more substantial than the spoken one, a point reiterated when, upon discovering a technology for lighting fires, Edgar uses pages of Shakespeare to feed the flames.

Likewise, Godard's technique of drawing attention to a sexual pun that would have been obvious to a Jacobean audience consists of the Freudian procedure of fracturing (into seemingly unnecessary particles) Cordelia's famous reply to Lear, a word that also functions as his shocked repetition of her response. In distinction to its Shakespearean source, {NO THING} returns to defy its repression: "words are one thing," says the Godard narrator in his most unctuous Speech Act moment, "and reality is another thing, and between them is no thing." {NO THING} is even transformed into an intertitle that introduces a later sequence. In so doing it references a cinematic track (the written word that in silent cinema functioned as narrative segmentation) that largely disappeared with the onset of synchronized dialogue in 1927. Moreover, in radically refashioning a play that stages a multiplicity of madnesses, real and feigned, Godard's linguistic tactic slyly invokes a trenchant critic of Foucault's social conception of madness, the redoubtable Derrida, whose notion of trace {NO THING} echoes: from a broken word, Godard summons the attributes of a broken silence.

Nor is this the only violence he enacts on natural language. In pursuing his trope of adaptation as deformation, Godard also distorts spoken words by playing with their sounds. At the start of his journey of rediscovery, we notice Will Jr. lurking awkwardly in the dining room of a posh hotel, eavesdropping on a young woman and her much older escort. Appearing to forget the governing Platonic rationale that knowledge must be remembered (rather than merely acquired through experience), he wonders whether her presence enhances his powers of recollection: "As you which, As you what," he gropes, and then utters a triumphant "As you like it." He pauses to thank the young woman for this sudden access of memory. Evidently a Cordelia to the older man's Lear (Don Learo), albeit a rather desperate one who assures her father that she is incapable of matching the effusions of loyalty her espoused sisters have dispatched to him by telegram, she turns to Will to thank him for having just saved her life by lighting her cigarette. "Are you making a play for my daughter?" inquires this punningly-possessive Lear.

In contrast to Don Learo's verbal facility and Will's garrulousness, Godard's Pluggy remains profoundly inarticulate. When we first encounter him, he sits reciting the opening lines of Sonnet 138, mangling the "truth" of "made of truth" so badly that it sounds like "trust." The verbal duplicity can hardly be a coincidence: another such slippage, in the form of the homonymous pun "made/maid," is to figure significantly in the film. When Shakespeare Jr. finally locates Pluggy, having been led to him by the infantile Edgar, he blurts out: "I am trying to recover the work of my ancestor. I understand that you have been working here on this problem, doctor"—to which Pluggy, after turning Will's pencil around to impede his obsessive, logomanic note-taking, responds, "The trouble with what you are looking for is that it does not exist." The natural consequence of this observation is that whether because his existence is predicated on words, or because Lear declares that he has been hanged, the Fool must cease to exist. In our final encounter with Pluggy, he is on the point of collapse, over-burdened by the strain of completing another of his experiments, the film we have been watching. Before expiring, still defending the primacy of the image in film, he calls out repeatedly for a certain "Mr. Alien." The Alien fast appears and happens to be the most overtly avant-garde of the 1970s crop of American *auteur* directors, Woody Allen, who as the character Alvy Singer in his *Annie Hall* (1977), had undergone extremes of alienation when forced to endure Hollywood.[16]

While Pluggy's disappearance is a narrative necessity, it must also, according to Freud's description of the return of the repressed, reflect the Oedipal imperatives of his progeny. In Godard's case, the progeny he envisions are essentially those born in 1968 with the rise and fall of the student protest movements whose aftermath included a profusion of theories that overtly stigmatized the *politique des auteurs* as a residual vestige of Modernism.[17] In *King Lear* he takes issue with two such responses to the *Cahiers'* position. The first branch of the post-*auteur politique* he addresses is that of Roland Barthes, who in 1969 wrote to proclaim "The Death of the Author," an obituary that invited Michel Foucault's prompt, if equally dismissive, rejoinder, "What is an author?" A second and, for Godard, still more wounding attack was that leveled by the emerging school of Situationists inspired by the publicity stunt-like successes of Guy Debord.

King Lear is, of course, separated from the events of 1968 by almost a generation. However, not long before Godard conceived the project, he had been offered fresh provocation by the posthumous publication of Barthes's *Camera Lucida*, which remains one of the most influential critical treatises on still photography. One of Barthes's points of departure is that in contrast to the moving image, the still image allowed its spectator time for contemplation and considered analysis, thus modifying the *studium*—the intended substance of a photograph — by the play of recollection and by some sign of the chance intrusion of reality, a visual discrepancy or *punctum* that pierces through the discourse of the photographer and provides the image with an unintended life of its own.[18] Refusing to speak of a photograph of his mother, whose death occasioned the book, and dwelling on the capacity of photographs to record the transitory and ephemeral, Barthes makes the case that the photograph is the closest human approximation to capturing a moment of time, a crystallization of the present that a hundred years into the future would represent a long-dead now; a transience accorded respect by silence.[19]

Godard demands — rather than begs — to differ. In making a case that moving images can render stillness with all the pathos Barthes grants to the fixed image, Godard incorporates images of numerous photographs, paintings, and drawings into *King Lear*, among them images of paternal monstrousness and contrasting ones of paternal benevolence (such as Francisco de Goya's allegory of Time, *Saturn Devouring His Children*, or Rembrandt van Rijn's idealization of forgiveness, *The Return of the Prodigal Son*). Chris Marker had previously made a film composed entirely of still photographs, the influential *La Jetée* (1963), whose medium-specificity revealed itself in two barely-noticeable camera movements. The author of those photographs, however, happened to be Marker, who made them for the purpose of the film. In contrast, by the time he made *Le Gai Savoir* (*The Joy of Learning*) in 1968, Godard was already juxtaposing found photographs and experimenting with the notion of assembling meaningful filmic sequences of them (just as Esfir Schub and Dziga Vertov had done with filmed news footage in the 1920s).[20] At one point, when Godard's voice has taken on the documentary voice-of-God function as *King Lear*'s narrator, a still photograph invites the commentary: "a picture. Sometimes you could put it in film. It will not transform itself in contact with other images." This is no doubt meant ironically in light of Marker's film, but the allusion to Barthes — contradicting him by using words to suggest their opposite — today seems more an expression of suspicion towards an over-rigorous semiology than a belated denunciation: after all, the narrator's assertions more generally call into question the 1960s Structuralist notion of the "shot" as the basic unit of film, an argument proposed and later abandoned by Metz and other film semiologists writing in the wake of Barthes's early analyses of narrative structure.[21] Yet by functioning as what Barthes terms "anchorage," the words themselves help pin down the meanings of the still photographs Godard translates into cinematic shots. Two images drawn from opposite ends of the "high" and "low" cultural spectrum, a reproduction of *Judith with the Head of Holofernes* and a pornographic still of a woman revealing the secrets of her sex, occur in succession, bridged only by the narrator's comment about visual analogy: "It is a resemblance of connection." The nod to the montage theories of Sergei Eisenstein and Dziga Vertov is no less a gesture to Barthes and to Freud, who terms such paths to connection "condensation."

Whereas Godard's debate with Barthes remains respectful, his response to the Situationists is scathing. Having advocated plagiarism and misappropriation as potent forms of resistance to the pervasiveness of proprietary capitalism, they rather illogically charged Godard with stealing Debord's techniques (Price 66–68). His response in *King Lear* is an outflanking maneuver, a mis-(s)use of the Situationist concept of *detournement*, the Dadaesque kidnapping or hijacking of an existing aesthetic object and its radical recontextualization.[22] One of the pretexts for the film's existence is that it is not Godard's but a realization of the *King Lear* film Orson Welles had struggled to make in his last years. Consequently, the *King Lear* we end up with claims not to be Shakespeare's Shakespeare (or critics' perception of Shakespeare's Shakespeare) but Welles's Shakespeare. Godard also pretends, elaborately, that Situationism is thrust upon him, in that in *King Lear* the preponderance of intertexts associated with "high culture" (Modernist literature and film, a drawing by Rubens, paintings by Titian, Renoir and Goya, a fresco of *The Annunciation* by Piero della Francesca, and so on) have as their aesthetic excuse his unwilling conformity to the dictates of his producers, the "Jewish gangster" (i.e., Hollywood studio executive) enforcers of the demands of a commercial medium. Yet far from desecrating the cited texts, Godard draws on their expressive power to explore the tension between the imperatives of aesthetic individuality and the obligations of fidelity to an adapted text on the one hand, and the simultaneously productive and fatal irreconcilability of art and commerce on the other. For convenience, as if they are footnotes to a filmic essay, Godard organizes such references into sets or clusters of citations. Some of these footnotes are plagiarisms of his *oeuvre*.

Deaths of the Father

One particularly apropos citational cluster, a pantheon consisting of a series of still images of film directors with Welles granted pride of place, provides a conspicuous instance of this tendency. The sequence is reminiscent in its list-like character of Andrew Sarris's ranking of important *auteurs*, itself the result of a certain tendency acquired from the early writings of Godard and the *Cahiers* critics. The gradual dissolution of the *politique des auteurs* and its general failure to transform cinema into something other than (and to) commerce, its eventual decline into a system of rankings, in fact reveals another Freudian dimension to Pluggy-esque disgruntlement. Godard's deliberately distracting (and obviously mock-serious) self-portrait is not so much that of a betrayed leader as that of a discredited, fallen high priest, so that the rediscovery of cinema in *King Lear* implies renewal, suggesting that, like the New Testament in relation to the Old, the reborn cinema surpasses and supplants what it brings to fruition. Welles's death becomes synecdoche, standing for the death of the *auteur* as independent filmmaker, his failure to complete his *King Lear* symbolic of the extinction of the New Wave with the coincident demise of one of its father figures.[23] Welles had suggested Carl Theodor Dreyer's *The Passion of Joan of Arc* (1928) as his cinematic model for *King Lear*, and if Godard's extensive allusions to Dreyer recuperate Welles's ambition, then adaptation for him is akin to Hamlet acting in apparent conformity with the Oresteian directives of his betrayed father, feigning a maddening textual digressiveness only to place the unfeigned Godard in an *auterist* line of succession. (In a famous footnote to his introduction of the Oedipus complex Freud had, of course, dismissed the idea that Hamlet hesitates to kill Claudius because of an inability to act, insisting instead that his unconscious impedes his killing the man who, by eliminating his father and taking his place, had brought to light his own childhood fantasy) (*Interpretation* 288–89).

Godard simultaneously envelops a number of fathers in an Oedipal embrace. The procession of *auteurs* (Bresson, Renoir, Pagnol, Pasolini, Truffaut ["perhaps"], Visconti, Cocteau, Lang, Guitry, Tarkovsky), each referred to by a first name (as a saint would be) by the Godard narrator voice, suggests an inevitable progression, just as the kings and prophets of the Old Testament herald a messiah. Welles is granted a sub-gallery of his own, his most famous roles reprised as reproduced production stills in a book through whose leaves Godard's own hand keeps flipping. The photographs alternate with illustrations of famous works of art. Godard cannot finish turning all the pages since the last page has to be Welles's absence (a blank leaf?) juxtaposed with a frame of Godard's completion of his film. The realization of Welles's *oeuvre*, however, implies a secondary conceit. The *detournement* of the early sequence of *Korol Lir* carries the *Lear* narrative to the point where the monarch prompts Cordelia to claim her third of the kingdom, which is the point at which Godard's retelling begins. Restoring the arts (including the youngest, cinema) after the Last Judgment of Chernobyl thus necessitates Godard's appended continuation in fulfillment of the New Testament promise of salvation; indeed, more than once *King Lear* cites Fra Angelico's fresco of *The Annunciation*, God's guarantee of human redemption. The strategy of filiation that *King Lear* pursues, one that reenacts a narrative of self-sacrifice, is to transform the start of Kozintsev's real film into the start of Welles's fictive one.

An even more elaborate instance of quotation, however, reveals the author of these nested texts to be none other than Godard himself. Towards the end of *King Lear*, Cordelia begins to reenact Joan of Arc's scenes from Dreyer's film. It is a referential strategy that alludes not only to the same director's 1945 *Day of Wrath*, an allegory of the condemnation of a woman innocent of witchcraft that was made during the Nazi occupation of Denmark, but also to an *auteur* who was deeply influenced by Dreyer, Ingmar

Bergman, who embedded a witch's execution into his own interpretation of Revelation in *The Seventh Seal* (1957).[24] The scenes Godard's Cordelia, Molly Ringwald, reenacts also happen to be those observed by Anna Karina (in the role of Nana) in his darkly Zola-esque *Vivre Sa Vie* (*My Life to Live*, 1962). Early in the film Nana tells a friend that rather than sharing dinner she wants to see a film, one that turns out to be *The Passion of Joan of Arc*. There, she appears to have a premonition (regrettably unheeded) that she is witnessing the foreshadowed spectacle of her own degradation. Godard quotes a chunk of the film, cutting from a close-up of Joan's tears on being told that she should prepare herself for death, to a close-up of Nana with tears welling in her eyes. The quoted sequence is a famous one, for Dreyer had so brutal-ized his Joan, Renée Falconetti, subjecting her to physical and emotional ordeals parallel to the saint's, that he could reputedly command her tears at will. There is no such sense of ominous premonition — except for those with unimpeded memories of the world of the *auteurs*—in Ringwald's reenact-ments of Falconetti's gestures or her increasing physical resemblance to Joan. Even so, Godard's double citation (of himself and of Dreyer) doubly reca-pitulates the Christian theme of redemptive suffering, and his appeal to Freud's idea of a Hamlet-Oedipus complex turns out to be a commentary on intertextuality itself. In seeming to contaminate a text by interleaving it with others, he transforms Joan from a figure that Shakespeare treats ambiva-lently as both saint and witch into an allegory of cinematic martyrdom. The film's overarching conceit, that it is postmodernism's homage to Modernism and thus allegory masquerading as quasi-documentary pastiche, turns out to be a Gnostic prayer for redemption.

Deaths of Modernity

In periodizing the work of *auteurs*, Godard also associates their work with particular visual, and even literary, styles. In the invented Welles book, for example, we encounter a reproduction of Jan Vermeer's *The Girl with the Pearl Earring*, with an emphasis on the pearl (we see it twice, the second being a closer view). This again is an instance in which Freud provides a key to Godard, whose allusion to Morelli's analytical method alerts us precisely to such details as earlobes. Although juxtaposed with an image of Welles as Macbeth, the repeated image probably alludes to another of his Shake-spearean assumptions, and hence to one of Othello's last lines regarding the base Indian throwing a pearl away worth more than all his tribe, the tribe being the artisans in charge of film production, the discarded pearl Welles himself. The reference is not coincidental: Welles's meteoric career, from celebrated experimental theatre and radio production director, to peripatetic studio has-been struggling to finance his films, validates Godard's use of him as a figure who bridges the Euro-American divide in what Wollen characterizes as the second of cinema's expressions of modernity.

Likewise, Godard enlists another talismanic figure, Woody Allen, to serve as a bridge between the initial manifestation of a *politque des auteurs* and the emergence of the more commercially-oriented film school trained *auteurs* in Hollywood's hedonistic 1970s. No doubt Allen's Shakespeare credentials also played a role in his presence as Alien. In *A Midsummer Night's Sex Comedy* (1982) Allen made numerous allusions to Shakespeare (even borrowing the incidental music by Mendelssohn that was put to good use in the Warner Bros. 1935 version of *A Midsummer Night's Dream*). He had also played a cameo as himself in Paul Mazursky's *Tempest* (1982) in which a starstruck Miranda (Ringwald) spots him atop a grand staircase. When Allen magically appears in *King Lear* he sports a Picasso t-shirt. In undertaking to salvage Godard's film, he tacitly accepts the loss of Hollywood's production values and is reduced to joining edited footage with needle, thread, and safety pins as if he were suturing the spatially-fragmented objects of a Cubist painting. The citation of Picasso is not casual: in referring to the iconic arch–Modernist among painters, Godard also hints that his own fragmentation of space and time has a Modernist rather than postmodernist precedent.

Part of Allen's editing process seems to involve his rendition of Sonnet 60, although unlike Godard's Pluggy he gets ten carefully selected lines. Allen is first seen in a state of despondency, prior to entering the editing suite, and musing in voice-over on the impossibility of his task. His first line, "Like as the waves," refers both to cinematic waves and to Virginia Woolf's textual strategy in *The Waves*, a copy of which (in a figuration of its absent author, whose death occurred by drowning) seems at one point in danger of being swallowed by the advancing tide. Perhaps because she, too, is iconic in her status as part of the Modernist literary vanguard[25], the visual analogy to Picasso is mirrored in an auditory connection to her prose-poetry. Allen's reading of the first line inevitably recalls the soothing, poetic Woolf voice-over that has accompanied the white-robed Cordelia, who leads a pale horse before the shot-gun wielding Learo overtakes her.[26] The wise female narrator, who in voice-over utters the more meditative lines of Shakespeare's Fool, eventually turns into the novelist's voice when it intones a monologue given to Bernard, the character in *The Waves* who serves as Woolf's alter-ego ("And in me too the wave rises. It swells; it arches its back. I am aware once more of a new desire, something rising beneath me like the proud horse whose rider first spurs and then pulls him back"). On the moviola Allen, his voice doubled by an out-of-synch technician, revivifies the proud horse in slow motion, in a manner reminiscent of Eadweard Muybridge, whose experiments in the 1880s in animating and projecting a galloping horse made cinema itself an inevitability. Yet Allen's reading of Shakespeare's sonnet ends not with a sense of new beginning but with the line that voices the film's final, funereal "nothing" ("And nothing stands but for his scythe to mow").[27] The film ends, in fact, in a manner reminiscent of the close of Godard's earlier commentary on Hollywood's production system, *Le Mépris* (*Contempt*, 1963), with an expanse of water. Learo sits, shotgun in hand, requiring no surrogates to kill Cordelia, an unrepentant Hollywood gangster contemplating a panorama of wave-less waters even as Cordelia lies stretched over a rock in an image reminiscent of the neo-primitivist virgin sacrifice of *The Rite of Spring*.

It may not be coincidence that Woolf's serene, prematurely-silenced voice is at the furthest extreme from that of another celebrated novelist, Norman Mailer, who had helped craft Godard's story and who, originally, was to be his Lear. Godard retains some of the footage of his assumption of the role: clearly disconcerted, Mailer heckles and kibitzes, at one point even demanding that the director call "action." Godard replies evasively from behind the camera and temporizes. For Mailer the final straw comes with Godard's demand that he kiss Kate, his daughter, who assays Cordelia. This precipitates his departure, but not before making a remark that Godard either doctors (omitting the final "hand") or simply reproduces. In the latter case it would be an extremely interesting instance of the phenomenon to which Freud grants the longest chapter in *The Psychopathology of Everyday Life*, a "slip of the tongue."

Deaths of the Daughter

Godard prefaces the Mailer debacle with a number of intertitles that could, potentially, frame the action of *King Lear*: {*A Picture Shot in the Back*} announces a title card, and then {*King Lear, Fear and Loathing*}, or, alternatively, {*King Lear, a Study*}, perhaps even {*An Approach*} or {*King Lear, a Clearing*}. Mailer's disillusionment grows to the point where, queasy with his role as an over-familiar *pater familias*, he demands: "Why does she take my hand, instead of me taking her?"

Replaced by a raspy-voiced Burgess Meredith (a one-time victim of the House Un-American Activities Committee and Hollywood's blacklisting), Mailer still leaves a discernible trace. In his own voice Godard comments: "It was not Lear with three daughters. It was Kate with three fathers: Mailer as star, Mailer as a father, and me as a director. Too much indeed." Their departure makes room for Godard to be more literal, in that the motivation for the insistent repetition of Cordelia's "No-thing" becomes evident later in the film when a hotel chambermaid reacts in shock to what she sees on the bed sheets in the room shared by Learo and his daughter. Shakespeare's use of "nothing" ("nothing comes from no-thing"), in fact, legitimates just such a reading of the play, even if Godard seizes on it to draw a broader analogy.

Godard is not alone, by any means, in finding incest lurking in the back-stories of Shakespeare's plays. Freud certainly had a hand in this cinematic rereading of Shakespeare's fraught father-daughter relationships, since Laurence Olivier credits his cinematic version of *Hamlet* (1948) to Ernest Jones's working-out of a footnote in *The Interpretation of Dreams*.[28] Even more explicitly, Zeffirelli's elegant 1990 envisioning of Denmark — from the circularity of Elsinore's walls to the uterine crypt in which Hamlet delivers his celebrated meditation on mortality (in the presence of his father's sarcophagus) — as the corrupt womb of the sexually rapacious and predatory Gertrude accounts for a fulminant desire that extends both to her husband's brother and her son. More subtly, Bill Murray's unctuous, suggestive Polonius in Almereyda's *Hamlet* (2000) seems (over)determined to handle his daughter. Nor is the obvious *Hamlet* the only play to invite such cinematic commentaries. Walter Pidgeon's Prospero-figure, Morbius, in Fred Wilcox's *Forbidden Planet* (1956) illustrates the true morbidity of an unrestrained id — so identified in the film itself — that has as its eventual object the subjugation of the superego and the violation of the incest taboo with a nubile Alta (Miranda). More recently it has been offered as an explanation in a sympathetic account of the Goneril and Regan characters in Jocelyn Moorhouse's *A Thousand Acres* (1997), while in *As You Like It* (2007), Kenneth Branagh leaves it as a potentiality when Duke Frederick confides his decision to banish Rosalind as if offering Celia an enticement. Yet the most apposite prior instance of such a suggestion occurred with Ringwald, who as Mazursky's Miranda finds John Cassavetes (Phillip Demetrios-Prospero), imposing himself on her in a rather sensuous dance.

In Godard's per-version of the play it is not sons (Edgar and Edmund are but minor presences), but daughters who are at issue, with invented male progeny (such as Will Jr.) serving as a derisive metaphor for pure textual lineages. From the start, the Freudian displacement allows the comic to play out against the tragic: the idea of the sacrifice of the son (Isaac and Jesus) finds itself repeated in the iconography of Cordelia's ritualized death and in the repeated references to a Christian eschatology drawing on St. Paul and the book of Revelation.

In her martyrdom, Cordelia becomes a figure of an art movement defiled, born from the *cinéphile's* addiction to the classical period of Hollywood's studio filmmaking, and violated by the money-mania of that very system depicted by Godard as having fallen into incestuous decline. If Godard's purpose in *King Lear* is to integrate documentary images extracted from cinematic performances and reproductions of other images, then he is transforming genres that claim to record reality, *pace* Plato, into a catalogue of meta-fictions of the film's status as a fictional retelling of a play. For such a conceit to work, Welles, Dreyer, and a select group of *auteurs* must become integral to the new document in order to dispel the pretense of the latter being either a documentary about Shakespeare's play or a fictional version of that play. *King Lear* is thus rescued from any impulse merely to reproduce Shakespeare, and is instead reconfigured as part of an account of the unmaking of Welles's putative *King Lear* and of Godard's "post-apocalyptic" revivification of the project. Unlike Cordelia's virgin knot, Godard's rules of allegory-by-citation remain unbroken: in the face of relentless pressure by commercial cinema, the French New Wave must lose her innocence *en route* to a death transfigured as a promise of resurrection into a new kind of cinema.

Notes

1. See *Moses and Monotheism* 66–71.
2. I am here drawing on the historical theses of Freud's preliminary essays in *Moses and Monotheism* and particularly on the section devoted to "The Return of the Repressed" in the concluding essay (see, especially, 159–176).
3. For a comprehensive account of Freud's passion for classical antiquities, see Gamwell and Wells.
4. See Freud, *The Complete Letters* 264–267, and, for example, the letters sent in October in the same volume (267–273), that of October 27 being his first epistolary account of his thoughts about Hamlet and Oedipus.
5. See Roettgen 384–421.
6. See the letter of 22 September 1898 in *The Complete Letters* 326–327.
7. I am drawing this surmise from Peter Gay's biography (314–317).
8. Carlo Ginzburg devotes a justly celebrated essay, "Clues, Myth, and the Historical Method," to the use of such insignificant details by historians and practitioners of other disciplines.
9. The way to some of my conclusions has, of course, been illuminated by Peter Donaldson's discussion of Godard in *Shakespearean Film / Shakespearean Directors*.
10. Freud was by no means alone in distinguishing between voluntary and involuntary memory. As Miriam Hansen points out, having extolled the potentialities of new media (particularly cinema) to diminish the elitist aura of high art, Walter Benjamin revised his opinions with the onset of Fascism in the 1920s, becoming increasingly concerned by the capacity of technological media to disturb the balance between voluntary memory (recollection) and involuntary memory (remembrance) by vastly expanding the archive of the former (see Hansen 45). Benjamin, himself, seems to be responding to Proust.
11. Of Freud's recognition of artists' intuitive understanding of the workings of the unconscious see, for instance, his correspondence with Wilhelm Jensen about his novella *Gradiva* ("Delusions and Dreams" 3–86), and the observations in Gay (268–274, 314–317, and 320–322).
12. See, in particular, Freud's letter of 6 January in which he hypothesizes that Moses was killed in a "popular rebellion" never having "heard the name of Jahve," but

that in the same process he described in *Totem and Taboo*, the return of the repressed demonstrates that "the strength of religion lies not in its *material*, but in its *historical truth*" (*Complete Letters* 204–208).

13. For a more extended treatment of the *Cahiers'* conception of the *auteur* see my chapter "Reconstituting *King John*" in *Shakespeare, Film Studies, and the Visual Cultures of Modernity* (75–94).

14. Note that this observation constitutes far more than casual analogy: like Freud's version of the Oedipus myth, paternity itself is seen as dangerous, and the fragility of the Edgar-like text can be discerned in earlier screen adaptations: Peter Brook, for instance, eliminates the Gloucester subplot entirely from his 1953 televised version of *King Lear* (co-directed by Andrew McCullough), which starred Orson Welles. For Donaldson's larger argument see 189–223.

15. For a discussion of Kozintsev's use of allegory, see my introduction to *Shakespeare, Film Studies, and the Visual Cultures of Modernity* (12–14).

16. In *The Psychopathology of Everyday Life*, Freud devotes the longest chapter (74–139) to slips of the tongue, and he once again cites the example of "Signorelli" to disprove an earlier linguistic theory of the phenomenon. Slips resulting from the proximity of sound patterns in speech that cause disturbance in the flow of sound are relatively uncommon, the more likely cause being a disturbance emanating from outside the utterance, from unconscious procedures of condensation, displacement, wish-fulfillment, and repression. In summoning an outsider, like himself, but one who has reconciled himself to Hollywood's commercial imperatives, the Alien substitutes in language and fact for the film's legitimate completion.

17. In observing that cinema has undergone two distinct phases of Modernism, Peter Wollen places Godard at the center of the second that culminates in the French New Wave (155–174). The question of whether Godard is, in fact, a Modernist, has long remained in issue (see, for instance, Loshitsky, "More than Style"), with Fredric Jameson famously accusing him of postmodern "nominalism" (see 190–192).

18. See, especially, 25–27. I have treated Barthes's work in relation to Benjamin and the emergence of early documentary filmmaking in the article "The Birth of a New Realism." In contrast to the normal practice of his famously elliptical style, Barthes defines *studium* and *punctum* as they apply to each of his distinctions, and while I have summed up his general intent in "Birth" his most encompassing definition comes as a revelation near the end of *Camera Lucida*: "At [the beginning of this book] I thought that I could distinguish between a field of cultural interest (the *studium*) from that unexpected flash that sometimes crosses this field and that I called the *punctum*. I now know there exists another *punctum* ... no longer of form but of intensity.... Time, the lacerating emphasis of the *noeme* ("*that-has-been*"), its pure representation" (93–94).

19. Note, for example, that Kaja Silverman and Haroun Farocki have discussed Godard's experiment in *Vivre Sa Vie* (*My Life to Live*, 1962), of reversing the normal emphases of sound cinema — in which the moving image and dialogue tracks dominate — so that "every sound and image is equal" (2). So, too, the equal importance granted in *King Lear* to silences and, at times, the lack of the "expected" images.

20. Brian Price, for instance, notes that early in the film Godard binds together a seemingly paratactic series of found stills with a syntactically coherent string of words: "The Lords of Imperialism have Transformed Technological Progress and Sexuality into Instruments of Repression" (see 68).

21. During the late 1960s and early 1970s he and Pier Paolo Pasolini, collaborators in *RoGoPaG* (1963), developed opposed notions about the nature of signs in the cinema. However, Godard's commentary on the semiotics of word and image in *King Lear* treats even symbolic signs as part of a language system, in that signs are modified by the signs adjacent to them (icons in paintings, shot relations in film, and so on), a concept Pasolini

termed "contamination." Observe that here the narrator's words function analogously to the opening sentences of Jacques Derrida's "The Law of Genre," when he states: "Genres should not be mixed. I will not mix genres."

22. Price has observed that Godard's practice of taking familiar images out of context and using them repeatedly in differing associations in *Le Gai Savoir* consciously mimics the Situationist strategy of *detournement*, but that the plagiarism of the plagiarists while adhering to his established stylistic repertoire actually functions as a critique of their rejection of authorship.

23. Welles's protracted attempts to fund the film, which he had conceived as an experiment in genre to be filmed exclusively in close-ups, approximating Dreyer's use of them in *The Passion of Joan of Arc* (1929), can be found, for instance, in Rosenbaum (see 170).

24. Admittedly, neither Godard nor Bergman achieve the systematicity of Olivier Messiaen, whose *Quatuor pour le fin du Temps*, written in Stalag 8A in the Silesian town of Görlitz, and performed by fellow inmates on January 15, 1941, gives a verse of Revelation musical form; but then their purpose is interpretation rather than representation.

25. In *Mimesis*, Erich Auerbach's magisterial summation of the realisms that have emerged in Western literature since Homer, Virginia Woolf is placed at the beginning of the end of that great tradition (see *Mimesis* 525–553).

26. The cinema seems to have appropriated the horse, one of the sacrificial emblems of Indo-European folk cults, as one of its recurrent symbols of life, fertility and rebirth, as the films of Alexander Dovzhenko, Andrei Tarkovsky and Govindan Aravindan attest.

27. It might also be remembered that in some famous passages confirming the speculation that no woman of his age could have written Shakespeare's plays, Woolf described the conditions under which women lived and labored then and afterwards, including the lack of education, a lack of cultural expectation, and even the lack of personal space (in a remark that gave one of her books its title, *A Room of One's Own*, in which she creates a fantasy of Shakespeare's unfulfilled sister). He deserved this sister, for beyond these considerations, too, was Shakespeare's difference from all the male writers of his time and afterwards: "All desire to protest, to preach, to proclaim an injury, to pay off a score, to make the world the witness of some hardship or grievance were fired out of him and consumed.... If ever a human being got his work expressed completely, it was Shakespeare" (see 43–59).

28. See Jones, "The Oedipal Complex." Olivier revealed his wholehearted endorsement of Jones's analysis to Kenneth Tynan in an interview included as a supplement to the Criterion *Hamlet* edition.

Works Cited

Auerbach, Erich. *Mimesis: The Representation of Reality in Western Literature*. Trans. Willard R. Trask. Princeton: Princeton University Press, 1953.

Barthes, Roland. *Camera Lucida*. 1980. Trans. Richard Howard. New York: Hill and Wang, 1982.

_____. "Death of the Author." *Image-Music-Text*. 1969. Trans. Stephen Heath. New York: Noonday Press, 1997. 142–148.

Derrida, Jacques. "The Law of Genre." *Glyph* 7 (1980): 202–232.

Donaldson, Peter. *Shakespearean Film / Shakespearean Directors*. Boston: Unwin Hyman, 1990.

Foucault, Michel. "What Is an Author?" *Language, Counter-Memory, Practice*. Ed. Donald F. Bouchard. Trans. Donald F. Bouchard and Sherry Simon. Ithaca, NY: Cornell University Press, 1980. 124–127.

Freud, Sigmund. *The Complete Letters of Sigmund Freud to Wilhelm Fliess, 1887–1904*.

1985. Trans. and ed. Jeffrey Moussaieff Masson. Cambridge, Mass.: Harvard University Press, 1995.

_____. "Delusions and Dreams in Jensen's *Gradiva*." *Writings on Art and Literature: Sigmund Freud*. Ed. Werner Hamacher and David E. Wellbery. Stanford: Stanford University Press, 1997. 3–86.

_____. *The Interpretation of Dreams*. 1900. Trans. and ed. James Strachey. New York: Avon Books, 1965.

_____. "The Moses of Michelangelo." *Writings on Art and Literature: Sigmund Freud*. Ed. Werner Hamacher and David E. Wellbery. Stanford: Stanford University Press, 1997. 122–50.

_____. *Moses and Monotheism*. 1939. Trans. Katherine Jones. New York: Vintage Books, 1967.

_____. *The Psychopathology of Everyday Life*. 1901. Trans. and ed. James Strachey. New York: W.W. Norton and Co., 1965.

_____. *Sigmund Freud and Lou Andréas-Salomé Letters*. Ed. Ernst Pfeiffer. Trans. William and Elaine Robson-Scott. New York: Norton, 1966.

Gamwell, Lynn, and Richard Wells, eds. *Sigmund Freud and Art: His Personal Collection of Antiquities*. Binghampton: The State University of New York, 1989.

Gay, Peter. *Freud: A Life for Our Time*. New York: Norton, 1998.

Ginzburg, Carlo. "Clues: Roots of an Evidential Paradigm." *Clues, Myths and the Historical Method*. Trans. John and Anne Tedeschi. Baltimore: The Johns Hopkins University Press, 2005. 96–125.

Guneratne, Anthony. "The Birth of a New Realism: Painting, Photography and the Advent of Documentary Cinema." *Film History* 10.2 (1998): 165–187.

_____. *Shakespeare, Film Studies, and the Visual Cultures of Modernity*. New York: Palgrave Macmillan, 2008.

_____. "'Thou Dost Usurp Authority': Beerbohm Tree, Reinhardt, Olivier, Welles, and the Politics of Adapting Shakespeare." *A Concise Companion to Shakespeare on Screen*. Ed. Diana Henderson. Malden, MA: Blackwell Publishing, 2005. 31–53.

Hansen, Miriam. "Benjamin and Cinema: Not a One-way Street." *Benjamin's Ghosts: Interventions in Contemporary Literary and Cultural Theory*. Ed. Gerhard Richter. Stanford: Stanford University Press, 2002. 41–73.

Jameson, Fredric. *Postmodernism, or, the Cultural Logic of Late Capitalism*. 1991. Durham, NC: Duke University Press, 1994.

Jones, Ernest. "The Oedipus Complex as an Explanation of Hamlet's Mystery: A Study in Motive." *American Journal of Psychology* 21.1 (1910): 72–113.

King Lear. Dir. Jean-Luc Godard. Perf. Burgess Meredith, Molly Ringwald, Peter Sellars, and Woody Allen. 1987. Videocassette. Xenon Entertainment, 1992.

Loshitsky, Yosefa. "More than Style: Bertolucci's Postmodernism versus Godard's Modernism." *Criticism: A Quarterly for Literature and the Arts* 34.1 (1992): 119–142.

Price, Brian. "Plagiarizing the Plagiarist: Godard Meets the Situationists." *Film Comment* 33.6 (1997): 66–69.

Roettgen, Steffi. *Italian Frescoes: The Flowering of the Renaissance*. New York: Abbeville Press, 1997.

Rosenbaum, Jonathan. "The Invisible Orson Welles: A First Inventory." *Sight and Sound* 55 (1986): 164–71.

Silverman, Kaja, and Harun Farocki. *Speaking about Godard*. New York: New York University Press, 1998.

Wollen, Peter. *Signs and Meaning in the Cinema*. Bloomington: Indiana University Press, 1972.

Woolf, Virginia. *A Room of One's Own*. 1929. Fort Washington, PA: Harvest Books, 1989.

11

"The Promised End" of Cinema: Portraits of Apocalypse in Post-Millennial Shakespearean Film

CAROLYN JESS-COOKE

Claims of the "promised end" of cinema have sounded throughout every upheaval during the history of film production, from Thomas Edison's denunciation of the seventh art as having no future (Israel 288) to Jean-Luc Godard's quip at the rise of the "New Hollywood" blockbuster, "I await the end of cinema with optimism" (Milne 210; cf. Lewis). In keeping with a host of manifesto-movements such as the French New Wave, New German Cinema, and the short-lived Dogme 95, cinema's innovators and *auteurs* announced the death of one cinematic phase and the arrival of the new to champion their own discrete brand of originality. Suffice to say, cinema's end is a *recurrent* event, one that is to be expected and, indeed, greeted with a certain amount of optimism if aesthetic energies are to be recharged at each technological, cultural, and ideological transition. By considering apocalyptic constructions of perpetual youth in Christine Edzard's *The Children's Midsummer Night's Dream* (2001), and post-apocalyptic affirmations of aesthetic "new-ness" in Dogme 95's *The King Is Alive* (2000), this paper examines the ways in which Shakespeare's texts are employed to articulate notions of an impending "end" of artistic and cultural production, in the same moment as Shakespeare serves as a legitimating negotiator of a new aesthetic system, indeed, a new cinema, at the commencement of the twenty-first century.

The discourses of "post-ness," conclusion, and apocalypse that have governed the aftermath of traumatic events during the previous century have "posted," to use Derrida's terminology, delayed sensibilities of trauma to the current moment, resulting in an urgency to re-present past-ness and the contingencies of "the end" (Derrida, *Post Card* 65). Cinema's most recent apocalyptic "end" seems to me to be premised in part on the throng of diegetic copies in the form of prequels, sequels, and trilogies, that have dominated the box office in recent years, which some critics have viewed as forcing the cinematic aesthetic into a terminal catatonia (Hoberman; Kael). Although the sequel is predominantly viewed as a diegetically-deteriorating profit-making scenario, I argue that a much more timely and compelling ethos underlies the cinematic reification of what Freud called "the compulsion to repeat" (Freud, "Beyond the Pleasure Principle" 30). The sequel's apocalyptic musings, moreover, are located in apocalypse's dichotomous signification of both the aftermath of the end and the *beginning* of that end. Deriving from the Greek *apokalypsis*, apocalypse translates as the unveiling, or revelation, of forthcoming events, and is particularly concomitant with Gérard Genette's cogitations on the sequel as a proleptic, or forward-looking, paradigm (177). *Post*-apocalypse, as James Berger points out, focuses on what is left, or *what comes after* cataclysm, and subscribes to what Genette calls analeptic continuation, a retrospective motion towards an originary diegesis (Berger 5; Genette 177). This clarification helpfully illuminates the filmic constructions of "before" and "after" the end of an aesthetic, and perhaps the more subtle configurations within that aesthetic of cathartic mediations.

I go on to approach the investment in notions of "before" and "after" throughout apocalyptic discourses in terms of the specifically filmic, and exceedingly current, tropes of prequelization and sequelization. Insofar as apocalypse contends with notions of pre-ness or "beforeness," I regard prequelization as a paradigmatic manifestation of apocalypse, exporting apocalypse's revelatory and "unveiling" dimensions to a system of narrative origins. Edzard's *The Children's Midsummer Night's Dream*—which employs over three hundred schoolchildren under the age of twelve to perform Shakespeare's *A Midsummer Night's Dream*—arguably constructs the child as an emblem of prequelization, a fixed figure of discursive immobility. The child in this production appears to me to reside within a frozen site of beginnings, that is, a locality filled with the Benjaminian notion of "a present which is not in transition, but in which time stands still and has come to a stop" (Benjamin 262). Titania and Oberon's argument in the play causes the seasons to be thrown into disarray, and is represented in the film, I think, by the theatrical *interior* forest that is caught in a perpetual "childing autumn" (2.1.112). By situating the forest inside the theater, Edzard's comment on cinema is analogous to Jean-Louis Baudry's observation of cinema's return of the spectator "to a primitive narcissism," or the return to the mirror stage of the Imaginary, which culminates in "the transfusion of the interior out into the exterior" (Baudry 313). In other words, the cinema screen contains no less than the projection of the spectator's infantile subconscious. Titania and Oberon's "dissension" (2.1.117) is translated cinematically to exert likewise confusion upon exterior and interior modes, resulting in the natural world inhabiting Edzard's theatrical domain. Literally pulled outside in, Shakespeare's play is additionally configured here according to the tension between "prequel" and "original," resulting in the figure of the child as less performing, and more prophetically *announcing*, Shakespeare's play. Unable to develop naturally because of the suspension of temporality within a paradigm that is rooted in anticipation, the child's habitation of an "Eden" is reviewed as emphatically apocalyptic, to the degree that apocalypse displaces progress with prophecy. The representation of an apocalyptic state in this production contrives Shakespeare's play as "unveiled," in the same moment as Shakespeare's play is preceded by a prophetic, originating "prequel."

At the beginning of the film, the puppet show performance of *A Midsummer Night's Dream* is interrupted by a young girl (Jamie Peachey), who rises to her feet and utters Hermia's lament: "I would my father looked but with my eyes" (1.1.56). From this point on, the children's rendition of the play displaces the puppet show, recalling the Amazonian conquest alluded to at the play's opening in a spectatorial context. The child represents "the Imaginary signifier" as cognized by Christian Metz, and may further be seen to embody the relationship between cinema screen and spectator that returns the spectator, however temporarily, to the moment of infantile union with the mother (Metz). The revelatory sense of a beginning that pervades apocalypse is experienced every time we go to the cinema, I think, insofar as cinema "makes us babies again ... by plunging us back in memory to that moment of identification with [the mother]" (Eberwein 42; cf. Fischer). The prequel's engagement with the spectatorial experience in this context points to the Imaginary as an apocalyptic condition, whereby the mirrored configurations of the infant's identity indicate a continually recycling state of "beforeness" wherein the film's spectator is constantly "sutured," or implicated within a series of shot/reverse shots, with his or her experience and (repressed) memories of the Imaginary (cf. Silverman; Oudart).

From the outset, Edzard's montage exhibits what Patricia Parker has observed as "structures of preposterous reversal in Shakespeare" (Parker 36). Parker's cogitations of "pre-" as inhering "beforeness," and as a reversal of the trajectory of the "original" and its sequel, are captured by the film's opening series of shot/reverse shots. Cutting systematically from the puppets to the youthful audience, the opening montage sequence underscores the subsequent reversal of the children and puppets in a parent-child context. The children's requisition of the play replaces the puppets' performance, just as the puppets replace the children's parents, setting Edzard's production as a whole into Oedipal dialogue with Shakespeare's text. Presiding over the Symbolic terrain captured at the moment of the children's citation of the play, the child's missing father is represented by Shakespeare's play, whilst the mother — the Imaginary — is captured by Edzard's theater/forest. Indeed, Edzard's construction of the theater according to early modern concepts of physiology suggests the theater in this connection as a feminized body inhabited by the children. The Aristotelian concept of the body as composed of four elements — earth, fire, water and air — that informed Elizabethan ideas of anatomy is signaled by the film's set design (Schoenfeldt 2, 8, 78). Edzard's theater incarcerates representatives of earth (the theatrical forest), water (small ponds which frame a fake moon), air (represented by mist and disintegrating fairies), and fire (represented by the lantern, acting as the moon), arguably to function as a substitute for an absent physical entity.

The film's transformed theater underlines two crucial forms of origins: firstly, Biblical origins in the form of the play's reference to the Garden of Eden narrative from the Old Testament, and, secondly, as a *body* within which the children are contained. This duality is signalled by the children's costumes at this point in the film, whereby their navy school uniforms are shunned for Elizabethan dresses in shades of red and green. The color green connects the children to their viridescent milieu. Red simultaneously gestures towards the theater's construction as a womb, evoking the blood red walls of this environment and simultaneously linking the exterior to the interior. The film's semiotic recapturing of this notion further corresponds to the wholeness of the Imaginary and its subsequent fracture by the appearance of a crescent moon. Reflected in a pond as Titania (Rajouana Zalal) and her fairy crew make their entrance, the moon is additionally treated as the "sign of the times" that so informs apocalyptic rhetoric, a mark of temporal transition that signifies the commencement of the end (cf. Berger 6). Once it is whole the crescent moon registers, as Mark Thornton Burnett has pointed out, "the end of one life-phase and the onset of another" (Burnett 169). An apocalyptic symbol prophesying *both* the end and a beginning, the moon epitomizes the fractured wholeness of the Imaginary that accompanies the child's entrance into the Symbolic.

The moon in Edzard's *mise-en-scène* conveys the play's "cold fruitless moon" (1.1.73) which is responsible for "that which [withers] on the virgin thorn" (77). Although Edzard's forest contains vegetation that is far from withered, the suggestion is that the "virgin thorn" is the child. Swiftly occupied by the natural world in the form of a theatrical "forest," the verdant interior of Edzard's theater suggests, in view of the chaotic seasons in the play, the perpetuation of spring, the perpetuation of youth. Titania's reference to the "green corn" who "hath rotted ere his youth attained a beard" (2.1.94–95) suggests the children as forever "pre-," always *almost* at their destination. Unlike Langston Hughes's poetic ruminations of the dried up, festering "sore" that becomes of "a dream deferred" (Hughes 1324), the child's utterly apocalyptic dream (that defers, no less, the Real) is entirely in keeping with André Bazin's notion of cinema as "change mummified," an aesthetic predicated upon the urge "[t]o preserve [life] artificially" (Bazin 9). For the dream that the child inhabits is not an organic, mortal temporality, but a locality in which the cinematic condition of the Imaginary is played out, projecting infantile memories upon adult fantasies. The staged puppet performance, moreover, evinces Freud's comments on "screen memories" whereby an "early memory is used as a screen for a later event" in the sense that the "memory" of the puppet performance becomes conflated with (and, of course, anticipates) the children's forest performance, suggesting the forest as a "screen" of the past (Freud, "Psychopathology" 28–29). Triggered by the puppet's performance, the children's collective unconscious begins to fill the theater. Freud regards infantile memories as recollections that substitute for other significant impressions, giving shape, as it were, to repressed desire. When questioned about his memories, a patient admits to Freud that he "amalgamated ... two sets of phantasies" to create a childhood memory (Freud, "Screen Memories" 315). Similarly, Hermia recalls the "dream" "with parted eye" (4.1.186). The forest "dream" in the film is arguably the children's aggregated screen memory of the puppet performance, the apocalyptic moment of the Real and the recreation of the Imaginary.

The play's portraits of progression and temporal upheaval are undercut by the evident artificiality of Edzard's forest, which denies the sense of rotting and decay that accompanies the play's portrait of altered temporality, and, like the unconscious, "exists *outside* time" (Freud, "Note" 213, my emphasis). The children's green outfits also underline notions of surrogacy and copies, for the color green at this point evokes the green light of a photocopying machine. The signature color of the Wachowskis' *Matrix* trilogy (1999, 2003), green was famously employed two years prior to Edzard's production in *The Matrix* to capture the film's absorption with Baudrillard's notion of simulacra. In this film, and according to the Baudrillardian text featured in the film (*Simulacra and Simulation*) the matrix itself is a copy, a replicated illusion of a natural environment and, indeed, a *reality* that evokes Edzard's imprisoning "womb." In *The Matrix* the mechanical "wombs" in which human beings are "grown" by late twenty-second century machines are patterned after the female womb: the point of all origins, it might be said, is proffered as a "sequel" to an irretrievable original. By gesturing towards and perhaps replicating this ideology, Edzard's film figures the children as both "originals" and copies. Indeed, the exchange between the children and the puppets here underlines that even the "prequel" is, at base, a copy of a copy. Like the humans that are "grown" in mechanical matrices in *The Matrix*, the child as copy here is arguably caught in a cycle of cinematic and mechanical reproduction, returning only to the copy and never to the original. In this light, apocalypse is confirmed as a copy of prior narratives of cataclysm, the cathartic manifestation of previous social traumas that is projected upon futurity to predict, and somehow defer, the return of "the end." In both spectral and "mortal" forms, the children in this production incarnate apocalypse as a spectatorial experience in which we are all participants. Furthermore, cinema is posited as the apparatus whereby anxieties provoked by each *fin de siècle* and social upheaval, as well as our repressed infantile memories, are assembled within a montage that both defers and advertises the sense of an ending.

In contrast to this sensibility, cinema's "rebirth" in the aftermath of historical transitions is pronounced by new wave cinemas, which frequently frame their movements towards a renewed aesthetic within a manifesto. Manifesto-movements such as Dogme 95 trade upon cinema's "promised end" to conceive of a "new" cinema that is, paradoxically enough, almost invariably premised on the reconstruction of an aesthetic that is rooted in the past. The last manifesto of the twentieth century, Dogme 95, was launched by a body of Danish filmmakers (Lars von Trier, Thomas Vinterberg, Søren Kragh-Jacobsen, and Kristian Levring) at the international symposium on the centennial anniversary of the Lumière Brothers' primary cinema screening in Paris, which was held on 22 March 1895 and not 28 December 1895 as was originally believed. With echoes of prior manifestos resonating throughout their "Vow of Chastity," Dogme's aim is to create original, innovative methods of film production free from the restraints of genre, Hollywood, music, and special effects. Dogme's fourth venture, *The King Is Alive*, directed by Kristian Levring, portrays cinema as at the brink of a post-apocalyptic aesthetic state, taking its cue from the portraits of death and apocalypse in *King Lear* to capture cinema's barren aesthetic at this historical juncture. Put briefly, I argue that the Dogme phenomenon is a pointed reactionary movement against the sequel phenomenon, treating Shakespeare's text as a document on aesthetic death that mediates anxieties about the dearth of "new-ness" in recent cinema. Set in Namibia, the film eschews conventional production methods and modalities save three digital video cameras and eleven actors who perform a version of *King Lear* (rewritten from memory by one of the team) in the middle of the African desert when their coach travels hundreds of miles in the wrong direction and subsequently runs out of fuel. Although concepts of transformation, death, and apocalypse have been examined in *Lear* at length, Levring's film tackles these concepts in terms of the redemption of "original" cinematic movements, signalling the apocalypse, or rather the aftermath, of an apocalypse, and of originality (Wittreich). The king *is* alive, it seems, by virtue of the revivification of Lumière purity, and the re-establishment of cinema's nineteenth-century origins at the beginning of the new millennium.

Dogme's philosophy is enforced in the film by a stridently post-apocalyptic cinematography. "New-ness" is translated in terms of the cinematic infantilism proffered by Dogme's manifesto *and* in terms of the apocalyptic end of cinema that has preceded its rebirth. At times Levring's camera lurks in the corner, capturing the tensions within the group from a low-angle shot like a child watching its parents argue. On another occasion the camera lingers on Ray (Bruce Davison) as he accepts the reality of his predicament, jump-cutting from his apparent acquiescence to childlike despair to adult stoicism. When Catherine (Romane Bohringer) carries the gas-lamp by her side at night (to damage tins of carrots in order to poison Gina [Jennifer

The tragically lost cast of characters in Kristian Levring's *The King Is Alive* (2001) wander in the wasteland of the Namibian desert (Photofest).

Jason Leigh]), the camera skulks along behind her knees, both to absorb the available light and to assimilate the "beast-like" position that Catherine has now descended to, morally creeping on all fours as she descends from "the intellect" to the murderess. Levring's cinematography subscribes to past styles and even past films to redefine its point of departure, for example, soaking up Namibia's tangerine dunes *à la* Anthony Minghella's *The English Patient* (1996), which visually connects the human body to Africa's wastelands. Levring evokes not so much the human body but Shakespeare's textual "corpus," as Courtney Lehmann observes, the remainder of which is recaptured in spectral form by cinematic incarnations (Lehmann 4–24). It is *Shakespeare* in this production that features as the remnant of historical and post-apocalyptic memory, whose texts provide the *tabula rasa* upon which new historical diegeses can palimpsestuously be inscribed.

The death of the sequel phenomenon is imagined in the film by the death of the "uncanny." The characters' "doubling" as performers of Shakespeare's play and actors in Levring's film connects Freud's comments on the "idea of the 'double'" in his description of *unheimlich* to the sequel insofar as the "double" here is likened to the sequel, the unmitigated spectral *doppelganger* (Freud, "Uncanny" 235). Doubling, Freud observes, is concomitant with denying death, and at first the performance of the play in the film offers the tourists a means of preventing this end. As the film develops, however, the double is coterminous with *causing* or anticipating death, becoming "the uncanny harbinger of death" (Freud, "Uncanny" 235). Gina, for example, dies twice: once as "Cordelia," and finally as Gina. She is also murdered "twice": by both Catherine (who feeds her poisonous tinned carrots) and Charles (who strangles her). That Catherine "doubles," to an extent, the role of Cordelia in the same moment as she murders Gina/Cordelia is further significant. Gina and Catherine are (unlikely) friends at the film's outset, and both are candidates for the role of Cordelia and the role of Henry's (David Bradley) daughter-figure. Catherine tells Gina (in French) "I'm fed up with you sticking to my ass," and rejects Henry's offer of Cordelia's role (which he subsequently gives to Gina), a decision she appears to regret throughout the rest of the film. Cutting free of Gina, the "primary narcissism" of Catherine's double is at last "surmounted," causing the double to "revers[e] its aspect" (Freud, "Uncanny" 235). At this point Catherine's survival depends on the *death* of the double, resulting in Gina's murder. The death of Catherine's double, I suggest, registers Dogme's emphasis on the death of the "sequel" as a necessary event if unique-ness, originality, and actuality are to be propagated.

Derrida has commented that "'Come' ... is in itself the apocalypse of the apocalypse; '*Come*' is apocalyptic. Our *apocalyptic now*" (Derrida, "Apocalyptic Tone" 94, his emphasis). This notion is inherent in the play, for Lear says, "Come, come; I am a king" (4.4.193). Derrida further proffers that "'Come' is only derivable, absolutely derivable, but only from the other, from nothing that may be an origin or a verifiable" (Derrida, "Apocalyptic Tone" 94). In this connection, Dogme is not an origin; it is the aesthetic redemption — almost an *homage* — of former patterns of filmic production from which future films are intended to derive. From this point on, Levring's film appears to suggest, death is displaced by perpetual new-ness. In preparing for his end, further, Lear embodies what Helga Nowotny has described as an "extended present," throwing into disarray the natural order of time (Nowtony 43). Paul Ricoeur's comments on the "arrow of time," an inversion of natural temporal progression, demonstrates how "the repetition of a story, governed as a whole by its way of ending, constitutes an alternative to the representation of time as flowing from the past toward the future." In so doing, this "alternative" enables us "to learn to read time backwards" (Ricoeur 6–7). Hence Dogme's revivification of the New Wave. The play's series of ends alters the progression of time, pushing the margins of the present towards those of the past and future. This sense of "now-ness" registers Lear's description as "an O without a figure" (1.4.168), for, as Richard M. Gale observes, "the 'now' is a *limit* of time (for it is the beginning of one and the end of the other)" (18). The "new wave" championed by Dogme, then, is the "now" wave, the movement that underlines the current moment, disengaging this age from any sense of "post-ness" or memory of the past.

Perhaps to indicate this notion, the modes of linearity constructed in Levring's film — most aptly by the bus journey — towards a filmic end are arguably beginning-bound. As Timothy Corrigan posits, "Apocalyptic closure might be defined as a terminal form of closure in which the narrative has traveled somewhere, but not to where it began" (Corrigan 138). When the group are found, at last, by Namibian soldiers as they sit around a camp fire, a succession of flashbacks compare each of the passengers as they have become with what, or who, they were at the film's beginning. The transition from one state of being is precisely the film's design: *Lear* has changed them, and for the most part the transformation has been a catastrophic yet necessary one. Not closure, but transition and aesthetic rebirth are denoted at the film's end. Lear's imagined prevention of future sequels is, according to this interpretation, an attempt to prevent the "end of all being," including his own. Like Cronos, who swallowed his offspring to prevent the prophecy of his dethronement being fulfilled, Lear's wish to dry up the wombs of his daughters (rendered in the film by Gina's implied morning sickness and subsequent death) is a call for a deferral of the end. Having passed through the temporal, cultural, and aesthetic apocalypse, the twenty-first century spectator can, like Levring's cast at the end of the film, dream of "what ought to be, or of what one day may be" (Wittreich 32).

Levring's film ultimately treats apocalypse as concomitant with eschatology, projecting all towards an unforeseeable, inevitable end that infects the present and the past with its dragging gravity, whereas post-apocalypse is charged with ideals of renewal and revivification. Dogme is arguably haunted not so much by the ghost, but by the Barthelmean "dead father" of diegetic reproduction that precipitates an apocalypse of the cinematic aesthetic by repeating images (Barthelme), narratives, genres, and production methods of the past throughout futurity until all trace of an origin is washed away in a tide of simulacra, a frenzy of postmodernism which "denies the idea of knowable origins" (Woods 3). Hence Dogme's dated, signed and certified seal of authentication and originality. Indeed, the "broken apocalypse" (Kermode 88) in the play can be read as Lear's sense of "nothing-ness" that culminates in his asking "who is it that can tell me who I am?" (1.4.205). The Fool's reply, "Lear's shadow" (1.4.206), underlines the "child-changèd" (4.7.17) king as deprived of identity, robbed of genealogy. The new wave of innovation that has "turned to muck," drowning under the weight of sequels that, like Lear, drag out their narrative mortality well beyond its "two hours' traffic" (*Rom.*, Prologue.12), is provided by regained originality that is authenticated and announced here by the performance of Shakespeare's text.

The formulations of apocalypse and post-apocalypse in these productions feature Shakespeare in the construction of cinema's end to authorize those "new" methodologies of aesthetic production and appropriation, treating the Bard's plays as manifesto-documents that anchor cinema's inception *not* in its late nineteenth-century *Cinématographic* forms, but in early modern culture. The post-millennial sequel phenomenon is responded to by negotiating the commentaries of "nothing new" and "[t]he second burthen of a former child" (Sonnet 59.1,4) in Shakespeare's texts, whilst the restoration of an apparently flagging aesthetic is initiated by methods that are *not* new, but which redefine and reconnect post-millennial spectators to the moment. Although sequels, prequels, and their respective theoretical paradigms ostensibly threaten to drown cinema in narrative confusion and decay, it would appear that their endorsements of apocalyptic and post-apocalyptic discourses enable a more thorough understanding of the processes of memory, trauma, and catharsis, at the same time as crystallizing the interstices and dialogues between early modern and post-millennial culture in the context of "now-ness." From this vantage point, one can begin to re-assess the cinematic aesthetic, and indeed the present moment, as an *un*deferred encounter that will not "dry up" or "stink," but that will have, in Derrida's words, "not even the post or the *envoi*, [but] *posts* and *envois*" (Hughes 1324;

Derrida, *Post Card* 65). The displacing of decay with rebirth, the post-apocalyptic plurality of ends and beginnings, then, is surely something to be optimistic about.

Works Cited

Barthelme, Donald. *The Dead Father.* New York: Zone, 2002.

Baudrillard, Jean. *Simulacra and Simulation.* Trans. Shelia Faria Glaser. Ann Arbor: University of Michigan Press, 1994.

Baudry, Jean-Louis. "The Apparatus: Metapsychological Approaches to the Impression of Reality in the Cinema." *Narrative, Apparatus, Ideology.* Ed. Philip Rosen. New York: Columbia University Press, 1986. 299–318.

Bazin, André. *What is Cinema?* Trans. Hugh Gray. Vol. 1. Berkeley: University of California Press, 1967.

Benjamin, Walter. *Illuminations.* Ed. Hannah Arendt. Trans. Harry Zohn London: Fontana, 1992.

Berger, James. *After the End: Representations of Post-Apocalypse.* Minneapolis, MI: University of Minnesota Press, 1999.

Burnett, Mark Thornton. ""Fancy's Images": Reinventing Shakespeare in Christine Edzard's *The Children's Midsummer Night's Dream.*" *Literature/Film Quarterly* 30.3 (2002): 166–70.

The Children's Midsummer Night's Dream. Dir. Christine Edzard. Perf. Derek Jacobi, Jamie Peachey, and Danny Bishop. 2001. DVD. Squirrel Films, 2006.

Corrigan, Timothy. *A Cinema Without Walls: Movies and Culture after Vietnam.* New Brunswick, NJ: Rutgers University Press, 1991.

Derrida, Jacques. "Of an Apocalyptic Tone Recently Adopted in Philosophy." *Semeia: An Experimental Journal for Biblical Criticism* 23 (1982): 63–97.

_____. *The Post Card: From Socrates to Freud and Beyond.* Trans. Alan Bass. Chicago and London: University of Chicago Press, 1997.

Eberwein, Robert. *Film and the Dream Screen: A Sleep and a Forgetting.* Princeton, NJ: Princeton University Press, 1984.

Fischer, Lucy. *Cinematernity: Film, Motherhood, Genre.* Princeton, NJ: Princeton University Press, 1996.

Freud, Sigmund. "Beyond the Pleasure Principle." *The Standard Edition of the Complete Psychological Works.* Ed. and trans. James Strachey. Vol. 19. London: Hogarth, 1995. 19–30.

_____. "A Note on the Mystic Writing-Pad." *The Standard Edition of the Complete Psychological Works.* Ed. and Trans. James Strachey. Vol. 19. London: Hogarth, 1995. 227–32.

_____. *The Psychopathology of Everyday Life. The Standard Edition of the Complete Psychological Works.* Ed. and Trans. James Strachey. Vol. 6. London: Hogarth, 1995. 1–279.

_____. "Screen Memories." *The Standard Edition of the Complete Psychological Works.* Ed. and trans. James Strachey. Vol. 3. London: Hogarth, 1995. 301–322.

_____. "The Uncanny." *The Standard Edition of the Complete Psychological Works.* Ed. and trans. James Strachey. Vol. 17. London: Hogarth, 1995. 217–252.

Gale, Richard M. Introduction. *The Philosophy of Time: A Collection of Essays.* Ed. Richard M. Gale. London and Melbourne: Macmillan, 1968.

Genette, Gérard. *Palimpsests: Literature in the Second Degree.* Lincoln: University of Nebraska Press, 1997.

Hoberman, James. "Ten Years That Shook The World." *American Film* 10 (1985): 8.

Hughes, Langston. "Harlem." *The Norton Anthology of Poetry*. 4th ed. Ed. Margaret Ferguson, Mary Jo Salter, and Jon Stallworthy. London and New York: W. W. Norton, 1996. 1324.

Israel, Paul. *Edison: A Life of Invention*. New York and Toronto: John Wiley & Sons, 1998.

Kael, Pauline. "Why Are Movies So Bad? or, The Numbers." *Taking It All In: Film Writings 1980–1983*. New York: Holt, Rinehart and Winston, 1984. 8–19.

Kermode, Frank. *The Sense of an Ending*. New York and Oxford: Oxford University Press, 2000.

The King Is Alive. Dir. Kristian Levring. Perf. Jennifer Jason Leigh, David Bradley, and Bruce Davison. 2001. DVD. Pathé, 2002.

Lehmann, Courtney. *Shakespeare Remains: Theater to Film, Early Modern to Postmodern*. Ithaca and London: Cornell University Press, 2002.

Lewis, Jon. "The End of Cinema as We Know It and I feel...: An Introduction to a Book on Nineties American Film." *The End Of Cinema As We Know It*. Ed. Jon Lewis. New York: New York University Press, 2002. 1–10.

Metz, Christian. *Psychoanalysis and Cinema: The Imaginary Signifier*. Trans. Celia Britton. Bloomington, IN: Indiana University Press, 1982.

Milne, Tom. *Godard on Godard*. London: Secker and Warburg, 1972.

Nowotny, Helga. *Time: The Modern and Postmodern Experience*. Cambridge: Polity Press, 1994.

Oudart, Jean-Pierre. "Cinema and Suture." *Screen* 18.4 (1977–78): 35–47.

Parker, Patricia. *Shakespeare from the Margins: Language, Culture, Context*. Chicago: University of Chicago Press, 1996.

Ricoeur, Paul. *Time and Narrative*. Trans. Kathleen McLaughlin and David Pellauer. Vol. 1. Chicago and London: University of Chicago Press, 1983.

Schoenfeldt, Michael C. *Bodies and Selves in Early Modern England: Physiology and Inwardness in Spenser, Shakespeare, Herbert, and Milton*. Cambridge: Cambridge University Press, 1999.

Shakespeare, William. *The Norton Shakespeare*. Ed. Stephen Greenblatt, Walter Cohen, Jean E. Howard, and Katharine Eisaman Maus. New York: W. W. Norton, 1997.

Silverman, Kaja. "Suture." *Narrative, Apparatus, Ideology: A Film Theory Reader*. Ed. Philip Rosen. New York: Columbia University Press, 1986. 219–35.

Wittreich, Joseph. *"Image of that Horror": History, Prophecy, and Apocalypse in* King Lear. San Marino, CA: Huntington Library, 1984.

Woods, Tim. *Beginning Postmodernism*. Manchester: Manchester University Press, 1999.

About the Contributors

Melissa Croteau is an associate professor of literature and film studies at California Baptist University. She has spoken on Shakespeare and film at numerous international conferences and serves on the board of *Americana: The Journal of American Popular Culture*. Recent publications include an edited volume for Press Americana entitled *Reel Histories: Studies in American Film* (2008) and an essay in *Shakespeare's World/World Shakespeares: The Selected Proceedings of the International Shakespeare Association World Congress Brisbane, 2006* (University of Delaware Press, 2008).

Kim Fedderson is a professor of English at Lakehead University and dean of its satellite campus in Orillia, Ontario. He is the co-author of *A Case for Writing* and has published articles on rhetoric, critical theory, pedagogy, and recent cinematic adaptations of Shakespeare's plays.

Carl James Grindley is an assistant professor of English at Hostos College of the City University of New York. Recently, his work on film has appeared in *Film & History* and in the collection *The Medieval Hero on Screen* (McFarland, 2004). Grindley has spoken on film at more than a dozen international conferences in Europe and the United States and has taught at Yale and the University of British Columbia.

Anthony R. Guneratne is an associate professor of communication at Florida Atlantic University. He is the author of *Shakespeare, Film Studies, and the Visual Cultures of Modernity* (Palgrave, 2008) and has published extensively on film history and historiography, the interrelations of various art forms and media, and issues of transnationality, diaspora, and postcoloniality in literature and cinema.

Carolyn Jess-Cooke is a senior lecturer in creative writing at the University of Northumbria. She is author of *Shakespeare on Film: Such Things as Dreams Are Made Of* (Wallflower, 2007*), Film Sequels: Theory and Practice from Hollywood to Bollywood* (Edinburgh University Press, 2009), and co-editor with Constantine Verevis of *Second Takes: Critical Approaches to the Film Sequel* (SUNY, 2009). She is also an award-winning poet.

Courtney Lehmann is an associate professor of English and film studies at the University of the Pacific. She is the author of *Shakespeare Remains: Theater to Film,*

Early Modern to Postmodern (Cornell University Press, 2002) and co-editor with Lisa S. Starks of *Spectacular Shakespeare: Critical Theory and Popular Cinema* and *The Reel Shakespeare: Alternative Cinema and Theory* (Fairleigh Dickinson University Press, 2002).

Gretchen E. Minton is an assistant professor of English at Montana State University in Bozeman. Her publications include articles on Shakespeare, the English Reformation, and contemporary drama and film. She is the co-editor of the Arden *Timon of Athens* third series and is working on a book about Shakespeare's contemporaries on film.

Alfredo Michel Modenessi is a professor of literature and translation at the National University of Mexico. He has published books and articles on English and American theater, translation, cinema, and Shakespeare in Mexico, Brazil, Spain, the UK and the United States. His stage translations include plays by Shakespeare, Marlowe and many modern playwrights.

J. Michael Richardson's publications include *Astrological Symbolism in Spenser's "The Shepheardes Calender"*; *The Existential Joss Whedon* (and J.D. Rabb; McFarland, 2007); contributions to *The Spenser Encyclopedia*; and articles on recent cinematic adaptations of Shakespeare's plays. He teaches at Lakehead University in Ontario, Canada.

Adrian Streete is a lecturer in English at the Queen's University of Belfast. He is co-editor of *Refiguring Mimesis: Representation in Early Modern Literature* (University of Hertfordshire Press, 2005) and has published in journals such as *Literature and History*, *The Review of English Studies*, and *Textual Practice*.

Richard Vela is a professor of English at the University of North Carolina at Pembroke. A co-author of *Shakespeare into Film*, he frequently writes on Shakespeare, film, and the literary and filmic connections between Mexico and the United States. His awards include the Ford Foundation Fellowship, the Danforth Foundation Fellowship, and the North Carolina Board of Governors Award for Excellence in Teaching.

Ramona Wray is the author of *Women Writers of the Seventeenth Century* (Northcote House, 2003) and the co-editor of *Screening Shakespeare in the Twenty-First Century* (Edinburgh University Press, 2006), *Reconceiving the Renaissance: A Critical Reader* (Oxford University Press, 2004), *Shakespeare, Film, Fin de Siècle* (Macmillan, 2000) and *Shakespeare and Ireland: History, Politics, Culture* (Macmillan, 1997). She has published essays and articles on early modern women's autobiography, Renaissance reading practices, editorial history, Shakespeare on film and pedagogy.

Index